EMERGENCY MEDICINE CLINICS OF NORTH AMERICA

Medical-Legal Issues

MATTHEW M. RICE, MD, JD, LTC, MC, GUEST EDITOR

VOLUME 11 • NUMBER 4 • NOVEMBER 1993

W.B. SAUNDERS COMPANY
A Division of Harcourt Brace & Company
PHILADELPHIA   LONDON   TORONTO   MONTREAL   SYDNEY   TOKYO

W.B. SAUNDERS COMPANY
A Division of
Harcourt Brace & Company

The Curtis Center
Independence Square West
Philadelphia, PA 19106-3399

The *Emergency Medicine Clinics of North America* is also published in translated editions by the following:

Spanish   McGraw-Hill/Interamericana de Espana
Manual Ferraro 13
28036 Madrid, Spain

The *Emergency Medicine Clinics of North America* is covered in *Index Medicus, Excerpta Medica,* and *BIOSIS.*

EMERGENCY MEDICINE CLINICS OF NORTH AMERICA   ISSN 0733-8627
NOVEMBER 1993   Volume 11, Number 4

The *Emergency Medicine Clinics of North America* (ISSN 0733–8627) is published quarterly by W.B. Saunders Company. Corporate and Editorial Offices: The Curtis Center, Independence Square West, Philadelphia, PA 19106-3399. Accounting and Circulation Offices: 6277 Sea Harbor Drive, Orlando, FL 32887-4800. Second class postage paid at Orlando, FL 32862, and additional mailing offices. Subscription price is $82.00 per year (US individuals), $99.00 per year (US institutions), and $109.00 per year (foreign individuals or institutions). Foreign air speed delivery for all *Clinics* is $8.00 per issue. All prices are subject to change without notice. POSTMASTER: Send address changes to the *Emergency Medicine Clinics of North America*, W.B. Saunders Company, Periodicals Fulfillment, Orlando, FL 32887-4800.

Customer Service: 1–800–654–2452.

The editor of this publication is Sandra W. Hitchens, W.B. Saunders Company, The Curtis Center, Independence Square West, Philadelphia, PA 19106-3399.

Printed in the United States of America.

GUEST EDITOR

MATTHEW M. RICE, MD, JD, LTC, MC, Chief, Department of Emergency Medicine, Madigan Army Medical Center, Tacoma, Washington

CONTRIBUTORS

DAVID T. ARMITAGE, MD, JD, FAPA, Associate Chairman, Department of Legal Medicine, Armed Forces Institute of Pathology, Washington, DC; and Clinical Professor of Psychiatry, Uniformed Services University of the Health Sciences, Bethesda, Maryland

R. JACK AYRES, Jr, JD, REMT-P, Associate Clinical Professor of Hospital Administration and Emergency Medicine, University of Texas Southwestern Medical Center at Dallas; and Director, Emergency Legal Assistance Program, Parkland Memorial Hospital, Dallas, Texas

JOHN D. DUNN, MD, Director of Emergency Services, Brownwood Regional Medical Center, Brownwood, Texas

FRANK T. FLANNERY, MD, JD, LTC, MC, USA, Chairman, Department of Legal Medicine, Armed Forces Institute of Pathology, Washington, DC

JAMES E. GEORGE, MD, JD, FACEP, President, Emergency Physician Associates, Woodbury; Partner, the Law Firm of George, Korin, Quattrone & Blumberg, Woodbury; Attending Physician, Department of Emergency Medicine, Underwood-Memorial Hospital, Woodbury; and the Emergency Medicine Residency Program of the University of Medicine and Dentistry of New Jersey–School of Osteopathic Medicine, New Jersey

RICHARD L. GRANVILLE, MD, JD, Deputy Chairman, Department of Legal Medicine, Armed Forces Institute of Pathology, Washington, DC

GREGORY L. HENRY, MD, FACEP, Chief, Department of Emergency Medicine, Beyer Hospital; Clinical Assistant Professor, Section of Emergency Medicine, University of Michigan; and Vice President, Emergency Physicians Medical Group, Ann Arbor, Michigan

THOM A. MAYER, MD, Director of Emergency Medicine, Department of Emergency Medicine, Fairfax Hospital, Falls Church, Virginia

DAVID M. SIEGEL, MD, JD, FACEP, FACP, FCLM, Chief Medical Officer, NES, Inc., Tampa, Florida

DANIEL J. SULLIVAN, MD, JD, FACEP, Chairman, Department of Emergency Medicine, Ingalls Memorial Hospital, Harvey; and Assistant Professor of Emergency Medicine, Cook County Hospital, Chicago, Illinois

GARY M. TOWNSEND, MD, JD, Medicolegal Consultant, Consultation Case Review Branch, Army Health Professional Support Agency, Office of the Surgeon General of the Army; and Department of Legal Medicine, Armed Forces Institute of Pathology, Washington, DC

CECE L. WOOD, JD, Corporate Counsel, Oklahoma Health Care Corporation, Oklahoma City, Oklahoma

CONTENTS

Preface   ix
Matthew M. Rice

**Historical Perspectives on Law, Medical Malpractice, and
the Concept of Negligence**   819
Cece L. Wood

> This article provides an overview of the origins and influences
> that contributed to the evolution of medical malpractice from its
> ancient beginnings to the present. Specifically, emphasis is given
> to the current theory of negligence and the concepts of duty,
> breach of duty, causation, and damages.

Consent and Refusal of Treatment   833
David M. Siegel

> The emergency physician is often faced with consent problems for
> emergency patients. Many different types of consent exist that are
> applicable in different circumstances. The emergency physician
> must be able to deal with difficult scenarios involving incompe-
> tent patients, minor patients, and patients who refuse treatment.
> Documentation in these situations is critical.

Minors and Emergency Medicine   841
Daniel J. Sullivan

> This article reviews medical-legal issues with regard to minors as
> they apply to the practice of emergency medicine. The topics of
> consent to treatment, refusal of care, child abuse, and medical
> malpractice are addressed. A working knowledge of these areas
> helps the emergency physician to avoid confusion, avoid delays
> in management, and maintain the safety of children.

Legal Considerations in Prehospital Care   853
R. Jack Ayres, Jr

> This article presents an overview of several major legal issues in
> contemporary prehospital health care delivery and emergency
> medical services. It includes review and analysis of medical-legal
> issues in medical control, patient consent and treatment; modern
> emergency medical services communications; discussion of medi-
> cal-legal concerns in regard to patient destination choice, diver-
> sion, and transfer; and an analysis of theories of recovery includ-
> ing a review of selected case histories.

Emergency Medicine, Psychiatry, and the Law   869
David T. Armitage and Gary M. Townsend

> The emergency department physician must assess, initiate treat-
> ment, and arrange for the disposition of patients whose presenta-
> tion reflects disordered thinking, emotions, and behavior. Unique
> diagnostic, management, and medicolegal challenges must be met
> daily. Understanding the issues inherent in the various stages of
> involvement with such patients helps reduce medicolegal risk and
> facilitates the provision of appropriate health care.

The Emergency Department Medical Record   889
James E. George

> Emergency physicians are overwhelmed by the load of medical
> record documentation in the emergency department. This article
> reviews the important reasons for better documentation and to-
> day's increasing regulatory requirements in medical record docu-
> mentation.

**Risk Management and High-Risk Issues in Emergency
Medicine**   905
Gregory L. Henry

> Risk management in the emergency department is defined in this
> article. The health care professional should focus on the health
> and best interests of the patient.

**The National Practitioner Data Bank: An Overview for the
Emergency Physician**   923
Richard L. Granville and Frank T. Flannery

> This article reviews the Health Care Quality Improvement Act,
> Title IV of Public Law 99-660, which was passed by the US Con-
> gress in 1986. The Act offered immunity to professional review
> societies of hospital and other health care entities, and persons
> serving on or otherwise assisting such bodies. It is believed that
> professional review actions will further the quality of medical care
> and provide due process safeguards for the health care provider.

Future Legal Issues in Emergency Medicine   933

John D. Dunn and Thom A. Mayer

> This article analyzes past legal trends in emergency medicine with
> an effort to project those trends and current developments into
> future legal issues that will confront emergency physicians and
> emergency departments. Special emphasis is placed on insurance
> trends and professional liability insurance developments along
> with medical malpractice claims past, present, and future. Also
> discussed in this article is the health care industry environment
> and ways that it might affect future legal challenges for emer-
> gency medicine.

Cumulative Index   953

Subscription Information   Inside back cover

Erratum

The August 1993 issue of the *Emergency Medicine Clinics of North America*
contained an error in the contributors list for Joseph E. Kutz, MD. Dr.
Kutz's correct affiliation is Clinical Professor of Surgery (Hand) and
Clinical Professor of Surgery (Plastic and Reconstructive Surgery), Uni-
versity of Louisville, School of Medicine; and Director, Christine M.
Kleinert Fellowship in Hand Surgery, Louisville, Kentucky.

FORTHCOMING ISSUES

February 1994

> THE PREGNANT PATIENT
> Lynette Doan-Wiggins, MD, FACEP, *Guest Editor*

May 1994

> CHALLENGES AND CONTROVERSIES IN TOXICOLOGY
> Marsha D. Ford, MD, FACEP, and
> Jonathan S. Olshaker, MD, FACEP, *Guest Editors*

August 1994

> EMERGENCY CARE OF PATIENTS WITH INDWELLING DEVICES
> J. Alan Morgan, MD, MAJ, MC, and
> Lawrence B. Stack, MD, *Guest Editors*

RECENT ISSUES

August 1993

> THE HAND IN EMERGENCY MEDICINE
> Dennis T. Uehara, MD, FACEP, *Guest Editor*

May 1993

> HEMATOLOGIC/ONCOLOGIC EMERGENCIES
> Gregory P. Moore, MD, FACEP, and
> Robert C. Jorden, MD, FACEP, *Guest Editors*

February 1993

> ADVANCES IN TRAUMA
> John A. Marx, MD, FACEP, *Guest Editor*

November 1992

> SOFT TISSUE EMERGENCIES
> Carey D. Chisholm, MD, FACEP, and
> John M. Howell, MD, FACEP, *Guest Editors*

PREFACE

Emergency care providers are confronted each working day with medical challenges and dilemmas that are frequently stressful and thought provoking. But this excitement of our specialty seems to pale in comparison with the anxiety-provoking medical-legal concerns we routinely face. The potential for a medical malpractice claim to be filed against emergency physicians is great, and the mere psychological impact from a suit can be devastating to the individual. This fear of medical malpractice claims can be significantly reduced through knowledge and a continued understanding of the legal system and the legal issues surrounding emergency care. For years, lawyers have been learning more about medicine. It is appropriate that physicians, out of interest and necessity, are learning more about law.

Hopefully, this edition of the *Emergency Medicine Clinics* will provide all of us with some important information. The authors have provided traditional as well as thought-provoking material, and I am grateful to them for their efforts and product. But this work merely touches on a complicated and tricky area of our profession, and we must apply local statutes and modern realities in formulating appropriate standards of medical practice. Providing the best medical care with reason, judgement, and compassion is the primary consideration for our patients because we must live with ourselves, no matter what a court later decides.

MATTHEW M. RICE, MD, JD, LTC, MC
Guest Editor

Department of Emergency Medicine
Madigan Army Medical Center
Tacoma, WA 98431-5000

HISTORICAL PERSPECTIVES ON LAW, MEDICAL MALPRACTICE, AND THE CONCEPT OF NEGLIGENCE

Cece L. Wood, JD

> This is a journey . . . most doctors and patients don't like to think about. It's
> where reality breaks on the shore of ideals, where lives are lost or broken
> and human frailty held up for public examination[9]

The history of medical malpractice law is clearly not straightforward and succinct. It has evolved through time, encompassed in the development of law itself, with a multitude of influences from various origins. Much of it has been lost or buried with our predecessors. Fortunately, bits and pieces of its elusive past have surfaced from the depths of historical literature. This article will attempt to put some of those pieces together to provide a glimpse of its interesting evolution.

THE INTRODUCTION OF LAW AND THE PRACTICE OF MEDICINE

Self-preservation is the root of existence for all living things. So it is not surprising to learn that throughout early history, humans evolved as social beings, within communities, dependent upon a system of practices, customs, and norms imposed upon its members—"laws" created to ensure amicable cohabitation and provide for its members' mutual protection and well-being. As these customs, practices, and norms grew in

---

From the Corporate Counsel, Oklahoma Health Care Corporation, Oklahoma City, Oklahoma

---

number, members of the communities began compiling them together in writings, calling them "codes."[28]

As an additional means of self-preservation and enhancement of human life, primitive humans also practiced medicine, in a variety of forms and manners, to heal the wounded and cure disease.

"Witch doctors," "medicine men," and "shamans" (titles likely held by the older, more experienced members of native tribes or clans) served their members by means of potions, magic spells, appeals to supernatural beings, common sense, the "laying on of hands," and "other various auditory, visual, and olfactory effects."[2] Although their training and indoctrination often allowed them to escape criticism by proclaiming an adverse result as the "will of the God," they were not exempt from violent retribution by their "medical malpractice" victims or the victim's family members when their errors were apparent.[2] Hence, the relationship between law and medicine began.

The same considerations given for developing codes to protect the members of the communities from crimes such as maiming and murder were eventually carried over to the practice of medicine, to protect the public from inept and careless practitioners.[12] This transition appears to have occurred in a number of cultures.

ORIGINS OF INFLUENCE ON MEDICAL MALPRACTICE LAW

One of the oldest and first-known codes to reflect strong concerns for the quality of medical care was the Code of Hammurabi, developed by the King of Babylon around 2200 BC. Pursuant to this code, unrestrained, personal violence against medical practitioners was replaced by more appropriate and synonymous forms of retribution. Specifically, if a doctor treated a man with a knife and the man died, the doctor's hand was cut off.[11]

The ancient Mosaic Code of the Israelites advocated a similar concept by demanding "an eye for an eye, tooth for a tooth."[17] However, by the eleventh century, the idea of monetary compensation for "damages," " . . . equivalent to the difference in value of the injured person before and after the incident if he were a slave being sold (for six years of service),"[2] became more tenable to the Israelites based on the necessity to preserve optimal manpower in their relatively limited population.

In Greece, Hippocrates, the "father of medicine," was known to have discussed many medical-legal issues, and he ultimately promulgated an oath governing the conduct of physicians and surgeons about 460 BC[12] known as the "Hippocratic oath." That oath states in part, "I will follow that system of regimen which, according to my ability and judgment, I consider for the benefit of my patients. . ."[12] Today, it still plays a vital role in the tradition of the medical profession.

The Justinian Code, AD 529 to 564, also made attempts to control medical practitioners. "The Code called for, among other things, an examination to test the physician's professional competency, a limitation on the number of physicians, and penalties for malpractice."[28]

Each of these cultures developed legal concepts for malpractice that were carried through time and have contributed to, or had an impact on, malpractice law as we know it now. However, the development of the form and principles of law used today in America can actually be traced back to early England.

THE DEVELOPMENT OF A LEGAL SYSTEM

Tribes of conquering Anglo-Saxons initially created two distinct institutions of law designed to maintain order within their communities—the "blood feud" and the act of "lynching."[6]

The killing of a member of a clan by another provoked retribution in the form of a feud between the two clans. The feud was a lengthy process, nurtured through generations of members of the clan, rarely without end—short of the clan's extinction.[6]

Lynching, on the other hand, was a form of law used by the community as a whole. Culprits of criminal acts suffered violent retribution, through mandatory lynching, if their criminal acts were witnessed. The "hue and cry" of the victim was the only trial that existed for the culprit.[6]

After William the Conqueror succeeded in his conquest of all of England in 1066, Henry I established dominion over the land.[2] A feudal system was implemented in which the king granted parcels of land to vassals in exchange for their loyalty and military service to him, as king. This system provided the king opportunity to organize and replace the rather chaotic system of laws with his own, and gradually the Anglo-Saxons adapted to a more civilized system of justice in which money took the place of vengeance in a feud, lynchings were outlawed, and select members of the community assumed the responsibility of serving as jurors or "finders of fact."[6] These jurors were entrusted to determine the facts about incidents through their own investigative efforts and to make allegations of wrongdoing against an individual based upon their discoveries. This formative process established the basis for what we know as the "grand jury."

During the reign of Henry II, a system of royal courts was created that offered trials by jury, as a legal right, to resolve disputes.[6] There were two forms of trial in these courts: "compurgation" and "ordeal." The rarest of the two, "compurgation," was reserved for the elite of the classes and was based on the accused's sworn innocence, and his or her veracity and "good repute," as elicited by the testimony of friends. "Ordeals" operated within the realm of the supernatural and were more commonly used for those accused of crimes. In ordeals, guilt or innocence was believed to be determined by signs from God. "The principal ordeals were these: the accused would carry a hot iron in bare hands, dip his arm in boiling water, or be bound and plunged into a pond or stream. . . . After several days . . . if the burn was healed, the accused was innocent; if it festered, he was guilty. In [the] ordeal by water, if the accused sank, he was innocent; if he floated, he was guilty—a no win proposition."[6]

Fortunately, the Catholic Church abolished trial by ordeal and replaced it with a second type of jury, smaller in number, albeit compilsed of some of the same members that sat on the larger jury that initially made the accusations of guilt. By the middle of the fourteenth century, the two juries finally evolved into separate entities with titles: the accusatory jury, the larger of the two, became known as "the grand jury," and the smaller was known as the "petit jury."[6]

Throughout the developmental period, the royal courts also established a variety of procedural rules for its courts. One such rule mandated that the offenses to be charged against an individual had to be in the form of a specific "writ" before the aggrieved party could be heard by the court.[23] A "writ" consisted of a written order issued by a judicial court or official in the name of a sovereign, requiring the individual to whom it was addressed to perform or cease the performance of a specified act that the sovereign acknowledged as being inappropriate. This rigid procedural requirement kept many individuals out of the courts and provided them no remedy because the act that the aggrieved party was alleging did not conform exactly to the language contained in a pre-existing writ. Owing to the perceived injustice brought about by the system, the king's chancellors began to intervene and provide equitable remedies. The chancellors were mostly ecclesiastics, and the "equity" they rendered "was initially regarded more as an administrative function of the executive branch of the government, rather than a separate judicial system."[6] This intervention by the chancellors met little opposition until they began stepping in to prevent the prosecution of actions against some individuals, and the enforcement of some judgments rendered by the courts. Sir Francis Bacon reportedly provided a solution for this dispute between the courts and the chancellors that allowed the two systems to coexist peacefully, without threatening the authority of the other. From that point forward, "the chancellor could enjoin a party from enforcing a judgment, but could not affect the judgment itself, nor the court which rendered it."[6]

THE ESTABLISHMENT OF COMMON LAW

Concurrent with the development of the court system was the creation and accumulation of a vast body of recorded decisions rendered by the courts in both civil and criminal trials. "This body of decisions, and the custom of applying those prior decisions of the royal courts to new cases, [established what] became known as the 'common law' . . .,"[23] and the actual practice of "following the precedent" or "stare decisis" was one of the Romans' contributions to this system of jurisprudence.[2] The same body of recorded decisions (common law) that was created by the royal courts in England was subsequently brought over to the American colonies and used to establish the basis for the American legal system as we know it today.

PROFESSIONAL LIABILITY UNDER COMMON LAW

A few of the early English medical malpractice cases were brought against practitioners in the form of criminal proceedings. The earliest mention of professional liability in England involved a physician in Britton around 1290. The case raised allegations of malpractice, but at that time no distinction was made between those practicing legitimate medicine and quackery.[3]

In the attempts to find theories of law and remedies to satisfy the parties involved, the concept of "negligence" began entering into the court's decisions, and it was not long before the notions of "duty" and "standard of care" were recognized as well.

BASIS OF LIABILITY: TORT

The term *tort* was derived from the Latin word *tortus*, meaning crooked or twisted, and was later associated with a "body of law" that redressed wrongs other than breaches of contract.[1] Tort actions were created to protect individuals' interest in being free from harm. The duties of conduct that give rise to tort actions are imposed by the law and are primarily based upon social policies rather that upon the will or intentions of the parties involved.[22]

As previously mentioned, to gain access to the court, those who considered themselves wronged were required to comply with the procedure of filing a "writ," pleading the facts of their case. Two writs served as the basis for actions in tort: the "action of Trespass" and "the "action of Trespass on the case" (also known as "Trespass" and "Trespass on the case," respectively).[22] "Trespass was . . . for all forcible, direct and immediate injuries, whether to person or to property . . . for the kind of conduct likely to lead to a breach of the peace by provoking immediate retaliation. Trespass on the case . . . developed somewhat later, as a supplement to the parent action of Trespass, was designed to afford a remedy for obviously wrongful conduct resulting in injuries which were not forcible or not direct."[22] An excellent example of Trespass is that of a man throwing rocks at a neighbor's house and ultimately breaking a window. Under those circumstances, the wrongdoer would not only be tried for criminal actions as a breach of the king's peace but also would be required to repair or pay for the repairs to the damaged house, a civil action. But what if, in addition, some of those rocks rolled off the roof onto the street below and caused a horse to stumble and throw the rider, breaking the rider's leg?[23] The narrowly drafted writ of Trespass did not apply to all possible injuries the rock thrower might cause in the future, based on the initial act of throwing the rocks. Therefore, the writ of "Trespass on the case" became applicable, so that the rider would be able to seek redress for injuries against the rock thrower as well.

From this early beginning over 600 years ago, the theory of tort law was born. Despite the fact that writs of "Trespass" and "Trespass on the case" were intended to emphasize the "causal sequence" and distinguish between "direct" and "indirect" injuries, that artificial classification has almost completely been abandoned, and we now look instead to the *intent* of the wrongdoer.[22] Hence, the terms "intentional tort" and "unintentional tort" (also called "negligence") were coined, and both theories still provide basis for malpractice liability today. However, it would still be a while before an action in Trespass on the case (negligence) would stand alone as a separate and distinct tort. In the meantime, it would be challenged by another type of legal action that appeared conducive for suits against physicians.

THE CONTRACTUAL BASIS OF LIABILITY FOR NEGLIGENCE

Initially, within the contractual context, "[n]egligence, as carelessness in the performance of some affirmative act which caused harm . . . was not the prevalent conception."[10] The concept of negligence was applied only in terms of "the 'nonfeasance' [failure to perform] of individuals charged either by contract or statute with a duty of care."[10] This was the case, under early English common law, with physicians, who were essentially regarded as members of a public calling, similar in nature to ironsmiths or innkeepers. They had a duty to serve all comers, and their liability was defined accordingly.[15]

With the rise of commercialism, the physician's role changed, and the legal premise for liability focused on the contract itself. The physician's "undertaking" came to be regarded as the true foundation on which to base an action. In essence, if a physician undertook, for a fee, to provide medical services, and failed to do what was promised, there was an actionable wrong, not because the law obligated the physician to provide the services (as was the case for public callings), but because the physician had agreed to assume the obligation toward the patient (a breach of the contract).

In 1374, things were to change even more drastically when "an obscure malpractice case came along and set the precedent upon which rests all Western malpractice litigation."[9] This case was reported to be the first recorded decision of its kind in all of England. A chief justice, John Cavendish, heard the case before the Court of the King's Bench. A well-respected London surgeon, John Swanlond, treated the crushed and mangled hand of Agnes of Stratton. Her hand ultimately was severely deformed and she sued Dr. Swanlond. The case was brought to the court under a breach of contract theory. The standards established by the Hippocratic oath were applied, and the court ruled that if the surgeon performed well, exercising the extent of his abilities with due diligence, that he should not be held culpable.[31] In other words, the court did not limit the scope of its consideration to whether the physician had performed his services under the contract, but rather the court scrutinized the quality of the services rendered, based upon the physician's assumed duty under the contract, as well as the legal duty that was imposed upon him to exercise some degree of care to everyone whom he treated. This decision established the precedent for applying the negligence concept under a contractual theory to cases of "misfeasance" (poor performance) by the practitioner. It served as a true stepping stone in the development of the English legal system in that it provided a means of bringing an action similar to "Trespass on the case," which traditionally could not be brought without a concurrent action in "Trespass," and allowed it to stand alone. Thus, if aggrieved parties could get their negligence cases into court under a contractual theory, they could seek redress that they would have been denied otherwise.

The blurred lines of distinction between actions in contract and tort subsequently created somewhat of a dilemma for the courts. Ultimately, in 1615, Sir Edward Coke, referred to as the "father of the common law," decided a case that laid the foundation in English common law to allow an action against a physician for negligence to be brought under a theory other than contract. He stated, " the law gives the party sufficient remedy to recover . . . for default of performance, or for negligence in the performance."[8] For the first time, negligence cases were acknowledged as being capable of standing alone, without a primary action in Trespass and outside the contract, and the lines of distinction between the two were renewed.

Another significant contribution made by the court in Dr. Swanlond's case was the following analogy, which Cavendish entered in his written opinion: "If a smith undertakes to cure my horse, and the horse is harmed by his negligence or failure to cure in a reasonable time, it is just that he should be liable."[9] By using that analogy, the court said, in essence, that however ably and however diligently doctors might perform their professional duties, that particular level of ability and diligence might not be enough.[12] Thus, it laid the framework to establish the standard of the "ordinary reasonable/prudent physician," which ultimately led to a turning point in the history of malpractice law.

THE EMERGENCE OF NEGLIGENCE IN AMERICAN LAW

Given that American laws were derived from the common law established in England, it should be no surprise that "[t]he development of negligence as the dominant standard of civil liability in tort within the American law during the first half of the nineteenth century paralleled . . . the English experience . . . the writ system, with its distinction between trespass and case, was in general use in the United States, and

American lawyers had many of the same problems as their English brethren in deciding whether a given action should be brought under one writ or another. Furthermore, negligence was a shadowy concept, with but a secondary position in the tort law."[10]

The first recorded case of malpractice in the United States arose in Connecticut in 1794, not long after the Revolution. Judgment was rendered against the physician on the theory that his "undertaking . . . to perform a mastectomy safely and skillfully was ignored . . . in that his professional performance was unskillful, ignorant and cruel, 'contrary to all the well known rules and principles of practice in such cases' "[12] resulting in his patient's death. The surviving husband was awarded 40 pounds, for the loss of his wife's companionship.[12]

By the mid 1800s, various courts within the United States had enunciated standards of professional conduct for tort actions "which to some extent still adhered to the contractual basis for liability, injecting the 'ordinary prudent doctor' standard, but not quite willing yet to adopt that standard wholly to the abnegation and exclusion of the contractual basis for liability."[12] In an eloquent interpretation of "standard of care" under a tort theory of liability in 1832, Chief Justice Tindal stated, "every person who enters into a learned profession undertakes to bring to it the exercise of a reasonable degree of care and skill; he does not undertake if he is . . . a surgeon . . . that he will perform a cure, nor does he undertake to use the highest possible skill. There may be persons who have a higher education and greater advantage and competent degree of skill and you will not say whether in this case the injury was occasioned by the want of such skill in the defendant. The question is, whether this injury must be referred to the want of a proper degree of skill and care in the defendant or not."[32] Negligence as a separate and distinct basis of tort liability was recognized in the United States about 1825, and by 1850 it had become ingrained as the primary theory of recovery in unintentional tort actions.[4]

THE CONCEPT OF NEGLIGENCE

Since attaining its status as an independent cause of action in tort law, negligence has also been provided with a variety of definitions. *Black's Law Dictionary* defines it as "the omission to do something which a reasonable man, guided by those ordinary considerations which ordinarily regulate human affairs, would do, or the doing of something which a reasonable and prudent man would not do."[1] Under all tort theories, liability is typically imposed on the basis of fault. All medical malpractice actions are predicated on an allegation that the patient, who claims injury, was owed some duty by the physician, and that the duty was breached, resulting in injury. It is important to recognize that the use of negligence as a criterion of liability in medical malpractice cases actually serves to limit liability, because the physician can escape liability for harm unintentionally caused if his or her conduct was found not to have been negligent.[10]

Over the years, American courts have dissected out the basic principles of negligence and developed long-standing and fluent decisions in the case law. The results have established somewhat of an adversarial system in which the aggrieved party (plaintiff) must prove, by a preponderance of the evidence, four essential elements for a judgment of negligence and, hence, liability to exist against the accused party (defendant). These elements include a pre-existing duty, a breach of that duty, damages, and a causal link between the breach of the duty and the damages that resulted. It is extremely important to understand each of these elements and the issues raised by them.

Does a Duty Exist? If So, to What Extent?

The first challenge that arises in a negligence action against a physician is ascertaining whether a duty exists and, if so, what that duty entails. Typically, before a duty can exist, a physician must undertake the responsibility to provide care. In other words, some relationship must exist between the physician and the patient. Usually, there is a greater duty imposed upon the professional than the patient. It has been recognized that a physician who is called upon to treat an ill person without a previous or defined obligation may refuse to provide treatment and, therefore, has no duty to treat.[14] Once the physician has agreed to care for, begun to care for, or possibly even established a rapport with the patient, however, the physician may acquire a duty of care relative to his or her act.[13, 18, 27] By assuming that responsibility, the physician by implication warrants that he or she possesses, and the law places upon him or her the duty to possess, that degree of education and training that is ordinarily possessed by other physicians under the same or similar circumstances. An emergency physician owes each patient the duty to possess and bring to bear on the patient's behalf, that degree of knowledge, skill, and care usually exercised by reasonable and prudent practitioners under similar circumstances, given the prevailing medical knowledge and the available resources.[7] A specialist owes a higher degree of care to the patient than does a general practitioner.[20] The emergency specialist is not required to exercise the highest degree of skill and care possible, but must use the degree of skill and care ordinarily exercised by physicians within that same specialty.[5, 30] In that regard, physicians may be held liable for failure to know what they are doing, if a reasonably prudent physician would have known, or they may be liable if they know what to do, but for some reason do not do it carefully or omit doing it at all.[21]

This does not mean to imply that negligence is limited to situations involving carelessness, because that is not the case. Negligence also encompasses situations in which a physician who does not possess adequate skills to perform a procedure is remiss in failing to recognize that he or she is not capable of treating the patient, and performs the procedure anyway, rather than referring the patient to a specialist. Such care may have, in fact, met the highest possible standard, but it could still be considered negligent for lack of diligence in referring the patient. Within this context, there exists one caveat. If a patient's condition could be jeopardized by referring the patient to a specialist or a better-equipped facility, a duty may require the physician to do the best possible, given the training and equipment available under the circumstances (i.e., an emergency).

In addition, due care may also require a treating physician to contact prior treating physicians for information or instructions. This can be demonstrated in the following case.

Case

An elderly man was brought to the emergency room following a motor vehicle accident. The patient appeared somewhat dazed and had minor cuts and abrasions. The physician elicited a history of "a blood clot sometime ago" for which the patient was taking "a blood thinner." Owing to the physician's concerns about internal injuries and bleeding, the patient was admitted to the hospital for 24 hours of observation and his Coumadin was discontinued. The following day, the physician's concerns about internal injuries were ruled out, and the patient was discharged home without a prescription for Coumadin, but was instructed to "follow up with the doctor who prescribed the Coumadin." Two weeks later, the patient was returned to the emergency room with a diagnosis of pulmonary embolus. Subsequent inquiries, made to the prior treating physician, revealed that the patient is a poor historian, has suffered multiple deep venous thrombosis, and had been placed on Coumadin therapy for the remainder of his life. An additional point, demonstrated in this example is that if a patient presents to an emergency room seeking assistance, a duty is implied to assist, even if that means only to evaluate.

Another important aspect of the duty a physician owes to patients is the obligation to keep abreast of new developments in medicine, because only in doing so can a physician assert as a defense that his or her action or failure to act followed the practices and treatment methods commonly employed by peers.

Breach of Duty: Was the Standard of Care Met?

Once a duty has been established, the next step toward establishing liability is to prove that the duty was breached. This requires a showing by the patient that the physician did something contrary to the recognized standard of medical practice within the community (or state, or region, in accordance with the requirements of the law within the jurisdiction in which the case is being raised), or neglected to do something by that standard. A majority of malpractice cases revolve around some phase of the diagnosis and treatment of an ailment or condition.[25]

More often than not, proving the breach of a duty will require professional equals to testify that the standard of care was met or not met.[19] Frequently, these experts are called upon because of their expertise within the same specialty as for the defendant physician.[16] Occasionally, the court will allow a breach to be proved through the use of and reference to well-established standards and regulations that have been articulated by professional organizations such as the Joint Commission on Accreditation of Healthcare Organizations or the American Medical Association, or published in professional textbooks or journals (i.e., *Rosen's Concepts in Emergency Medicine* or *Emergency Medicine Clinics of North America* and so on).[24]

Damages: Was There Injury or Loss?

This is often the next question asked in a medical malpractice action. The patient or surviving family members must establish that damages exist. This can be demonstrated on a personal, emotional, or economic basis.

To establish damages on a personal basis, the aggrieved party must prove a loss of life, physical injury/disability, or deterioration of the patient's condition/quality of life, any of which would satisfy the requirement. Emotional damages such as "distress" are acknowledged and thus are compensable in some jurisdictions, but not all. An example of a case in which emotional damages might be awarded would be a situation in which a wife takes her husband to the emergency room with complaints of chest pain, his vital signs are taken by a triage nurse, and the couple is sent to a waiting room, where, while waiting, the wife subsequently watches her husband die after no one responds immediately to her cries for help. However, the most common and frequently utilized means of determining the damages a patient claims he or she has suffered is by placing a value on it in terms of the pecuniary (monetary) loss a patient has suffered as a result of a physician's negligence, whether it be lost wages, present and future medical expenses, or special equipment needed for daily living and special care. Without damage, negligence cannot be established.

Proximate Cause

The fourth and final element of a negligence action is called causation or proximate cause. Causation is the process of building a bridge between the negligent act or omission, on the part of the physician, and the damages suffered. In other words, once the elements of duty, breach of duty, and damages have been established, the patient must prove, by a preponderance of the evidence, that the physician's breach *caused* the resulting damages claimed by the patient. The requirement of proof between cause and effect is known as the legal concept of "proximate cause." No matter how negligent a physician may have been, harm must be shown to have resulted from the negligence before judgment can be awarded in favor of the aggrieved party.

Sometimes causation is evident, as is demonstrated in the following case.

Case

A child was brought to the emergency room and sedated to manipulate a forearm fracture. To place the splint, hot water was used to dip the plaster, causing the plaster to set up fast and release intense heat. This intense heat caused second- and third-degree burns on the child's forearm, which were later discovered after the child recovered from the effects of sedation.

The cause of the burn and subsequent skin grafting is apparent in this example (*res ipsa loquitur*—the thing speaks for itself), so damages would be awarded.

More often than not, causation is the most difficult of the elements to prove. In a case in which a patient is so ill or so severely injured that death may be imminent, if negligence occurs in the course of treatment and the patient dies, damages will not be awarded unless the survivors who bring the action can prove that the deceased probably would have survived in the absence of the malpractice. A similar dilemma can occur when a patient presents with an underlying condition of which he or she may or may not be aware at the time of the consultation. Under these types of circumstances, it is often difficult to determine if a poor result in treatment was the result of the physician's negligence or the patient's pre-existing condition. Therefore, before any patient can recover damages, he or she must eliminate the pre-existing condition as the probable cause of the failure to recuperate fully. This can tremendously complicate the determination of proximate cause.

If there is a possibility of two or more causes for a bad result in treatment, the judge or jury is charged with the responsibility of choosing between them, or determining percentages of the attribution of cause of each contributing factor, if permissible. The patient bears the responsibility of proving, by substantial evidence, that there is a reasonable probability that the physician's negligence was the cause of the patient's injury. The expert medical witnesses who are employed to testify as to the duty or standard of care often also provide their opinions and assist with testimony on causation. It is important to recognize that allowing judges and juries such discretion to weigh the credibility and testimony of witnesses can sometimes leave them vulnerable to the persuasive arguments and testimony elicited, which may, in turn, serve to sway them emotionally or alter their judgment in some fashion. Unfortunately, although the courts remain mindful of this possibility and exercise their authority to limit it, it is often beyond the control of the system.

SUMMARY AND CONCLUSION

Since the dawn of human history, the inherent morbidity and mortality of human beings has made the diagnosis and treatment of human disease a high-risk profession. The ancient risk of physical retribution against the physician has been replaced by the modern risk of economic indemnity or compensation. Monetary settlements and awards are at times so huge that they may result in personal bankruptcy and professional disgrace.[2]

This article should not discourage health care providers from continuing their pursuits, but encourage them to enhance their knowledge about how and why medical malpractice has developed. It has been intended to facilitate the "prudent practitioner" with a more thorough understanding of some of the elements of negligence that have caused concerns in the past and will certainly create new concerns as science continues to drag the law in its wake.[29]

References

1. Black HC: Deluxe Black's Law Dictionary, ed. 6. St. Paul, West Publishing, 1990, pp 1032, 1489
2. Blackman NS, Bailey CP: Liability in Medical Practice: A Reference for Physicians. New York, Harwood Academic Publishers, 1990, pp 7–11, 39
3. Britton: Homicide. Edited and translated by FM Nichols. London, MacMillan, 1864, p 34
4. Brown v. Kendall, 60 Mass. (6 Cush.) 292, 1850
5. Bryant v. St. Paul Fire and Marine Ins. Co., 382 So. 2d. 234 (La. Ct. App. 1980)
6. Bufkin CE: The malpractice situation: Historical background and present status. Journal of the Mississippi State Medical Association 26:289–295, 1985
7. Carter v. Ries, 278 S.W.2d. 487, 489 (Mo 1964)
8. Court of King's Bench, 2 Bulst. 332; 1 Roll Rep. 124, 80 E.R. 1164 (1625)
9. Edwards F: Medical Malpractice: Solving the Crisis. New York, Henry Holt & Co, 1989, pp 1, 15
10. Epstein RA, Gregory CO, Kalven H Jr: Cases and Materials on Torts, ed 4. Boston, Little, Brown, 1984, pp 73–74, 120
11. Gadd CJ: Hammurabi and the End of His Dynasty, rev ed. (Ancient History, vol. 2, ch 5). New York, Cambridge University Press, 1965
12. Gordon VM: The origin, basis and nature of medical malpractice liability. Connecticut Medicine 35:73–77, 1970
13. Gray v. Davidson, 15 Wash 2d. 257, 130 P.2d. 341 (1942)
14. Hurley v. Edingfield, 156 Ind. 416, 59 N.E. 1058, 53 A.L.R. 135 (1901)
15. King JH Jr: The Law of Medical Malpractice in a Nutshell, ed 2. St. Paul, West Publishing, 1986, p 2
16. Krause v. Bridgeport Hospital, 169 Conn. 1, 362 A.2d. 802 (1975)
17. Legal Medicine: Legal Dynamics of Medical Encounters. The American College of Legal Medicine. St. Louis, CV Mosby, 1988, p 35
18. McNevins v. Lowe, 40 Ill. 209 (1866)
19. Noel v. King County, 48 Wash. App. 227, 738 P.2d. 692 (1987)
20. Park v. Chessin, 88 Misc. 2d. 222, 387 N.Y.S.2d. 204 (1976)
21. Pike v. Honsinger, 49 N.E. 716 (1898)
22. Prosser WL: Law of Torts. St. Paul, West Publishing, 1964, pp 28–29, 634
23. Reed EA: Understanding tort law: The historic basis of medical-legal liability. Journal of Legal Medicine 5:50–53, 1977
24. Shilkret v. Annapolis Emergency Hospital Association, 276 Md. 187, 349 A.2d. 245, 254 (1975)
25. Sloan IJ: Professional Malpractice. Legal Almanac, Second Series. Dobbs Ferry, Oceana Publications, 1992, pp. 33–34
26. Smith J: Medical Malpractice. Psychiatric Care. New York, McGraw-Hill, 1986, p 2

27. Tucker v. Gillette, 22 Ohio C.C. 664, aff'd 67 Ohio S.Ct. 106, 65 N.E. 865 (1902)
28. Wecht CH: Legal medicine: An historical review and future perspective. New York Law School Law Review 22:873–903, 1977
29. Werthmann B: Medical Malpractice Law: How Medicine Is Changing the Law. Lexington, MA, Lexington Books, 1984, p xi
30. Whitehurst v. Boehm, 41 N.C. App. 670, 255 S.E.2d. 204 (1976)
31. Y.B. 48th Ed. III f. 6, pl. 11 (1369)
32. 1874: The Malpraxis Epidemic. Medical Times 7:51–52, 1972

Address reprint requests to

Cece L. Wood, JD
Corporate Counsel
Oklahoma Health Care Corporation
3300 NW Expressway
Oklahoma City, OK 73112

CONSENT AND REFUSAL OF TREATMENT

David M. Siegel, MD, JD, FACEP

Patient consent issues present some of the most complicated legal concerns for physicians, particularly emergency physicians. Any physician who has practiced emergency medicine for a substantial length of time has dealt with various types of consent for treatment problems. Emergency medicine, by its very nature, regularly produces situations wherein the physician must decide how and when to proceed with treatment with patients who may not give or are unable to provide consent. Frequently, the emergency physician sees patients who, given the time, would be able to consent, but are unable to do so within emergency time-frame limitations. The competing concepts that the emergency physician often must deal with are the need for medical therapy (immediate or urgent) versus the right of the patient to determine what treatment he or she should receive.

BACKGROUND OF CONSENT

When first questioned about consent or "informed consent," most persons would believe they understand these concepts. However, when analyzing and investigating these ideals, one finds it extremely difficult to define precisely what the term "informed consent" means. Many legal authors agree on the difficulty of explaining the concept.[2] Most individuals would concur that medicine should strive for fully "informed consent" as the ultimate standard. However, if that term is undefinable for all situations, or we are unable to provide this type of consent in any given patient scenario, the area becomes very problematic. The two com-

From NES Inc., Tampa, Florida

EMERGENCY MEDICINE CLINICS OF NORTH AMERICA

peting interests that appear in any definition of consent are how, and to what degree, physicians explain proposed care and the patient's right of self-determination.

It may be helpful to briefly trace the legal history of how the concept of consent has evolved. Originally, in American jurisprudence, a patient could "consent" to treatment merely by passive actions or lack of objections.[8] "Informed consent" developed later in American case law. Justice Cordozzo stated that "every human being of adult years and sound mind has a right to determine what shall be done with his own body."[11] Cordozzo couched the ideal of consent in terms of a tort (intentional wrong). Failure to obtain "adequate" consent would leave the physician liable for potential assault (fear of an offensive touching) or battery (intentional touching of another person's body without authorization).

Only after many years was the concept of consent described in terms of negligence theory rather than tort theory. Initially, consent was described in terms of the physician relating to the patient what the average reasonable practitioner would divulge. Later, in 1972, one important case helped to change the standard of disclosure in consent cases to that of a patient-based norm. *Canterbury v. Spence* stated "the scope of the physician's communication to the patient . . . must be measured by the patient's need, and that need is the information material to the decision."[3] This latter norm is what most jurisdictions now recognize as the ideal. The American Medical Association has also endorsed this theory, stating "the patient's right of self-decision can be effectively exercised only if the patient possesses enough information to enable an intelligent choice."[5]

TYPES OF CONSENT

Given the difficulty of defining "informed consent," one should not be surprised that there can exist many different types of consent, especially in the field of emergency medicine.

"Express" and "implied" are two general terms often used to categorize consent. *Express consent* describes a scenario wherein the person (here, patient) is aware of the proposed care, agrees to such, and overtly, in some manner, demonstrates willingness to proceed. Typically, this overt agreement takes the form of an oral or written consent. *Implied consent* refers to the situation whereby consent of the patient is inferred by the actions of the patient, without specific agreement. This may occur by specific deeds of the patient, such as standing in line for an immunization and then holding an arm out for the injection.

Most emergency patients provide *general consent* to treatment upon arrival to the emergency department. Usually, this takes the form of signing the emergency record and agreeing to evaluation and treatment. This type of consent indicates the patient's willingness to be seen and treated in the emergency department. One could not call this consent truly "informed consent," because the patient may have no idea of what care will be recommended. Certainly, the average patient has not "consented" to any conceivable treatment in the department, especially without explanation of the therapy.

Specific consent in emergency medicine would more likely approach the concept of informed consent in emergency practice. Specific consent for a treatment or procedure would characteristically be sought by the treating physician when a more invasive, risky, or complicated plan is proposed. Under the ideal scenario, the physician would discuss the benefits and risks of the therapy or procedure to the patient. The patient would then consent to or refuse therapy based on the information imparted by the physician.

The physician who performs the procedure or therapy should seek the consent. A discussion, ideally witnessed, should take place with the patient, exploring the risks and benefits. This should be supported by written documentation of the consent in the emergency department record or on any standardized form used for this purpose in the emergency department (witnessed as well).

An important point should be emphasized concerning this type of consent. The physician or hospital is not automatically "protected" from liability merely because a standard form or note appears in the record. The key ingredient is that the necessary information is verbally communicated to the patient to make an informed decision and that the patient comprehends the information communicated.

A related problem arises when one attempts to decide when a specific consent is needed in addition to the customary general consent obtained. There is no absolute rule or guideline. It is essentially a clinical decision. The treating emergency physician should consider the particular therapy or procedure and the relative risks or benefits: Is the therapy invasive? Does the treatment have potential serious complications? Is the treatment controversial or experimental? Most emergency physicians would not seek specific consent in addition to the general consent obtained to do such things as drawing venous blood samples, performing an electrocardiogram, or starting a routine intravenous line. However, most practitioners probably would seek specific consent, time permitting, to insert a Swan-Ganz catheter or a chest tube or to perform a lumbar puncture. Procedures or therapies that lie somewhere between these extremes in terms of risks or benefits are the questionable areas that demand individual clinical judgment in a given situation. In borderline cases, it is probably best, time permitting, to err on the side of more involved consent than less involved consent. This approach leads to a greater likelihood of protecting patient rights in situations in which the patient will not suffer medically from the delay necessitated by receiving additional consent.

Emergency consent is a rather common form of consent obtained for acutely ill patients. This situation describes a scenario wherein the normal consent standards are ignored because of a need to rapidly treat a critically ill patient. The legal logic permitting one to negate normal consent proceedings in these emergency situations involves the legal assumption that the average, reasonable, competent patient would agree to standard treatment in an emergency situation if the patient were able to consent.

All emergency physicians have cared for patients who are critically ill (e.g., in cardiac arrest) and who must be treated before even attempting to obtain consent. There usually is no problem in these situations as far as consent issues are concerned because of their obvious emergent nature. A problem may arise in scenarios wherein it is unclear whether a particular patient requires immediate treatment or can wait until consent is obtained. There are no clear-cut guidelines. This question is judged by the clinician on an individual case-by-case basis. In this category, the physician is well advised to proceed with reasonable emergency treatment and be concerned with consent issues later. The physician would be advised that only clearly indicated standard care should be given, and the physician should attempt to receive follow-up consent with the patient or relatives, when possible.

The physician may be placed in the unenviable position of determining if a true emergency exists only by evaluating the patient immediately, without consent. If doubt exists as to the patient's medical condition, the physician should obviously proceed to assess the patient. Only by such evaluation can the patient's status be determined. In addition, emergency medicine physicians are obliged to perform a medical screening examination on every patient who presents to the emergency department (Consolidated Omnibus Budget Reconciliation Act, COBRA).[4] This further complicates the scenario, especially in view of the particular consent issues raised in COBRA (such as patient consent to transfer).

The concept of *deferred consent* has also been proposed, for use primarily in research protocols involving critically ill emergency patients.[1] This technique facilitates beginning treatment protocols on unresponsive patients or those who cannot otherwise give consent. Retrospective consent is obtained at a later date, usually from a family member. This type of consent has not yet received widespread use. It remains to be seen how commonplace this practice, designed to encourage research studies, will become in view of the obvious potential patient consent and rights problems.

Abbreviated informed consent has been suggested as the standard to apply for emergency medicine physicians in daily practice.[12] This concept requires that the physician obtain the closest thing possible to "full informed consent," given the clinical condition and time constraints that apply. One can envision this consent running the gamut from minimal or no initial consent all the way to detailed oral and written consent, depending on the patient situation.

PROBLEM AREAS IN CONSENT

In emergency medicine practice, certain patient situations typically present problems with regard to consent. One area of concern when obtaining consent is the incompetent emergency patient. The patient may be unable to legally give consent because of an acute medical condition, intoxication, or mental condition. In this situation the emergency physician obviously will not be able to obtain a legal consent from the patient.

In cases wherein immediate medical treatment is indicated, the emergency physician should not hesitate to provide care. This situation is but a variation of the emergency exception to the need for consent.

A more problematic scenario commonly occurs in most emergency departments. A patient arrives in the department who is not in need of immediate medical care, but who may need some urgent attention (laceration repair) or further observation and evaluation to assess any underlying serious pathology. The intoxicated patient presenting with mild to moderate head trauma is an excellent example. This patient cannot give true consent for treatment. However, the emergency physician has an obligation to attempt to evaluate the patient and treat if necessary, even without consent. One can strongly argue that the patient in this condition is not even able to leave or "sign out" if a reasonable suspicion of serious injury or illness exists. The fact that the patient "refuses" to give consent in an intoxicated state does not mean the patient would do the same when mentally competent. The medical evaluation of such patients is difficult enough; the legal issues of consent and "refusal" of consent only add to the complexity of the case.

The emergency physician has options in these difficult cases. One option would be to allow the intoxicated patient to leave the department, "refusing treatment," and hope that no serious pathology exists. This choice places great risks of medical harm on the patient and the potential for legal liability on the physician and hospital.

A more complicated choice of actions might be to hold and observe the patient for a period of time in the emergency department. Repeat assessments might help to uncover underlying pathology. Also, after a prolonged period in the department, the patient may be able to give consent or true refusal to treatment, once alcohol or other drugs are cleared from the system.

Another type of incompetent emergency patient is the patient who is chronically in a mentally deficient state. These patients typically have others appointed to give consent for treatment. Usually, the person giving consent would be a family member (spouse, parent, sibling). When such a patient arrives in the emergency department, it is wise for the physician to determine who is responsible to consent for treatment in place of the patient. Be aware of the local statutes that may have particular mechanisms to select the caretaker. Generally, any immediate life-saving measures should be undertaken without regard to consent.

Patients who are minors also present consent problems for the emergency physician. Minors are legally incapable of giving consent. Typically, a *minor* is defined as a person who has not yet reached the age of 18 years. Parents or guardians usually give consent for treatment in these situations.

There are exceptions to minors not being able to consent for therapy. Emancipated minors (minors living alone or no longer dependent on parents for financial support) or minors who have graduated from high school, have been pregnant or had a child, or who have served in the armed forces are able to give consent. These general descriptions apply in many states, but some states have different legal definitions, which must be appreciated by the treating physician.

In addition, minors, by statutes in most states, may still be able to give consent for treatment in certain situations. Many jurisdictions allow minors to consent to treatment for mental illness, substance abuse, pregnancy, or venereal disease. The theory is that the societal need for these conditions to be treated lowers the strict standards for the patient to be able to consent. Emergency physicians should be aware of their local criteria for treatment of these patients, because they can represent a significant portion of an emergency department volume.

Many emergency physicians would also suggest that lack of time makes getting "adequate" consent impossible in many patient scenarios. If the lack of time available to get consent in any particular case is related to the critical nature of the patient, then this situation merely represents a variant of the emergency consent exception. If the physician cannot obtain the appropriate level of consent because of not being able to dedicate enough effort to explaining treatment (whether because of patient volume overloads, documentation needs, or staffing problems), then the physician is on tenuous legal grounds. The law might retrospectively decide lack of consent was proper in a medical emergency, but it may not condone the lack of seeking and obtaining "proper" consent merely for reasons of time constraints.

REFUSAL OF TREATMENT

In the United States, an adult, competent patient is free to refuse medical treatment, even to the point of opting for death over life-saving therapy.[10] Such patients may then legitimately refuse treatment of any kind in the emergency department. These types of refusals for treatment represent an excercise of patient rights and autonomy that must be respected. The emergency physician's duty, in this situation, is to document the circumstances of the case—ensure the emergency record reflects that care was offered to the patient, the risks of not receiving treatment were explained fully, alternatives (if available) were explained, and the patient declined care. The record must reflect the competency of the patient. Refusal should, ideally, be witnessed. The written evidence of the refusal may be placed in the emergency record or appropriate forms developed for this purpose. All of these elements define the situation of "informed refusal."

However, the courts have recognized the overriding right of the state to treat certain infectious or contagious diseases to safeguard its citizens, even in the setting of a patient's refusal of treatment.[6]

Consent questions have frequently arisen with regard to religious beliefs of patients, which may lead to problems for acute or life-saving therapy. The law recognizes religious freedom and the right of the competent adult to refuse treatment. However, even recognizing these rights, courts have occasionally intervened to provide life-saving therapy in such cases.

One such case involved a young adult who was a victim of a motor vehicle accident. The patient was a Jehovah's Witness. He needed emergency surgery and blood transfusions to live. Because the patient was unconscious, he could not consent to treatment. His mother refused to give consent for therapy. The hospital sought legal authority to transfuse and treat the patient. The decision of the hospital was upheld on legal appeal.[7]

It may be problematic to decide if a court would order treatment for a patient, over the patient's objections, in any particular case. A case-by-case analysis is necessary. According to Post et al,[9] certain factors may be taken into consideration when attempting to look at individual cases:

1. Whether the treatment will restore the patient to a normal life
2. Whether the patient's refusal to consent is suicidal or rather a desire to avoid bodily intrusion
3. Competence of the patient
4. Age of the patient
5. Presence or absence of dependent children

It is noteworthy that in analyzing these situations, the courts have ruled that the quality of the living situation, as opposed to the physical health of the patient, will *not* be considered.

SUMMARY

Clearly, a multitude of potential consent problems can exist for the emergency physician. It is difficult at times to balance the concepts of patient autonomy with the desire to provide optimal medical care. Experienced emergency physicians should be able to individualize the type of consent needed in a particular situation, based on a clinical evaluation of the case. Some general principles apply, but no strict rules can guide the physician in every case. Documentation of consent and refusal of treatment are critical for quality of patient care and legal liability reasons. Principles of what is good, "appropriate" legal consent usually follow from good medical care and strict concern for the patient's health and rights.

References

1. Abramson, et al: Deferred consent: A new approach to resuscitation research on comatose patients. JAMA 255:2466–2471, 1986
2. Appelbaum, Lidz, Meisel: Informed Consent—Legal Theory and Clinical Practice. Oxford, Oxford University Press, 1987
3. Canterbury v. Spence, 464 F 2d 772 (DC Cir., 1972)

4. Consolidated Omnibus Budget Reconciliation Act of 1985, Public Law No. 99-272, Tit X, 100 Stat. 82, 222–237 (1986)
5. Current Opinions of Council on Ethical and Judicial Affairs of the American Medical Association, Sec. 8.08 (1989)
6. Jacobson v. Massachusetts, 197 US 11, 25 S Ct 357 (1905)
7. John F. Kennedy Memorial Hospital v. Heston, 58 NJ 576, 279 A 2d 670 (1971)
8. O'Brien v. Cunard Steamship Company Limited, 154 Mass 272, NE 266 (1891)
9. Post, Peters, Stahl, et al: The Law of Medical Practice in Pennsylvania and New Jersey. Lawyers Co-Operative Publ Co, 1984, pp 374–375
10. Prince v. Massachusetts, 321 US 158, 64 S Ct 438 (1944)
11. Schloendorff v. Society of New York Hospital, 211 NY, 105 NE 92, 93 (1914)
12. Siegel: Legal Issues in Emergency Cardiac Care. In Emergency Cardiac Care. Chicago, Mosby–YearBook, in press

Address reprint requests to

David M. Seigel, MD, JD, FACEP
1065 Normandy Terrace Road
Tampa, FL 33602

MINORS AND EMERGENCY MEDICINE

Daniel J. Sullivan, MD, JD, FACEP

The emergency physician must be aware of several critical medical-legal issues with regard to minors. This article addresses four key areas: consent; refusal of care; child abuse; and medical malpractice. Other medical-legal topics applicable to both children and adults are covered elsewhere in this volume. Gaining knowledge in these areas empowers the emergency physician and helps to avoid confusion, delays in management, and, most important, helps to keep our children safe.

CONSENT

Consent in an "Emergency"

The law always implies consent for treatment of a child in the event of an emergency. A child's life and health should never be compromised by a delay in an attempt to obtain consent. Parental consent is not needed; it is assumed.[11] When time permits, attempts can and should be made to obtain consent by telephone. The medical record should reflect all attempts including those that are unsuccessful.

This notion of implied consent in an emergency is an exception to the general consent requirement. Two criteria must be met before it applies. First, the patient must lack competence to make decisions independently. The minor child is deemed incompetent as a matter of law; thus, the first criterion is established.

Second, an emergency must exist. The definition of "emergency"

From the Department of Emergency Medicine, Ingalls Memorial Hospital, Harvey; and
    Cook County Hospital, Chicago, Illinois

has not been determined nor agreed upon by all courts. Clearly, an emergency exists when immediate treatment is necessary to preserve a patient's life or to prevent permanent disability.[13] Similarly, immediate treatment to alleviate pain and suffering has been deemed an emergency.[20] When both criteria are met, care may be provided.

Recently, many states have broadened the definition of "emergency." Most states have case law or legislation providing a basis for treatment without parental consent when "prompt" treatment is necessary. The harm resulting from an "emergency" may be severe or slight. The physician need not be certain as to the actual eventuality of harm, but only that harm or injury is a reasonable possibility.[14] Thus, the emergency physician has broad discretion in this area. Generally, if the delay for the purpose of obtaining consent could adversely affect the child, the physician should initiate evaluation and management under the emergency exception to the consent requirement.

Check the law in your state. This area of medicine and law has important practical application. A delay in wound closure, delay in initiating treatment for bronchitis, or delay in examination for abdominal pain would be adequate criteria for initiating treatment. The minor who presents to the emergency department should be triaged and registered as would any other patient. Do not delay the evaluation by waiting for parental consent.

Thus, the emergency physician should be comfortable providing treatment in "emergency" cases. The likelihood of successful litigation against the emergency physician for not obtaining parental consent is remote. In fact, delay in an emergency for the purpose of obtaining parental consent may expose the child to risk of harm and may be considered negligent.

Other Exceptions to the Consent Requirements

Today, states recognize that although the general rule of parental consent should apply in cases involving younger children, exceptions may exist for certain categories of older minors. Through case law and legislation, most states have adopted, in addition to the emergency exception to consent of the parent or guardian, one of several additional exceptions.

The Emancipated Minor

The law recognizes the "emancipated minor," who, although below statutory age, lives apart from his or her parents, is self-supporting, and is not subject to parental control.[2] Also, a minor is considered emancipated if married, pregnant, or in the armed forces. The concept has evolved today to include college students, even when parents are completely responsible for paying the bills, and unmarried minor mothers.[1]

The emergency physician may take the representation of the minor at face value, provided that representation seems reasonable and sincere, and the provider has no reason to believe otherwise. No specific documentation of the minor's emancipation is required. The physician should believe that the information presented by the minor is reasonable.[15]

Mature Minors

The mature minor is another exception to the general rules regarding competency of a minor to consent to medical care. No cases have been reported within the past 30 years in which a parent successfully sued a physician for care of an adolescent without the parent's knowledge. In these cases, courts apply what has come to be known as the "mature minor" rule.

The legal principle is that if a young person (age 15 or older) understands the nature and the risks of proposed treatment, the physician believes that the minor patient can make an informed decision, that the treatment is for the minor's benefit, and that the treatment does not involve serious risk, the adolescent may validly consent to receiving it.[4, 16] If these criteria are met, the likelihood of exposure to liability for not obtaining parental consent is remote.

These patients may not fit the criteria for the emancipated minor exception. They may not be independent of their parents, but they are cognitively able to understand the risks and benefits of treatment. The age range varies from state to state, between 14 and 18 years of age, and depends upon individual maturity and state statutory requirements.[18]

Minor Treatment Statutes

Through the 1960s and 1970s, many states statutorily authorized treatment of minors. These laws are known as minor treatment statutes. The statutes differ from state to state, some providing for the minor's right to consent to all medical care, others providing for treatment only for certain medical conditions.

The general statutes provide a specific age, usually 16 years, at which a minor may be considered completely independent for all health care purposes, and treatment may be given as if the minor is an adult. All other states without a general consent statute have enacted provisions giving a physician the specific right to treat any minor for venereal disease. Many states have statutes permitting treatment of any minor for drug or alcohol problems, pregnancy, and psychiatric conditions.[5] Most of the venereal disease and alcohol and drug statutes forbid informing parents.[14] In such cases, the parents should not receive a bill for treatment.

Specific Situations Involving Consent With Minors

The Minor Presents With a Single Parent

When parents are divorced, parental powers are divided, and the custodial parent and the noncustodial parent may each have parental rights and duties. The emergency physician should be aware of the parental status.

If the parents are divorced or separated, the relationship of the child to the presenting parent, relative, or friend should be determined. The custodial parent retains the duty to provide the child with medical care and the right to give consent for treatment. Permission need not be obtained from the noncustodial parent.

If the parent without legal custody presents with a minor for medical care, the physician can assume that the accompanying parent with possession of the minor has authority to consent to treatment. Technically, that parent may not retain the right or duty to provide for medical care, but practically, medical care should be provided as necessary, and the likelihood of resulting liability is remote.

In joint custody arrangements, both divorced parents have an equal responsibility for making decisions that affect the child. Again, the emergency physician may assume that the parent has the authority to consent to treatment. The divorced parent requesting treatment for a child should represent, and the emergency physician should document, that the parent has the legal authority to give consent for the medical treatment requested.

If the child needs immediate treatment, or if a delay for the purpose of obtaining consent will adversely affect the child, the physician should initiate care. In cases in which treatment is elective or the risk of treatment is substantial, and parental status is uncertain, it may be appropriate to request that the parent produce written evidence regarding custody. The emergency physician is not likely to encounter this situation very often.

The Minor Presents With an Adult Who Is Not a Parent

If an emergency exists, or if prompt treatment is necessary, provide evaluation and treatment as necessary; the emergency exception to consent applies. The emergency physician may also provide treatment if the nonparent adult has guardianship or legal custody with the right to provide for the child's medical needs.

The Minor Resides in a Foster Home

If a child resides in an institutional setting or foster home, the natural parents may or may not have the legal right to consent to medical care for the child. Again, the emergency exception applies for emergent or prompt treatment. Several state statutes provide that the individual or institution with custody may consent to treatment for medical care. If treatment is not governed by statute, parents may need to consent for high-risk and elective procedures.

Minors in Detention Facilities

Parental consent is unnecessary for the routine medical care of minors in detention facilities. Again, the emergency exception applies. Parental consent should be obtained for high-risk or elective procedures.

Minors in Boarding Schools, Camps, and Related Institutions

Parents retain the right to provide for the medical care of children in boarding schools, camps, and other institutions. Typically, parents must sign a blanket consent form whereby the camp or school officials stand *in loco parentis* (in place of the parents) and may consent for routine medical care. This blanket consent does not cover nonemergency high-risk or elective procedures.

Runaway Minors

Children who run away from home, but plan to return to the home, are not emancipated and may not consent for their own medical care. Once again, the emergency and other exceptions may be applicable. However, an exception to the consent requirements may apply. Otherwise efforts should be made to contact the parents. If the runaway requires routine medical care and will not identify the parents, providing care is usually acceptable and carries low risk in terms of the physician's exposure to liability. However, in an elective or high-risk situation, legal counsel should be consulted before providing treatment.

REFUSAL OF TREATMENT

The Child Refuses Care

Unless a minor is emancipated, is a "mature minor," or has one of the special conditions covered by the treatment statutes, he or she is not cognitively or legally capable of giving or refusing consent for medical treatment. The 8 year old refusing a laceration repair is typically not a problem. Both the parents and physician agree on treatment, and the child is overruled.

Problems typically arise when the adolescent refuses care. This often presents a significant dilemma for the emergency physician. For example, a mother presents to the emergency department with her 16-year-old daughter. Mother states that she believes the child has had sexual intercourse, and she asks the physician to perform a pelvic examination. The 16 year old adamantly refuses examination.

The case clearly presents an ethical and legal dilemma. Arguably, the refusal of care should be respected. The 16 year old is probably old enough to understand her actions. She certainly understands the nature and purpose of the examination. State law supports the minor when presenting for sexually transmitted diseases or pregnancy. States are increasingly recognizing the minor's right to privacy. The emergency physician should evaluate and document the patient's developmental state and maturity. The child's refusal should be accepted under either the mature minor exception or may be covered under one of the specific treatment statutes with regard to pregnancy or sexually transmitted diseases.

Although the prior scenario seems relatively straightforward and low risk, these cases can be complex and there are many gray areas. For example, a 15-year-old boy with leukemia refuses a blood transfusion, a 17-year-old girl with vaginal bleeding and lower abdominal pain decides to leave against medical advice prior to evaluation for ectopic pregnancy. These are difficult issues, and one should not proceed without assistance from hospital administration or hospital counsel.

Parent Refuses Medical Care for the Child

Generally, state and federal courts support parental control over the basic matters affecting their children. However, when parental actions have resulted in inadequate medical care, courts in the United States have stepped in to decide between parent wishes and physician concerns.[3] Under the doctrine of *parens patriae* (the state's paternalistic interest in children),[2] the state will not allow a child's health to be seriously jeopardized because of the parent's limitations or convictions.[7] Parents do not have the authority to forbid saving their child's life. Courts invariably rule in favor of a physician who claims that a parent is denying standard medical care to a child.[7]

Under the doctrine of *parens patriae*, the state represents the best interests of the child. The state also looks to the child abuse and neglect statutes, which provide for protective custody when the child has not received medically indicated treatment.

Once again, the emergency physician is empowered by understanding the law. If parents withhold consent, and there is a life threat, the emergency physician should take temporary protective custody based on child neglect. It helps to explain to the parents that this is a medical obligation under the law, and you will immediately report to the hospital administrator, hospital attorney, and the local child protection agency. The parents will typically stand down and allow you to proceed with your mission. Even in situations in which the minor's life may not be threatened but is severely impaired, the courts usually will order medical treatment over the parents' objections.

If there is no life threat, and no potential for serious impairment, the parents' refusal should be respected. The refusal should be "informed" and well documented. In this context, "informed" means that one or both parents have a normal mental status, understand the risks of refusal, have had an opportunity to ask questions, and have decided to leave against your advice.

Remember that you are protected from civil and criminal liability under the child abuse and neglect statutes. You may be hesitant to take custody, but it should not be for fear of liability.

Parental Refusal Based on Claims of Religious Freedom

The First Amendment issue of religious freedom does not change the analysis. The typical example is the 14-year-old boy, victim of a car accident and with a lacerated spleen. He is in shock and needs blood. The emergency physician has typed and crossed the blood, and has contacted the surgeon to go to the operating room. The parents intercede and refuse to consent to the blood administration.

The courts have held that denying medical care to a child is not within the parents' First Amendment right of freedom of religion: "The right to practice religion freely does not include the liberty to expose . . . a child . . . to ill health or death. Parents may be free to become martyrs themselves. But it does not follow that they are free . . . to make martyrs of their children."[19]

The emergency physician should take temporary protective custody, provide care in such cases, and report to the appropriate individuals and agencies.

In more difficult cases, such as the management of the terminally ill, there are many ethical and legal uncertainties. In the previous car accident case, blood administration is clearly in the "best interest" of the child. But in other cases, such as a minor with leukemia and life-threatening anemia, the "best interest" analysis is far more difficult. Here the emergency physician must discuss the case with the family physician and may need to temporize until reasoned judgment from a larger group of decision makers can be brought to bear.

THE ABUSED OR NEGLECTED CHILD

Definitions

"Child abuse and neglect" is medically defined as nonaccidental injury to a minor child without adequate explanation and failure to provide for the needs of the child (medical, environmental, nutritional, educational, and emotional).

Legal definitions vary according to individual state laws.[6] Note the following legal definitions, which are typical of state laws throughout the country.

An "abused child" is any "unemancipated person under 18 years of age whose parent or immediate family member or any person who is responsible for the child's welfare, who resides in the same home as the child, or who is a paramour of the child's parent does one or more of the following:

1. Inflicts, causes to be inflicted, or allows to be inflicted upon the child physical injury, by other than accidental means, which causes death, disfigurement, impairment of physical or emotional health, or loss or impairment of any bodily function.

2. Creates a substantial risk of physical injury to the child by other than accidental means which would be likely to cause death [or] disfigurement. . . .
3. Commits or allows to be committed any sex offense against the child, as such sex offenses are defined in the Criminal Code. . . .
4. Commits or allows to be committed an act or acts of torture upon the child.
5. Inflicts excessive corporal punishment.[8]"

Equally important for the emergency physician is the state definition of the "neglected child":

A "neglected child" means any person "under 18 years of age whose parent or other person responsible for the child's welfare:

1. Withholds or denies nourishment or medically indicated treatment including food or care denied solely on the basis of the present or anticipated mental or physical impairment as determined by a physician acting alone or in consultation with other physicians.
2. Otherwise does not provide the proper or necessary support, legally required education, or medical or other remedial care recognized by law as necessary for a child's well-being, including adequate food, clothing, and shelter.[8]"

A practical definition that discriminates corporal punishment from abuse is that if the injury requires medical attention, it is child abuse.

Reporting Child Abuse

Emergency physicians must report child abuse, as must hospital administrators, nurses, emergency medical technicians, and social workers. Most reporting statutes require physicians to report to a state agency any *suspicion* of child abuse or neglect. The requirement to report is not discretionary.

The emergency physician may be exposed to civil liability for failure to report. Several states now have held physicians in malpractice for subsequent reinjury of a child abuse victim after physician failure to diagnose the syndrome in a prior examination and failure to initiate state intervention.[12, 17]

Immunity from Liability in Connection With Reporting

Emergency physicians have been sued for reporting child abuse and neglect. The cases range from allegations of defamation[10] to civil rights actions.[21] Most state laws provide physicians with complete immunity from civil and criminal liability. Some provide immunity whether the report is made in good or bad faith. Nothing can prevent the filing of a lawsuit, but the physician should prevail on a motion to dismiss.

Temporary Protective Custody

The key to the emergency department management of a child abuse case is understanding the law and taking swift and decisive action. Emergency physicians are empowered by the child abuse laws. In most states, a physician treating a child may take or retain temporary protective custody of the child without consent of the person responsible for the child's welfare under the following circumstances:

"1. The physician has reason to believe that the circumstances and conditions of the child are such that continuing in the child's place of residence or in the care and custody of the person responsible for his or her welfare, presents an imminent danger to the child's life or health; and
2. There is no time to apply for a court order under the state law.[9]"

"Temporary protective custody" is defined to mean custody within a hospital or other medical facility or a place designated for such custody by the state child protection agency, subject to review by a court. After taking protective custody, the physician must immediately make every reasonable effort to notify the person responsible for the child's welfare and must immediately notify the child protection agency. Typically, the physician then contacts the administrator in charge at the hospital, who is then responsible for the further care of the child in the hospital.

MEDICAL MALPRACTICE

The essential elements and other important aspects of medical malpractice are addressed elsewhere in this volume. Malpractice cases involving minors are different in just a few important respects, which will be addressed here.

The statute of limitations in malpractice cases involving minors is an extremely important issue. Every state has a statute of limitations for malpractice cases. Generally, a statute of limitations declares that no suit shall be maintained unless brought within a specified period of time after the patient's injury becomes apparent. For adults this period is usually 2 or 3 years.

Consider this hypothetic example. Dr. Smith failed to immobilize a C-spine dislocation on January 4, 1990, in Chicago. The patient was taken to the radiology department, had flexion and extension radiographic views, and was diagnosed as having quadriplegia. At the moment the neurologic injury occurred, the patient accrued the right to sue Dr. Smith. Illinois has a 2-year statute of limitations. Therefore, the patient has until midnight January 3, 1992, to file a claim against Dr. Smith. After that he has lost his right to sue.

In cases involving a minor, in several states, the statute of limitations is extended through the age of majority plus 2 or 3 years. For example, in Alaska, if our C-spine patient was 10 years old at the time of the injury, the statute of limitations would not expire until the child was 20 years old (age of majority plus 2 years). More than half the states use the age of majority plus 2 or 3 years. Other states use some age less than majority, and yet others use the same statute of limitations for both minors and adults. Consider the possibility that meningitis may be missed when a child is 1 month of age, and the lawsuit could be filed more than 22 years later.

The other important issue is that of damages in the malpractice suit involving a minor. Damage awards can be particularly large in such cases. The damage award typically addresses compensation of the parents for their added costs and foregone parental income associated with the extra care that a negligently injured child may require. Second, if the child sustains permanent injuries, he or she can usually recover whatever additional expenses may be associated with the injuries for the rest of his or her life, whether the damages are simply a small amount of foregone income or permanent institutionalization.

CONCLUSION

Understanding the law as it applies to minors is critical in the practice of emergency medicine. Too many hours are spent wondering if a child should receive treatment because the parent cannot be reached on the phone, and how to provide safety for the child abuse victim. A working knowledge of the information presented here will empower the physician allowing more rapid management decisions.

Please use care in applying these principles. There are 50 separate jurisdictions with different sets of laws and court cases. Generalizations can be made, but it is wise to review the law in your own jurisdiction and when time permits to request assistance from hospital administration and legal counsel.

References

1. Bach v. Long Island Jewish Hospital, 267 NYS2d 289 (NY 1966)
2. Black's Law Dictionary, ed 5. St. Paul, West Publishing, 1983
3. Bross DC: Medical care neglect. Child Abuse and Neglect 6:375–381, 1982
4. Carter v. Cangello, 164 Cal Rptr 361 (Cal 1980)
5. Cohn R: Minors' right to consent to medical care. Medical Trial Tech Q 31:286, 1985
6. Helfer RG, Kempe CH (eds): The Battered Child, ed 3. Chicago, University of Chicago Press, 1980
7. Holder AR: Parents, courts, and refusal of treatment. J Pediatr 103:515–521, 1983
8. Ill. Rev. Stat. ch. 23 ¶ 2053 (1985)
9. Ill. Rev. Stat. ch 23 ¶ 2055(a) (1985)
10. Johnfroe v. Children's Hospital, 537 S.2d 383 Louisiana Ct. of Appeals
11. Keeton W: Prosser and Keeton on the Law of Torts §§18 & 32 (5th ed 1984)
12. Landeros v. Flood, California Reporter, 2nd Series, vol 131, p 69, 1976
13. Luka v. Lowrie 171 Mich 122, 136 NW 1106 (1912)
14. Morrissey J, Hoffman A, Thorpe J: Consent and Confidentiality in the Health Care of Children and Adolescents: A Legal Guide. New York, Macmillan, The Free Press, 1986, pp 1–147

15. Morrison v. State, 252 SW2d 97, 103 (Mo 1952)
16. Munson CF: Toward a standard of informed consent by the adolescent in medical treatment decisions. Dickinson Law Rev 8:431, 1981
17. O'Keefe v. Osorio Medical Center Ltd. (Cook County Cir Ct July 26, 1984) No 79 L 14984
18. Rozofsky F: Consent to treatment: A Practical Guide, ed 2. Boston, Little, Brown, 1990, pp 255–351
19. State v. Perricone, New Jersey Reporter, vol 37, p 463, Atlantic Reporter, 2nd Series, vol 181, p 751, 1962
20. Sullivan v. Montgomery 119 So 2d 649 (La 1960)
21. Thomas v. Chadwick, No D010223 Cal. Ct of Appeals, 4th App. Dist

Address reprint requests to

Daniel J. Sullivan, MD, JD, FACEP
210 St. Michaels Court
Oak Brook, IL 60521

LEGAL CONSIDERATIONS IN PREHOSPITAL CARE

R. Jack Ayres, Jr, JD, REMT-P

As organized emergency medical services (EMS) in the United States enter their third decade of existence, new and evolving legal issues in prehospital health care reflect the unprecedented and complex changes observed in American economic, social, and political institutions.

MEDICAL CONTROL

The term "medical control" has historically held different meanings to different commentators.[8, 25, 30, 98] Although the American College of Emergency Physicians (ACEP) and the National Association of EMS Physicians (NAEMSP) generally agree that EMS should be under the direction and control of a qualified physician,[4, 6, 75] divergent views remain as to the particular roles and responsibilities of the medical director. Despite these differences, leading authors seem to have reached a consensus that, at a minimum, "medical control" should embrace each of the following subject areas.

First, the medical director must have a clearly defined legal and medical relationship to the EMS system as a whole, with specifically articulated medical and legal authority to carry out the responsibilities of the position. In the United States today there are a variety of EMS systems and models including private and public, "third service" and fire department, and paid and volunteer.[74] Depending upon the organization of the EMS system in which the medical director operates, the director may receive his or her medical and legal authority to act from a governing board, from company management, or from state or local

From the University of Texas Southwestern Medical Center at Dallas, Dallas, Texas government, or the individual may act purely as a private consultant. It is therefore advisable that any such relationship be reduced to writing[1] so that all parties mutually understand their respective duties and responsibilities, before one undertakes the position of medical director. The contract should also include any specific conditions of or limitations upon the medical director's authority. Such foresight will prove useful if controversy arises as to such matters in the actual medical management of an EMS system. A medical director should not assume responsibility for EMS providers if lacking proper authority over them.

A second legal concern in medical control is the relationship of prehospital health care providers to the system's medical director. Ideally, all the EMS providers in a given geographic jurisdiction would report to a single medical director, who would have centralized authority for training, continuing education, medical management, and quality assurance of the entire EMS system. Unfortunately, this goal has proved difficult to achieve within the American political structure. Legally, almost every state requires that any person who undertakes to invasively treat an illness or condition of the human body must be licensed to practice medicine. Because of this legal restriction, paramedics or advanced emergency medical technicians who provide invasive modalities of therapy can best be described as "physician surrogates" or "physician extenders."[4] In other words, these prehospital health care providers have no independent authority to provide invasive care except through and by means of their medical control physician's scope of licensure. By comparison, basic emergency medicine technicians, first responders, or first-aid practitioners frequently provide emergency medical treatment without direct physician supervision or involvement. Not infrequently, such basic-level providers are members of volunteer fire departments or rescue squads, which are essentially autonomous and not subject to direct medical control. As *de facto* EMS organizations continue to proliferate without medical control, effective EMS management and quality assurance become increasingly problematic and liability risks are compounded.

Another basic legal consideration in medical control is the nature of medical control itself. The National Association of EMS Physicians, in its *EMS Medical Directors' Handbook,* has developed an excellent analytic framework by which to evaluate and describe medical control.[75] *Prospective medical control* includes administration, training, protocol development, and system design and is categorized as "indirect" medical control.[75] *Immediate medical control* includes clinical and administrative support, patient care, concurrent review, and radio direction. These activities are categorized as "direct" medical control.[75] *Retrospective medical control* includes administrative activities such as run sheet review, quality control, and risk management. Such activities are also referred to as "indirect" medical control.[5] The use of such standardized terms should greatly facilitate professional communication on these subjects.

Regardless of the terms or categories used, there is undoubtedly significant risk of liability to the medical control physician. In general, such liability may be described as either vicarious, encompassing the medical control physician's liability for the acts or conduct of others, or direct, involving the physician's own actions. Because there is little case law in this area, it is difficult to predict with certainty the nature or ultimate outcome of such claims. Ordinarily, truly vicarious liability is already limited to formal legal relationships such as principal-agent and employer-employee. Rarely is the field EMS provider the true agent or employee of the medical control physician. However, a more plausible vicarious liability theory might involve the use of the legal doctrine of "borrowed servant." Under this doctrine, a defendant may become vicariously liable for the acts of a third person even though that person was not originally the defendant's agent or employee, if the defendant had the right or authority to control and direct the activities of the third party and in fact did so, even for a temporary period of time. It is not difficult to envision a scenario in which the plaintiff could claim that the field EMS provider was or became the "borrowed servant" of the medical control physician. In such a case, the medical control physician may be vicariously liable for the negligence of the EMS provider. In addition, the medical director may also have direct liability for negligence in on-line or direct medical control and perhaps for institutional or administrative negligence in the operation of the EMS system. A thorough exposition of these interesting issues is beyond the scope of this presentation. However, an excellent, more detailed discussion of this subject is available for those with a greater interest.[83]

A final and very important legal consideration in medical control is the availability of quality assurance and programs of risk management and claims prevention in prehospital health care. Despite nationwide calls for comprehensive quality assurance in EMS by both the ACEP and NAEMSP,[2, 76] such efforts have not been demonstrably effective. Governmental regulatory activity in EMS has proved somewhat haphazard and subjective in application, whereas private quality assurance has varied dramatically in actual effectiveness, depending upon the staff assistance available to the medical director and the director's personal willingness to engage in such frequently unpleasant activity. Other than the general state and local administrative regulations governing EMS providers, the only comprehensive safeguards designed to be effective in protecting the public from inappropriate conduct by EMS providers are only now being developed by the ACEP and NAEMSP.

This problem has been compounded both by the individual and combined effect of legislation relating to state and local governmental immunity and by so-called "Good Samaritan" legislation. In general, the state and its political subdivisions of government including the cites and counties are immune from suit or liability for claims of negligence arising out of their governmental activities. An exception may exist when such immunity has been waived by state law or the parties are otherwise subject to liability for such conduct under federal law. Many states have restricted the liability of state and local government and governmental employees under state law to claims arising out of the negligent use or operation of motor vehicles by the government or negligent use, maintenance, or conditions of the government's real or personal property.

"Good Samaritan" legislation provides additional broad immunity to any person who renders emergency care in good faith (sometimes even without distinction as to paid or volunteer status), unless the provider's actions constitute intentional misconduct or "willful" neglect. The combined effect of these statutes is such as to provide almost complete immunity from responsibility or liability for their actions to a number of EMS providers.[49] As will be discussed later in this article, such statutes in effect operate only to penalize the innocent citizen who may be the victim of incompetent prehospital medical care.

Although the overwhelming majority of EMS providers are competent and provide safe and effective care for their patients, there exists throughout the country a small minority of truly incompetent and dangerous EMS providers who have thus far escaped definitive administrative regulation, who have no meaningful medical control, and who, by virtue of immunity statutes, are effectively insulated from the corrective processes of the civil law. As the first priority of government must be to protect its citizens' lives and property, so the first priority of medical control and public policy involving EMS should be to identify and eliminate those individuals who function as EMS providers but lack the basic knowledge, skills, or training or even the willingness to become or remain truly competent. Absent internal reform, the only solution for this situation may be additional governmental regulation or changes in legislation to allow its correction through the courts, or both.

CONSENT

Several years ago, what some have subsequently referred to as the "Parkland Protocol" was developed to assist prehospital providers in determining the existence of required patient consent. In general, this system requires the provider to first determine if the patient is an adult or a child under applicable state law.[13, 14] As a second step, the provider then attempts to confirm the existence of patient consent at one of three levels: voluntary consent, involuntary consent, or implied consent. This methodology was subsequently adopted by the Department of Transportation in its curriculum and textbooks[97] and is now in use throughout the United States. Nonetheless, difficulties in prehospital determination of consent continue.

One recurring problem in consent involves the prehospital patient who presents with an altered sensorium and a life-threatening disease or injury that has an excellent prognosis with treatment, but who nonetheless refuses to consent to evaluation, treatment, or transportation to the hospital. Such patients may or may not have demonstrable mental illness in the form of thought or affective disorders, frequently are intoxicated as the result of recreational drug or alcohol use, and may or may not have corroborating "hard" signs of impending medical catastrophe. Some of these patients may even admit that their actions represent an overt attempted suicide or may admit to suicidal ideation. Based on the idiosyncrasies of the medical director, his or her legal training, and the vicissitudes of the local legal and political climate, EMS systems have responded to this challenge in different ways. Some systems routinely and openly forcibly transport and sometimes treat such patients against their will with or without law enforcement assistance. Although this practice has been repeatedly warned against by both physicians and EMS legal counsel, it continues unabated.[25, 92] At present, only Florida and California specifically provide the emergency physician with legal authority to order the involuntary treatment and transportation of patients in such circumstances.

A second approach to such patients is the administration of a simple mental status examination in the field. If alert and oriented as to time, place, and person, the patient is presumptively deemed to be competent to refuse treatment. In systems using this approach, a patient's refusal is then sometimes copiously documented by the EMS providers, and no further action is taken regardless of the gravity of the prognosis or other circumstances. Undoubtedly, this approach has resulted in an unacceptably high level of mortality and morbidity, even if one acknowledges the patient's right to make an incorrect or foolish medical judgment.

One system in the United States, Parkland Memorial Hospital in Dallas, uses 24-hour-a-day on-call medically trained legal counsel to interface with medical control and EMS providers to obtain court orders for treatment in such cases. Parkland estimates more than 100 "saves" of patients who would, in reasonable medical probability, otherwise have expired but for such intervention.[9] Some have argued against this approach as being too cumbersome and expensive, requiring too much contact with or dependence upon lawyers or judges, and involving staffing or training requirements that are unrealistic.

Another area of controversy in prehospital consent is the care and treatment of the terminally ill patient. Many such patients are now discharged home to die in an essentially informal hospice format.[15] Sometimes the attending physician has given private "do not resuscitate" (DNR) instructions to nursing or personal care personnel. Still other patients diagnosed with terminal illness have executed directives to physicians ("living wills") or durable powers of attorney that designate third persons to make health care treatment decisions for them should they become incompetent or otherwise incapable of making informed decisions. Although much has been written on these subjects,[3, 15, 79, 86] no clear consensus or standard of care has emerged for prehospital application. The problem in such cases centers around finding an appropriate method of honoring a patient's wishes, consistent with maintaining the integrity of the EMS system itself. Some systems have adopted protocols whereby any such documents or orders must be evaluated prior to any health care emergency by legal counsel for the EMS system as well as by the medical director. If approved, these patients are then placed on DNR status by the medical director, subject to rigid security measures. Other systems allow or encourage EMS providers to make individual medical or ethical decisions to provide or withhold resuscitation on essentially an ad hoc basis in the field with or without medical control. This approach would appear to violate current ACEP policies.[7] Others have argued that DNR orders, living wills, or durable powers of attorney should be routinely honored whether or not they have been previously evaluated for medical and legal sufficiency.[54]

Several states are in the process of attempting to address these issues by legislation specifically related to prehospital health care providers. The American Heart Association is also now in the process of reviewing its Advance Cardiac Life Support guidelines with regard to these subjects. Until protective legislation is securely in place and medical consensus is reached, it appears prudent to decline to honor prehospital DNR orders, living wills, or durable powers of attorney until their legal and medical viability has been previously determined by the medical director or his or her designate.

COMMUNICATIONS

Modern EMS communication now encompasses far more than radio or telephone communication by and between fire, police, EMS units, and medical control. It also involves communication by individuals requesting EMS assistance ("systems access") and other communication functions including public education, disaster networking, and the maintenance and transmission of medical records for hospital personnel and administrative records for EMS administration. Two such issues will be explored.

One of the primary concerns in medical/legal evaluation of EMS communications is safe and immediate system access for the public. In other words, "an EMS communications system must provide a mechanism by which any citizen with an urgent medical need can easily and reliably access emergency providers."[12] Throughout the United States, more and more communities have adopted the 911 universal access system for emergency communications. Now, more than ever, the public perceives access to appropriate emergency services as a *right* that governmental and EMS agencies have a duty to provide and protect. This belief is underscored by the fact that in many localities, particularly large urban areas, government has by state law or local ordinance prohibited emergency ambulance operations within its political subdivisions except as specifically authorized by the city or locality in which the provider operates. In such cases, the public has no other access to emergency assistance except through the EMS system. Not surprisingly, a considerable volume of litigation has occurred because of the actual or perceived abuses of the public's right to access emergency assistance. Regrettably, these suits include examples of serious communications errors in which an appropriate call for emergency assistance was ignored, overlooked, or inappropriately handled. Representative examples are collected in the discussion of civil rights cases that follow.

Legal issues involving emergency medical dispatch, although interrelated with issues of system access, also represent a discrete and independent subject area. "Emergency medical dispatching" as we know it today has been pioneered in substantial part by the creative genius of Dr. Jeff Clawson. Dr. Clawson has devised an elaborate and medically validated system of gathering and providing emergency medical information that includes overall medical control for dispatch personnel as to training, administration, management, and quality assurance. All of Dr. Clawson's protocols contain at least three components that must be rigidly adhered to in emergency medical dispatching: (1) a set of key questions that are asked the caller; (2) medically validated pre-arrival instructions; and (3) a dispatch priority system that includes determinant and recommended response code.[29]

Regrettably, some have confused the portion of Dr. Clawson's emergency medical dispatch system that includes call or dispatch prioritization with "call screening," a not necessarily medically controlled technique that has been used by some large municipalities. A significant distinction between the two approaches is that in "call screening," the dispatcher is given the option of not sending any response to a call for assistance, whereas in priority dispatching, the dispatcher has no such option. In practice, "call screening" has frequently been associated with a lack of viable medical control, as well as insufficient or incomplete training of dispatch personnel, and it has been used primarily as a method of cost savings to lessen inappropriate use of emergency equipment and personnel. Call screening carries with it the very real risk that a true emergency call will be inappropriately "screened," as ultimately occurred in a notorious case in Dallas in 1984. Such tragedies can result in catastrophic liability for the provider and the loss of credibility for the entire EMS system.

Dr. Clawson's emergency medical dispatch concept, including priority dispatching, is a medically designed and medically controlled system that is geared to have an effective impact on the crucial time interval between the initial request for assistance and the time that such assistance actually arrives. Some argue that it is not appropriate or cost-effective to have the full emergency medical dispatch system proposed by Dr. Clawson. Others argue that the standard of care in the United States may now require medically competent pre-arrival instructions as well as a rationally designed system to prioritize the needs of the public.[30]

ISSUES OF DESTINATION CHOICE, DIVERSION, AND TRANSFER

The prehospital patient's right or ability to choose his or her own treatment destination is a recurring medical and legal problem. Because EMS personnel, their medical director, and the medical control physician are finally responsible for the patient's care, treatment, and resulting welfare during the process of transportation, the ultimate decision as to the patient's destination must be the responsibility of the medical director or the physician who is providing direct medical control for EMS personnel, or both.

Many factors should be considered in formulating a destination policy. One of the foremost is the medical needs of the patient. As an example, it is entirely appropriate to require that all patients with certain categories of trauma be transported only to a certified trauma center, or that patients with highly specialized medical needs, such as neonates, be transported only to hospitals with neonatal intensive care units.

A second consideration in the formulation of such policies must be the resources of the EMS system itself, as well as the resources of the hospital(s) within the EMS system. In a basic life-support system, it may be necessary to transport all persons with unstable vital signs to the nearest fully staffed emergency department before transporting them elsewhere. Providers must be mindful that once the patient arrives at the emergency department of a receiving hospital, further transportation of the patient within the EMS system will probably be considered a "transfer" under both state and federal law, thereby requiring compliance with all such laws from the time of arrival at the initial hospital.

Another relevant consideration in such decisions is the wishes of the members of the local medical and hospital community regarding destinations and transfer of emergency patients. Such consideration should include sound concern for continuity of care issues implicit in an ongoing physician-patient or physician-hospital relationship. The destination protocol should appropriately address the rights and wishes of the patient and the patient's family. The medical director or the medical control physician, or both, should assume full responsibility with the patient, the patient's family, or the patient's physician for any transportation decision made in accordance with the protocol of the EMS system, as opposed to allowing the responsibility for such decisions to fall upon the EMS providers themselves.

Finally, destination protocols should be flexible in their application. For example, the patient's request to be transported a significant distance to a hospital where his or her physician practices perhaps can be honored if the system is not in an overload mode. In an overload situation, the medical control physician must balance due regard for the individual patient's wishes with the resources of the EMS system. Thus, the patient may be taken to the nearest appropriate hospital, where the patient can arrange a transfer to the hospital of his or her choice at a later time. Flexibility also involves matters of purely medical discretion relating to individual considerations of the severity of the patient's injury or illness, prognosis, and the availability of resources. If all other factors are equal, of course, the patient should be transported to the facility of his or her choice consistent with available EMS resources.[87]

As a consequence of decreasing economic resources, the unavailability of health insurance, and increasing violence, more and more emergency departments of major hospitals throughout the United States have either closed entirely or regularly adopt an administrative "diversion" protocol whereby the hospital during the period of "diversion" does not accept certain patients, because the receiving hospital is at or has exceeded its resource capability to care for such patients. Although diversion is technically distinct from the issue of patient transfer, there has been overlap in regulation of both subjects at both the state and federal levels. A very recent decision illustrates this concern. In *Johnson v. University of Chicago Hospitals*, 1992 W.L. 259404 (7th Cir., Ill.), the University of Chicago Hospital provided medical control for a paramedic unit that responded to a call involving an infant in full cardiac arrest. As the nurse serving as telemetry operator directed the paramedics as to the medical services to be provided, the paramedics advised her that they were only five blocks from the University of Chicago Hospital. However, it was on "diversion" status. The nurse, under authority of the medical director, directed the child to be taken instead to St. Bernard's Hospital, which had no pediatric intensive care unit. The child was treated in the emergency room, then transferred to Cook County Hospital, where the infant expired. Initially, the Court of Appeals held that when the paramedics under the medical control of the University of Chicago Hospital began to care for the patient, the patient had been "received" by the University of Chicago Hospital regardless of her physical presence there and, accordingly, any decision to transport the patient elsewhere was a "transfer" within the meaning of federal law. Although this decision was subsequently withdrawn on rehearing, it illustrates the potential relationship between diversion and transfer.

The issue of interhospital transfers has gained increasing political interest and also has generated a considerable volume of litigation in recent years. Motivated by numerous reports of "patient dumping" and "reverse dumping" in August 1986, Congress enacted Public Law 99-272, "The Emergency Medical Treatment and Active Labor Act," as a part of the Consolidated Omnibus Budget Reconciliation Act (COBRA).[108] As its acronym suggests, COBRA has mandated major changes in the legal responsibilities of emergency departments and emergency physicians throughout the country. In general, the statute requires any hospital with an emergency department that participates in the Medicare program to examine the patient without delay regardless of the patient's ability to pay, and if a medical emergency exists to render all necessary medical care to stabilize the patient. The act provides that a patient shall not be transferred without the patient's consent after full disclosure of the patient's rights, and in no case until the patient is stabilized, unless a physician certifies in writing that the risk of transfer is less than the risk of not transferring the patient. The transferring facility must confirm in advance the willingness of the receiving facility to accept the patient, must provide appropriate staffing and equipment to accomplish the transfer, and must provide certain medical records and laboratory studies that shall accompany the patient.

COBRA applies to all patients who come into the emergency department, whether or not such patients are eligible for Medicare benefits, prohibits any discrimination among patients based on ability to pay or reimbursement considerations, and contains so-called "whistle blower" protection for any physician, qualified medical person, or the hospital employee who reports a violation.[115, 116]

COBRA's enforcement mechanism is multifaceted and may be severe in application. Civil monetary penalties may be imposed up to $50,000 for each violation occurring on or after December 22, 1987.[109] Civil monetary penalties originally could be imposed only if there was a finding that the hospital or physician had "knowingly" violated a requirement under the act. In 1990, the act was amended to allow the imposition of such a penalty for even *negligent* violations.[110] In addition, any hospital that fails to meet the requirements of COBRA is subject to suspension or termination of its Medicare provider agreement.[107] The secretary may bar a physician from participating in the Medicare program for up to 5 years if the physician violates COBRA's provisions.[112] Civil monetary penalties may be imposed against both the hospital and the physician if indicated.

In addition, COBRA creates and authorizes private enforcement actions by any individual who suffers personal harm as a direct result of a hospital's violation of the requirements. COBRA allows suit in federal court to recover damages available under the law of the state in which the hospital is located.[113] Likewise, any medical facility or hospital that suffers financial loss as a result of another hospital's violation of COBRA may also sue for damages and equitable relief.[114] Many COBRA claims have been litigated.* Although a detailed discussion of the holdings of each of these cases is beyond the scope of this presentation, case law has helped to shape the application of the act, including questions of applicability to professional negligence claims, preemption of state law remedies and limitations, recoverability of certain types of damage, and other related matters. For example, a US District Court in Virginia recently held that state malpractice damage limitations upon the liability of charitable hospitals do not apply to federal COBRA patient-dumping claims.[41, 71] Other cases have been decided affirming the imposition of substantial civil monetary penalties against physicians for violation of the provisions of COBRA.[22] Many excellent references assist in analysis of the medical and legal implications of COBRA.[53, 57, 60, 91]

A number of states also have comprehensive "antidumping" statutes and administrative regulations that can also be enforced by state regulatory agencies or private individuals or both.[10, 78, 94] In addition, the common law of many states, even without federal or state statutory or administrative authority, recognized tort claims typically in negligence both against hospitals and physicians for inappropriate patient transfer.[24, 48, 64]

LIABILITY ISSUES

Potential liability for negligence claims by patients continues to be one of the primary concerns of EMS providers in the United States. Experience over the last 25 years reveals several common attributes of such claims.

---

* Refs. 18–21, 32, 33, 37–40, 42, 50, 55, 59, 61, 63, 65, 69, 71, 73, 88–90, 95, 96, 99, 102

First, claims are frequently associated with inappropriate and high-risk activity by EMS providers themselves. For example, the greatest single medical and legal risk in EMS systems today is the failure or refusal to treat or transport a patient who desires such treatment and transportation. In a very recent article that was editorially described as "probably . . . one of the most important articles that *Prehospital and Disaster Medicine* ever has published . . . ,"[80, 85, 103, 104] Dr. Paul Pepe and his group in Houston conducted a retrospective review of a number of consecutive EMS incidents in which an ambulance was called but the patient was not transported. This study both confirmed the fears expressed by other authors and made additional ominous findings. First, it found that 25% to 75% of total EMS responses involve no transportation of the patient. Second, it noted "recently, non-transport of patients has become a critical issue in EMS because it now accounts for 50% to 90% of litigation directed toward EMS."[104] Next, the study found that 30% of the patients surveyed could not remember whether the risk of the decision not to be transported, whether made by them or by the EMS provider, had been explained to them even though they might have signed a form acknowledging such information.[105] Ninety percent of the patients who expressed dissatisfaction with EMS in this study came from a group who had been refused service by the EMS providers. More seriously, the study "point(s) out the possibility that a potential error in prehospital triage by paramedics may have occurred in as many as 20% of the cases . . ." [in which a decision was made to decline to transport patients.] The authors concluded in their abstract that "serious, even fatal outcomes were identified in the follow-up of patients not transported by EMS." Although the authors did not have sufficient data to directly establish that such inappropriate conduct by EMS providers did in fact cause or contribute to cause the high ultimate mortality or morbidity they found, they did urge immediate research in the area.

Another example of gratuitous medical risk-taking by EMS providers is the failure to immobilize the cervical, thoracic, and lumbar spine of a patient who complains of neck or back pain, or who has suffered a mechanism of trauma for which such treatment is routinely indicated. Other frequent sources of liability to EMS providers are the occurrence of vehicle collisions, typically during emergency operations, and the failure of EMS equipment, typically as a result of inadequate or incomplete maintenance or inspection.

Second, claims appear to be associated with increased demand for service accompanied by a simultaneous diminution in funding resources. EMS providers seem to be expected to do more and more with less and less, but they are unable to do so. An overburdened, understaffed, and inadequately equipped EMS system is a design for legal disaster.

Third, increasing evidence suggests that some claimants are motivated to sue EMS providers for perceived indifference or hostile attitudes toward the patient or the patient's family. Many claimants have expressed frustration with the failure of the EMS system to respond effectively and positively to informal or formal complaints against EMS providers. Accordingly, some claimants feel the courts are the only forum in which they can vindicate their complaints or dissatisfaction with health care providers.[26, 77, 84]

Non–patient-related liability issues for EMS providers have also expanded in recent years. Increasingly, claims by EMS employees arising out of their employment relationship have been litigated.[17, 28, 34, 51, 52, 70] In addition, EMS employees have made claims against their employers for work-related injuries and exposure to contagious diseases, including HIV.[23, 27, 67, 68, 82] It would appear that such employment and administrative issues will continue to expand in the future.[36, 56, 81]

Some EMS claims have involved suits under federal law for alleged violation of the victim's civil rights. In general, federal law[106] provides that any person who acts under color of state law to deprive a citizen of the United States of federally created rights may be liable in damages. Such a suit may be brought in either federal or state court and is governed solely by federal law. Accordingly, state law defenses such as state governmental immunity or "Good Samaritan" immunity do not apply. Two such cases arose from serious allegations of misconduct in emergency medical dispatching,[11, 47] and another case arose out of destination selection issues.[35, 101] Other civil rights claims have been made in EMS-related contexts.[16, 45, 46, 62] To the surprise of many attorneys, such cases have frequently been decided against the civil rights plaintiff on the ground that the local government agency involved did not have any legal duty to provide emergency medical service or aid to the patient unless the state had actually caused the person's injury or illness, or unless the person was incarcerated. Given the increasing public dissatisfaction with the results of EMS operation in the United States today, and the rapidly changing political and judicial climate, it is highly probable that civil rights cases as well as liability cases generally against EMS providers will continue to increase both in number and in size.

Despite the potential for liability, EMS providers continue to successfully rely on "Good Samaritan" immunity to defend themselves from apparently otherwise meritorious claims of professional negligence.[58, 66, 93, 100] Governmental or sovereign immunity has also been used to prohibit the plaintiff from obtaining a recovery,[44, 72] although the states providing the qualified immunity may also provide ways to overcome it.[43]

CONCLUSION

As in any area of contemporary life, the legal considerations involved in providing prehospital care are numerous and often complex. Although the law may give the provider some protection from liability, proper planning and management can decrease the chance (and cost) of litigation while increasing the quality of care delivered to the patient and saving lives. Although no single presentation such as this can hope to provide all, or perhaps even most, of the appropriate legal guidelines for the day-to-day practice of prehospital health care, perhaps it can alert the professional to potential problem areas that may be identified and corrected before they become legal issues.

References

1. ACEP: Contractual Relationships. Position Summaries, American College of Emergency Physicians, 1990, III.9:23–24
2. ACEP: EMS Systems. Position Summaries, American College of Emergency Physicians 1990, Section I.5.
3. ACEP: Guidelines for "do not resuscitate" orders in the prehospital setting. Ann Emerg Med 17:1106–1108, 1988
4. ACEP: Medical Control in EMS. Position Summaries, American College of Emergency Physicians 1990, Section I.6, 4–6
5. ACEP: Medical Control in EMS. Position Summaries, American College of Emergency Physicians 1990, Section I.6, 157
6. ACEP: Principles of EMS Systems, A Comprehensive Text for Physicians. Dallas, American College of Emergency Physicians, 1989, pp 95–108
7. ACEP: Withholding Resuscitation in the Prehospital Setting. Position Summaries, American College of Emergency Physicians, 1990, Section I.11:11
8. American Academy of Orthopedic Surgeons: Emergency Care and Transportation of the Sick and Injured, ed 4. Park Ridge, IL, American Academy of Orthopedic Surgeons, 1987, pp 3, 18
9. Anderson RJ, President and Chief Executive Officer of Parkland Memorial Hospital, Dallas, Texas and the Board of Directors (personal communication)
10. Andrew L: Emergency transfers. Topics in Emergency Medicine 14:1–13, 1992
11. Archie v. City of Racine, 826 F.2d 480 (7th Cir. 1987) rev'd en banc 831 F.2d. 152 (7th Cir. 1987)
12. Augustine J, Paul P, Gustave P: EMS communications. *In* Kuehl AE (ed): The National Association of EMS Physicians: EMS Medical Director's Handbook. St. Louis, CV Mosby, 1989, p 54
13. Ayres RJ Jr: Patient consent and the law: Part 1, General principles. Journal of Emergency Medical Services 5(10):33–35, 1980
14. Ayres RJ JR: Patient consent and the law: Part 2, Special problems. Journal of Emergency Medical Services 6(1):39–41, 1981
15. Ayres RJ Jr: Current controversies in prehospital resuscitation of the terminally ill patient. Prehospital and Disaster Medicine 5:49–85, 1992
16. Bass by Lewis v. Wallenstein, 769 F.2d 1173 (7th Cir. 1985)
17. Baxter v. Fulton DeKalb Hospital, 764 F.Supp. 1510 (N.D. Ga. 1992)
18. Boyle v. Lauengco, 1991 WL 1563 (Ohio App. 1991)
19. Brooks v. Maryland General Hospital, Inc., 1992 WL 142690 (D. Md. 1992)
20. Bryant v. Riddle Memorial Hospital, 689 F.Supp. 490 (E.D. Pa. 1988)
21. Burrows v. Turner Memorial Hospital, Inc., 762 F.Supp. 840 (WD Ark. 1991)
22. Burditt v. U.S. Department of Health & Human Services, 934 F.2d 1362 (5th Cir. 1991)
23. Burke v. Sage Products, Inc., 747 F.Supp. 285 (E.D. Pa. 1990)
24. Burns v. Hussain, #TR-634076-7, Superior Court, Alamedia County, Ca., decided Feb. 20, 1991
25. Caroline N: Emergency Care in the Streets, ed 3. Boston, Little, Brown, 1987, pp 7, 324–325
26. Ciechon v. City of Chicago, 686 F.2d 511 (1982)
27. City of Ft. Lauderdale v. Lindie, 496 So.2d 168 (Fl. 1986)
28. City of Mesquite v. Moore, 800 S.W.2d 617 (Tex.App. Dallas, 1990 no writ)
29. Clawson J: Emergency medical dispatch. *In* Kuehl AE (ed): The National Association of EMS Physicians: EMS Medical Director's Handbook, St. Louis, CV Mosby, 1989, pp 59–90
30. Clawson J: Emergency medical dispatch. *In* Kuehl AE (ed): The National Association of EMS Physicians: EMS Medical Director's Handbook, St. Louis, CV Mosby, 1989, pp 81–85
31. Cleary VL: Prehospital Care: Administrative and Clinical Management. Rockville, MD, Aspen Publishers, 1987, pp 36, 68–71
32. Cleland v. Bronson Health Care Group, Inc., 917 F.2d 266 (6th Cir. 1990)
33. Collins v. DePaul Hospital, 963 F.2d 303 (10th Cir. 1992)
34. County of Hennepin v. Association of Paramedics, 464 N.W.2d 578 (Minn.App. 1990)

35. Curran WJ: The Constitutional right to health care. N Engl J Med 320:788–789, 1989
36. Daniels N: HIV-infected professionals, patient rights, and the switching dilemma. JAMA 267:1368–1371, 1992
37. DeBerry v. Sherman Hospital Association, 741 F.Supp. 1302 (ND Ill. 1990)
38. Delaney v. Cade, 756 F.Supp. 1176 (D. Kan 1991)
39. Draper v. Chiapuzio, 755 F.Supp. 331 (D Ore. 1991)
40. Evitt v. University Heights Hospital, 727 F.Supp. 495 (SD Ind. 1989)
41. Emergency Department Law 1992; 4:2–4
42. Gatewood v. Washington Healthcare Corp., 933 F.2d 1037 (D.C. Cir. 1991)
43. Green v. City of Dallas, 665 S.W.2d 567 (Tex.App. El Paso, 1984 no writ)
44. Griesel v. Hamlin, 963 F.2d 338 (11th Cir. 1992)
45. Hayes v. City of Chicago, 595 N.E.2d 144 (Ill. App. 1st Dist. 1992)
46. Heflin v. Stewart County, Tennessee, 958 F.2d 709 (6th Cir. 1992)
47. Hendon v. DeKalb County, 417 S.E.2d 705 (Ga. App. 1992, cert. den'd)
48. Hickson v. Martinez, 707 S.W.2d 919 (Tex.App., Dallas 1985, ref'd n.r.e.)
49. Higgins v. Detroit Osteopathic Hospital Corp., 154 Mich. App. 752, 398 N.W.2d 520, 68 ALR 4th 285 (1986) app. den. 428 Mich. 911
50. Hutchinson v. Greater S.E. Community Hospital, 793 F.Supp. 6 (DC 1992)
51. Jarrett v. Hill, 648 S.W.2d 170 (Miss. 1983)
52. Kierstead v. City of San Antonio, 645 S.W.2d 118 (Tex. 1983)
53. Krugh TD: Is COBRA poised to strike? A critical analysis of medical COBRA. Journal of Health and Hospital Law 23:161–175, 1990
54. Lazar RA: Letter to the Editor. Prehospital and Disaster Medicine 5:405–406, 1990
55. Lee v. Adrales, 778 F.Supp. 904 (WD Va. 1991)
56. Lo B, Steinbrook R: Health care workers infected with the human immunodeficiency virus: The next steps. JAMA 267:1100–1105, 1992
57. Lydon DR, Clara SR: Triage for emergency patients: Conflicting interests abound. Emergency Legal Briefings 3:76–79, 1992
58. Malcolm v. City of East Detroit, 180 Mich. App. 633, 447 N.W.2d 860 (1989) rev'd 437 Mich. 132, 468 N.W.2d 479 (1991)
59. Maziarka v. St. Elizabeth Hospital, 1989 WL 13195 (N.D.Ill. 1989)
60. McClurg AJ: Your money or your life: Interpreting the Federal Act against patient dumping. Wake Forest Law Review 24:173–237, 1989
61. McIntyre v. Schick, 795 F.Supp. 777 (E.D. Va. 1992)
62. Miller v. Szelenyi, 546 A.2d 1013 (Maine 1988)
63. Nichols v. Estabrook, 741 F.Supp. 325 (D N.H. 1989)
64. Ortiz v. Santa Rosa Medical Center, 702 S.W.2d 701 (Tex.App. 4th Dist. 1985, ref'd n.r.e.)
65. Owens v. Nacogdoches County Hospital, Dist., 741 F.Supp. 1269 (ED Tex. 1990)
66. Pavlov v. Community Emergency Medical Service, Inc., No. 129847 Michigan Court of Appeals, Sept. 8, 1992
67. Pepe PE, et al: Accelerated hearing loss in urban EMS fire fighters. Ann Emerg Med 14:438–442, 1985
68. Pepe PE, et al: Viral hepatitis risk in urban EMS personnel. Ann Emerg Med 15:454–457, 1986
69. Petrovics v. Prince William Hospital Corp., 764 F.Supp. 415 (ED Va. 1991)
70. Pickens v. Children's Mercy Hospital, 124 F.R.D. 209 (W.D. Mo. 1989)
71. Power v. Arlington Hospital, 61 U.S.L.W. 2134, 1992 WL 210588 (E.D. Va. 1992)
72. Ramsey v. City of Forest Park, 418 S.E.2d 432 (Ga. App. 1992)
73. Reid v. Indianapolis Osteopathic Medical Hospital, Inc., 709 F.Supp. 853 (SD Ind. 1989)
74. Reines D: The emergence of medical control. In Kuehl AE (ed): The National Association of EMS Physicians: EMS Medical Director's Handbook. St. Louis, CV Mosby, 1989, pp 10–13
75. Reines D: The emergence of medical control. In Kuehl AE (ed): The National Association of EMS Physicians: EMS Medical Director's Handbook. St. Louis, CV Mosby, 1989, pp 155–229
76. Reines D: Quality assurance in emergency medical services system. In Kuehl AE (ed): The National Association of EMS Physicians: EMS Medical Director's Handbook. St. Louis, CV Mosby, 1989, pp 213–229

77. Risks of poor communication. Hospital Risk Management 14:117–123, 1992
78. Rothenberg B: Who cares?: The evolution of the legal duty to provide emergency care. Houston Law Review 26:21, 61–62, 1989
79. Sachs GA: Limiting resuscitation: Emerging policy in the emergency medical system. Ann Intern Med 114:151–154, 1991
80. Selden BS, Patricia GS, Francis XN: Medicolegal documentation of prehospital triage. Ann Emerg Med 19:547–551, 1990
81. Severino v. North Fort Myers Fire Control District, 935 F.2d 1179 (11th Cir. 1991)
82. Shanaberger CJ: Infected on the job? Don't get stuck twice. Journal of Emergency Medical Services 16:91–93, 1991
83. Shanaberger CJ: Legal issues in medical control. In Kuehl AE (ed): The National Association of EMS Physicians: EMS Medical Director's Handbook. St. Louis, CV Mosby, 1989, pp 393–404
84. Shanaberger CJ: The sharing of responsibilities. Journal of Emergency Medical Services 11:58–59, 1986
85. Shanaberger CJ: Thorough assessments: Giving patients a fighting chance. Journal of Emergency Medical Services 9:81–86, 1990
86. Shanaberger CJ: When there's a living will, is there a way? Journal of Emergency Medical Services 15:70–72, 1990
87. Smith v. Medical Center East, 585 So.2d 1325 (Ala. 1991)
88. Smith v. Richmond Memorial Hospital, 243 Va. 445, 416 S.E.2d 689 (1992)
89. Stevison v. Enid Health Systems, Inc., 920 F.2d 710 (10th Cir. 1990)
90. Stewart v. Myrick, 731 F.Supp. 433 (D Kan. 1990)
91. Strobus J: Risk management for emergency physicians. Patient transfer update: Part I. Foresight, American College of Emergency Physicians, 20:1–6, 1991
92. Sucov A, et al: The outcome of patients refusing prehospital transportation. Prehospital and Disaster Medicine 7:365–371, 1992
93. Tatum v. Gigliotti, 80 Md. App. 559, 565 A.2d 354 (1989)
94. Texas Health and Safety Code. Sec. 241-027, Texas Regulations are contained in Title 25 of the Texas Administrative Code
95. Thompson v. St. Anne's Hospital, 716 F.Supp. 8 (N.D. Ill. 1989)
96. Thornton v. Southwest Detroit Hospital, 895 F.2d 1131 (6th Cir. 1990)
97. U.S. Department of Transportation, National Highway Traffic Safety Administration: Synopsis of Legal Considerations in Prehospital Care. Emergency Medical Care: I-13 to I-24
98. van de Leuv JH: Management of Emergency Services. Rockville, MD, Aspen Publ, 1987, pp 80–91
99. Verhagen v. Olarte, 1989 W.L. 146265 (SD NY. 1989)
100. Wicker v. City of Ord, 233 Neb. 705, 447 N.W.2d 628 (1989)
101. Wideman v. Shallowford Community Hospital, Inc., 826 F.2d 1030 (11th Cir. 1987)
102. Wilson v. Atlanticare Medical Center, 868 F.2d 34 (1st Cir. 1989)
103. Wright v. City of Los Angeles, 268 Cal. Rptr. 309 (Cal. App. 2 Dist. 1990)
104. Zachariah B, et al: Follow-up and outcome of patients who declined or are denied transport by EMS. Prehospital and Disaster Medicine 7:359–364, 1992
105. Zachariah B, et al: Follow-up and outcome of patients who declined or are denied transport by EMS. Prehospital and Disaster Medicine 7:362, 1992
106. 42 USC 1983
107. 42 USC 1395cc(b) (2)
108. 42 USC 1395dd
109. 42 USC 1395dd(d) (1) (A)
110. 42 USC 1395dd(d) (1) (A) (B)
111. 42 USE 1395dd(1) (B)
112. 42 USC 1395dd(d) (2) (B)
113. 42 USC 1395dd(d) (2) (A)
114. 42 USC 1395(d) (2) (B)
115. 42 USC 1395dd(i)
116. 42 USC 4207(i)

Address reprint requests to

R. Jack Ayres, Jr, JD
4350 Beltway Drive
Dallas, TX 75244

EMERGENCY MEDICINE, PSYCHIATRY, AND THE LAW

David T. Armitage, MD, JD, FAPA,
and Gary M. Townsend, MD, JD

In the assessment, management, and disposition of the psychiatric patient, the emergency department physician is confronted with unique medicolegal as well as diagnostic and therapeutic challenges. Emotional, mental, and behavioral symptoms may reflect easily overlooked organic causes. Dubin et al[12] studied approximately 1000 patients who were defined as "medically cleared" for further psychiatric evaluation. A substantial number of these patients were later found to have an organic basis to their psychiatric symptoms. At times, what appears to be a "physical" disorder such as coma or physical trauma may mask a primary psychiatric illness. To confuse the matter further, a patient may suffer more than one condition at the same time. Consequently, the emergency physician must conduct a broad-based "whole person" evaluation of a patient who may be uncooperative or even extremely violent. The emergency department staff may risk harm to themselves to conduct even a cursory evaluation of a patient whose behavior places not only the staff but other emergency department patients at risk of physical injury. The often chaotic atmosphere of the emergency department both

The opinions or assertions contained herein are the private views of the authors and are not to be construed as official or as reflecting views of the Department of Defense or its components.

From the Department of Legal Medicine, Armed Forces Institute of Pathology, Washington, DC; and Department of Psychiatry, Uniformed Services University of the Health Sciences, Bethesda, Maryland (DTA); and Consultation Case Review Branch, Army Health Professional Support Agency, Office of the Surgeon General of the Army; and Department of Legal Medicine, Armed Forces Institute of Pathology, Washington, DC (GMT) complicates the evaluation of, and is compromised by, a behaviorally disordered patient.

Factors that contribute to a staff attitude that a psychiatric patient represents a less desirable patient include the often involuntary circumstances of the patient's presence in the emergency department, the disruptive behavior, the likelihood of nonpayment for services rendered, and the often difficult and time-consuming requirements for disposition. Such an attitude can adversely affect the staff's ability to assess and manage the patient, placing them at increased medicolegal risk. The presence of law enforcement personnel and a need for physical or chemical restraints, or both, in a noncommunicative or abusive patient can challenge the physician's ability to obtain a reliable history and conduct an appropriate examination. Because many physicians working in emergency departments have had little formal training in the assessment and management of such situations, they are less confident than when dealing with trauma victims or patients with myocardial infarctions. Yet, it is both an ethical and legal axiom that no physician "should provide a service for which he has no training."[11] Competence in handling patients with neuropsychiatric symptoms is a skill required of the emergency physician. The American College of Emergency Physicians in its Emergency Care Guidelines (revised)[1] repeatedly refers to the requirement for skill and training with such comments as "physicians and nurses providing emergency care should have, at a minimum, the knowledge and skills necessary to provide appropriate initial evaluation, management, and treatment to patients who present to the facility with life-or-limb-threatening conditions. . . . A physician is ultimately responsible for the evaluation, diagnosis and recommended treatment of the emergency patient. . . . The emergency facility should be staffed by appropriately educated and experienced emergency care professionals, including a physician, during all hours of operation." That emergency department physicians must possess adequate knowledge and skills for assessment of psychiatric patients is supported by the fact that as many as 8.5% of patients who come to the emergency department present with neuropsychiatric complaints.[31] In addition, up to 65% of nighttime users of emergency department services in one urban setting were judged to have current or past psychiatric illnesses potentially relevant to their presentation.[31]

Of special concern to the emergency physician is the potential for violence by behaviorally disordered patients. Violent behavior in the emergency department exposes both patients and staff to potential injury. Fifty-seven percent of 127 teaching hospitals responding to a survey indicated that they had at least one threat of violence involving a weapon against a staff member in the 5 years preceding the survey, and 32% experienced at least one verbal threat each day.[23] The emergency medicine physician must be able to reasonably assess the patient's behavioral status and implement appropriate management.

Patients who have expressed or are considering suicidal behavior present to the emergency department under a variety of circumstances. Yet, recent research has shown that physicians in general are seriously deficient in knowledge about suicide risk factors and are ill prepared to intervene.[28]

Disposition of the psychiatric patient from the emergency department is frequently a vexing issue. Because involuntary commitment to a mental institution may be required, the emergency physician must be prepared to be part of the commitment process. Lack of knowledge of the law concerning involuntary commitment and lack of skill in assessing the need for involuntary commitment exposes the physician to legal action. Involuntary commitment deprives patients of their constitutional right of liberty. At the same time, patients who are psychiatrically ill and prone to injure themselves or others require active intervention. Judgments as to which patients are suicidal or likely to commit violence are subject to intense retrospective scrutiny when wrong. The emergency physician is frequently hampered in this area because facilities specifically designed for the treatment of the mentally impaired may be unavailable, overcrowded, or even resistant to accepting further patients. This is particularly problematic at night, or if the patient is underinsured. Establishing a dialogue with a suicidal patient or finding reliable sources of information about an uncooperative patient can certainly be time-consuming. But although the physician may be assisted by ancillary personnel, he must avoid the temptation of totally delegating the tasks necessary to the evaluation and treatment of psychiatric patients.

Despite all of the potential pitfalls confronting the emergency physician who cares for the psychiatric patient, the number of malpractice cases involving psychiatric treatment in an emergency department appears small. However, the cost of each case is often high. Karcz et al[22] found that only 1.5% (4 of 262) closed claims against Massachusetts emergency physicians involved psychiatric issues, specifically the release of suicidal or homicidal patients. These claims had the highest average indemnity of all emergency medicine claims—higher even than cases resulting from failure to diagnose chest pain, epiglottitis, or pediatric meningitis. The average legal expense, including indemnity costs, was $293,352. Armitage and Townsend (unpublished data) reviewed 5354 closed malpractice claims in the Armed Forces Institute of Pathology, Department of Legal Medicine's malpractice data base. They found 694 cases related to emergency department treatment, none of which involved substandard treatment of a psychiatric condition. Although such data are encouraging, medicolegal risks exist for the emergency department physician during each phase of care of the psychiatric patient, from admission to the emergency department through disposition.

ISSUES RAISED BY THE "CATEGORY" OF PATIENT

It may be useful for the emergency department physician to consider whether a particular patient presents voluntarily, involuntarily, as a minor, or as a physically absent person with whom the physician is dealing telephonically but who, nevertheless, can be legally viewed as a patient.

Each category confronts the physician with different medicolegal issues and their attendant risks.

In general, adult patients admitted to emergency departments are considered to have consented to an evaluation either expressly (in verbal or written form), by implication (by voluntarily requesting treatment), or imputedly (because a reasonable person in the same or similar circumstances would have sought treatment). Such consent is a general consent, however, and may not meet the requirements of informed consent. Granting of informed consent requires the mental capacity to understand the nature and consequences of the evaluation process and proposed treatment. This is legal competence. A mentally impaired patient, however, may lack this required element. The United States Supreme Court has declared that "an incompetent person is not able to make an informed and voluntary choice to exercise a hypothetical right to refuse treatment or any other right. Such a 'right' must be exercised for [the patient] . . . , if at all, by some sort of surrogate."[10] If a patient gives the appearance of being incompetent, the emergency department physician must seek permission to conduct anything more than an observational evaluation, unless the well-known exception involving immediate danger to life and limb obviates the required consent. Legally proper permission can be obtained only from a legal guardian who has been given authority to make such decisions, or by the order of a court that has declared the individual incompetent. Many emergency physicians request a responsible family member to authorize treatment in such circumstances. Such an authorization has no legal force, although it may, on a practical basis, protect the emergency physician from suit based on failure to obtain informed consent.

The reasonableness of the physician's action is the issue when a patient is unwilling or unable to provide an appropriate history. Good faith reliance by the emergency department physician on collateral sources of history should protect the physician from liability. It has been held, for example, that a physician has no obligation to independently determine whether history provided by family members is based on an ulterior motive detrimental to the patient's rights.[24] Even in a circumstance in which the physician's examination of a patient did not reveal evidence confirming the history provided by third parties as to the patient's propensity to violent behavior, the physician was held not to be liable for involuntary commitment. A societal need existed to protect others by further assessing the patient's potential for violence.[15]

An involuntary patient is one who does not wish to be seen in the emergency department, but who has been brought there at the behest of third parties such as family members or police or by court order.[25] Such a patient may be very suspicious, concerned about intrusive questioning or physical examination, and resistant to efforts made to ameliorate agitated or violent behavior. The involuntary patient often will not provide a necessary history including prior psychiatric treatment, current medications, or recent suicidal acts. The involved third party may have limited information, may be biased, or, may have ulterior motives for bringing the patient to the emergency department.

The physician may be obligated by the requirements of the EM-TALA (Emergency Medical Treatment and Active Labor Act—formerly called COBRA, the Consolidated Omnibus Budget Reconciliation Act of 1986)[13] to conduct at least a cursory examination of a noncompliant patient. The legislated goal is to ensure that any subsequent transfer is competently conducted, and that the patient or others are not placed at increased risk by such transfer. If the physician concludes that the patient is competent, the question arises as to whether the physician may be held liable for the technical battery of the unconsented examination. It is doubtful that a competent physician proceeding in good faith would be held accountable under such circumstances. Of real concern, however, is releasing the patient without examination, which could result in injury to the patient or third parties. Under EMTALA, any discharge is considered a "transfer" for which the physician and the hospital might be held liable.

Minors brought to the emergency department by family members may be considered a subset of involuntary patients or may be reasonably cooperative. If cooperative, it is useful to go through the process of obtaining informed consent from the minor, if an adolescent, even though it may not be legally required. Should an issue arise in the future, a case is more comfortably defended when the physician has demonstrated good faith even beyond technical legal requirements.

Until recent years, patients under the age of majority have been legally viewed as unable to possess the capacity (and therefore competency) to consent to medical treatment. The responsibility for treatment decisions involving minors rested with their parents or legal guardians. In *Parham v. J. R.*, the United States Supreme Court stated, "Our jurisprudence historically has reflected Western civilization concepts of the family as a unit with broad parental authority over minor children. . . . Most children, even in adolescence, simply are not able to make sound judgements concerning many decisions, including their need for medical care or treatment. Parents can and must make those judgements."[27] *Parham* involved a case in which parents volunteered their minor child for psychiatric treatment against the child's wishes. The Supreme Court ruling allows parents to make decisions for their minor children but does not prevent states from allowing minors to make certain decisions for themselves. Further, in most jurisdictions, the requirement for parental input can be waived if the minor is considered emancipated or is seeking statutorily authorized medical advice for specific problems such as sexually transmitted disease, pregnancy, contraception, and in some cases treatment for mental disorders or substance abuse. It is strongly recommended that the emergency department have written procedures concerning the age of consent for various treatments of minors. In any circumstance other than true life-saving treatment of a minor, consent should be obtained from a parent or legal guardian. If it is not an emergent situation, consent must be obtained from the parent with legal custody. Should married parents disagree on giving consent, only the consent of one parent is required.

Minors (usually adolescents) brought to the emergency department for treatment of suicidal behavior, acute psychosis, or symptoms of substance abuse might not be accompanied by legal guardians. If they are brought by school personnel, the personnel should be queried as to whether they have written consent from the parents to authorize emergency care to the minor. Should a treatment be required that may have significant risks, the physician is wise to obtain a second opinion.

Treatment against the wishes of both the parent and the involved minor may be legally correct. A Pennsylvania court recently held that a mother's right to determine the appropriate treatment for her son who had made a suicidal gesture was not unconstitutionally infringed upon by subjecting the minor to involuntary inpatient psychiatric treatment. The court held that the state had an interest in ensuring the health, safety, and welfare of the minor, which "arose from the clear threat he posed to his own life" and that the mother's rights over her son were not absolute.[21]

Adult patients who are competent may waive their decision-making authority, that is, their right to informed consent. There is one qualification, however; patients cannot waive their decision-making authority "until their rights to be informed and choose have been explained to them."[5] The physician should be aware that an anxious, agitated, frightened, or seriously depressed patient may prematurely waive a right to informed consent merely to get the process moving. They should be gently, but firmly, encouraged to participate in at least a brief, pertinent discussion of evaluation and treatment issues. In the context of the psychiatric patient, consent to evaluation or treatment obtained under the threat of involuntary commitment is not voluntary.

Physicians dealing with potential or actual psychiatric patients may invoke the concept of "therapeutic privilege" to proceed with treating the patient without obtaining informed consent. Although this is a generally acknowledged exception to the requirement to obtain informed consent, physicians place themselves at extreme risk unless they have substantial competent evidence that information provided to the patient "would severely compromise the patient's health or ability to make an informed decision."[5]

Rendering telephonic advice to a patient may be viewed in law as establishing a doctor-patient relationship, exposing the physician to malpractice liability. This is especially true if, under the circumstances, a "reasonable person" would have a basis for believing that the telephonic service was available to the public and was provided in a professional context. Of particular concern is the emergency department that has an established suicide hot line. Such a department has a duty to the hot-line caller to provide a reasonable assessment of the caller's concern and appropriate advice and guidance as to how to proceed from that point. Personnel attending the lines should be knowledgeable concerning suicide and how to manage callers.[11]

ISSUES ARISING DURING THE EVALUATION PHASE

The emergency department physician is expected to be able to evaluate the physical and mental status of any patient brought to the Emergency Department to the extent necessary to prevent loss of life and limb, to ameliorate severe suffering, to obtain a competent consultation, and to accomplish a reasonable disposition. As previously noted, although it may be tempting to delegate assessment of annoying or undesirable patients to ancillary staff or allied personnel in the emergency department, it is unwise. Should any part of the assessment—such as history gathering from third parties, interviewing the patient, physically examining the patient, discussing issues of consent, and so forth—be performed by someone other than the emergency department physician, the physician is ultimately responsible for the adequacy of the performance of the delegated tasks, and for utilizing any information thereby gathered in reaching a management plan and disposition for the patient. An emergency physician should be as competent at conducting a mental status evaluation as he or she is at other medical assessment procedures. The level of skill must allow at least for initial emergency stabilization and treatment, even if the patient receives follow-up care from a specialist.

In a complex case reported by Fiscina,[14] an emergency department physician failed to conduct an adequate examination that would have determined that an alcoholic who was somewhat agitated, disoriented, and hyperventilating was suffering from lobar pneumonia rather than alcohol intoxication.

Although testimony as to the standard of care in emergency medicine cases involving negligence should come from emergency medicine physicians, it is not uncommon to find other specialists providing testimony. A psychiatrist might be allowed to testify regarding the assessment and mental status evaluation that a reasonably competent emergency department physician should be able to conduct. If a specialist in psychiatry gives evidence that the emergency department physician conducted his or her evaluation to the level of a reasonably competent psychiatrist, such testimony will be allowed and will generally provide a solid defense for the emergency department physician.

In a study regarding the use of a mental status examination by emergency physicians, Zun and Gold[35] found that 82% of physicians surveyed "perceived a need for . . . a short standardized [mental status examination] that would take less than five minutes to perform." The authors have pointed out that, unfortunately, the currently available abbreviated forms of the mental status examination, and even the formal extensive mental status examination itself, have not been validated for the emergency department. Fifty-seven percent of the physicians surveyed did not conduct a formal mental status examination in patients because of lack of time. This was true even though the majority of physicians were in agreement as to the indications for mental status examination. Many of the physicians used selected items from the formal mental status examination.

During the evaluation phase, or while awaiting final disposition, many patients require monitoring by emergency department staff. The predicament emergency department personnel may face is illustrated by the case of *Torres v. City of New York*.[33] Torres, dressed in a T-shirt, white pants, and socks but no shoes, approached a police officer and related that he had escaped from the King's County Hospital, where he claimed to be under treatment for a sexually transmitted disease. The officer convinced Torres to go to the emergency department at a nearby hospital. After informing the charge nurse that he considered Torres to be an escaped mental patient, the policeman left the emergency department to make telephone calls to determine Mr. Torres's status. The medical records indicated that vital signs were taken and that Torres complained of a penile discharge and pain in his back and throat. Torres walked out of the emergency department 14 minutes after he had arrived because he "felt the nurses and policeman were talking about him." Shortly thereafter, he jumped in front of a subway train, injuring his right leg.

By only a three-to-two majority, the court held that there was "no legal ground upon which the nurse or hospital could have restrained Torres." A strongly worded dissent, however, argued that "although the hospital had no legal right to detain the plaintiff, who appeared to be acting rationally, the jury could have found that in the exercise of reasonable care, [the nurse] should have made an effort to detain or reassure him, at least until [the police officer] had completed his telephone inquiries as to the plaintiff's status at King's County Hospital. Even a remote possibility of harm to a patient might be enough to pose an issue to the jury as to whether the hospital used reasonable care and diligence not only in treating but in safeguarding a patient, measured by the capacity of the patient to provide for his own safety." *Torres* was a close call and could easily have gone against the physician. The court noted that there had to be a legally sufficient reason to detain Torres, implying that the mere suspicion by a police officer that the patient was an escaped mental patient was not adequate legal grounds. Given the court's reluctance to find liability even retrospectively after a suicidal act, the same court might have found against the emergency department staff had Torres in fact been restrained and chosen to sue for false imprisonment, assault and battery, or a constitutional tort in view of the arguable infringement on his constitutional rights by medical staff acting with color of a governmental authority. One could also raise the question in this case as to whether a competent assessment of Torres had been done to determine his mental state and potential for harm to self or others. Given his apparent psychotic condition, had further evidence been elicited as to his deranged thinking and potential dangerousness, justification would clearly have existed for restraining Torres.

The crucial question during the evaluation phase is: What evidence exists from even a cursory observation or evaluation that justifies restraining and detaining the patient until a more complete assessment can be done? Staff would seem to be justified in detaining or restraining a patient whose history suggests previous violence and who appears acutely agitated, disturbed, and disorganized. Good faith restraint is easily defensible under such circumstances. In fact, more suits are brought and won for failure to restrain a patient than are brought or won for improper detention and restraint.

The evaluating physician should be alert for certain neuropsychiatric problems that may not be immediately obvious and that, if missed, place the patient or others at risk of injury. Certain disturbed parents, for their own disordered psychologic needs, induce factitious illness in their children. Parents may poison, lacerate, burn, or partially suffocate their child; induce vomiting with an emetic; or challenge a sensitized child with an allergen. These parents suffer from "Munchausen syndrome by proxy." Although this appears to be a rare condition, its existence and potential for harm to the child require the physician to consider it in the differential diagnosis. Repeated visits to the emergency department may eventually expose the situation for what it is.

Patients who complain of migraine headache, renal colic, or severe low back pain may be seeking drugs because of a substance abuse problem. Although not all such patients can be detected, it is incumbent upon the physician to assess the circumstances of the visit, the patient's symptoms, and physical findings with substance abuse in mind. If the evaluation was substandard and the physician failed to detect a drug-seeking patient or even contributed to that drug-seeking behavior by prescribing drugs of abuse, the patient will likely continue to abuse the substances. Being "allowed" to continue abusing substances may be injurious in and of itself.

The emergency physician should be alert for the patient whose symptoms are consistent with incipient withdrawal or intoxication. Their judgment may be compromised to the point of incompetence to drive, to conduct personal business, or to make decisions about health care.

Certain physical diseases masquerade as psychiatric disorders and vice versa. Examples include the neuroleptic malignant syndrome wherein disorientation, hyperthermia, and hypertension result from an unusual reaction to neuroleptic medications; panic disorder and anxiety attacks; drug and alcohol withdrawal and intoxication; encephalitis; cerebrovascular accident; myocardial infarction; metabolic and electrolyte disturbances; hypoxemia; head trauma; and seizure disorders. Patients with agitation secondary to organic mental disorder have been treated as if they were suffering anxiety. The foreseeability of harm in these circumstances is usually easy to demonstrate.

A medicolegal issue of particular importance to emergency physicians, but in a high state of flux and controversy, is that of elder abuse. Elderly persons brought to the emergency department by relatives or other third parties are often reluctant to explain what happened to them if they have been traumatized, starved, or not given proper care. Interview techniques are available to help such patients describe their plight. Patients do have a duty to cooperate. However, given the knowledge that elder abuse is becoming more frequent and that certain circumstances of assessment should lead the physician to consider elder abuse, negligent evaluation is of concern. A number of states are passing legislation in this area, including the requirement that suspected elder abuse be reported. At the present time, the laws are highly variable, irregularly enforced, and severely problematic to professionals. In view of the estimate that elder abuse occurs in approximately 10% of Americans over 65 years of age, the issue will continue to confront emergency physicians.[2, 7, 8]

During any evaluation phase, an emergency department physician must consider whether a duty to consult exists. In most cases, once the emergency department physician recognizes that a psychiatric problem is at hand, a consultation is almost invariably requested from a psychiatrist if one is available. Consultations are not requested when the emergency department physician feels quite competent with his experience, skill, and knowledge regarding psychiatric disorders, or when the usual disposition, after a reasonable assessment, would be to a psychiatric facility, which inherently involves specialist evaluation. Because it is every physician's duty to know the limits of his or her knowledge and skill, the emergency physician should request consultation from a psychiatrist when those limits are reached. The consultative process should make perfectly clear who will assume responsibility for continued assessment and care of the patient. The patient preferably should be personally evaluated by the consulting psychiatrist. Although telephone consultation does not violate the standard of care, the subtleties of evaluation of thinking, emotion, and behavior make it difficult to conduct an assessment telephonically. Emergency department physicians often complain that they do not have adequate or responsive psychiatric back-up. If such is the case, the Emergency Department or hospital must ensure that such consultation is available.

At the conclusion of the evaluation phase, the emergency department physician is often asked to provide information about the patient's condition, history, or even personal facts to third parties such as relatives and the police.[3] Although the pressures to reveal confidential information are considerable and may even seem necessary to affect an appropriate disposition of a patient, the physician should determine an individual's legal right to have the requested information. The physician's conclusion that a patient is mentally incompetent does not legally authorize a relative to have access to the patient's confidential communications, even if those communications were made in a less than fully cognitively responsible state. In fact, the patient's lack of judgment may have allowed certain facts to be revealed to the physician that would have been censored by the patient under other circumstances and were unnecessary to the physician's evaluation.

Release of confidential information is a different matter if there are state laws that require reporting child or elder abuse, or which create a duty to take actions to protect or warn identifiable third parties who may be in danger as a result of the patient's mental condition.

If there is no clear legal waiver for breach of confidentiality, some emergency departments have recommended obtaining informed consent to release information. But it has been argued that consent to release information, even if obtained, is rarely truly informed.[19] Physicians, themselves, may be ignorant of the impact of revealing certain information to others. The patient may be subjected to ridicule, loss of family respect, insurance or occupational problems, divorce, child custody contests, guardianship, and involuntary commitment actions. Furthermore, a patient who was fully cooperative with the emergency department physician and disclosed considerable personal information may be reluctant or embarrassed to refuse permission to disclose personal information to third parties such as family members, friends, police, or even other health care personnel. The patient may feel "pressured" to consent, thereby vitiating the "voluntary" requirement of informed consent.

But there are compelling state interests that justify limited disclosure to family members who are needed to aid in the patient's recovery. Society benefits from the increased functional capacity of a person whose care is improved as a result of such limited disclosure. Heimberg[19] advocates applying "the least onerous alternative" doctrine wherein only information *essential* to the family's understanding of the illness should be disclosed. Such data include but are not limited to prognosis, signs of the worsening or exacerbation of illness, primary and side effects of drugs, and any special requirements for protecting the patient and others from harm. Attitudes toward family members, fantasies, personal history, and content of delusions should not be conveyed unless they are specifically related to dangerousness.

Disclosure of information to police and other official governmental agents is justified to maintain the public health and safety, or to help police to increase "their ability to differentiate criminal, intoxicated and psychotic activity."[19] Disclosure, however, should be limited to information that directly affects the ability of police to deal with subsequent similar situations.

Heimberg[19] differentiates disclosure issues involved in passing information, on the one hand, to subsequent, directly involved health care providers who will care for the patient, and on the other hand, to ancillary emergency department staff who have no need to know details of a case. The latter need be informed only of facts directly related to whatever involvement they may have with a patient's case, which is usually extremely limited, if any. Idle curiosity is not to be tolerated.

The following hypothetical case illustrates the possible consequences of divulging confidential information. A husband brought his young wife to the emergency department because she had taken an overdose of acetaminophen. After completing an assessment, the physician met with the husband who asked what had caused his wife's actions. The physician related to the husband that his wife was pregnant by an extramarital affair and was severely depressed about it. The wife had not chosen to reveal this circumstance to her husband, who later severely abused her. The wife filed a claim for breach of confidentiality against the emergency department physician.

ISSUES INVOLVED IN THE TREATMENT/
STABILIZATION PHASE

Many of the points made concerning the evaluation phase can be additionally applied to the treatment/stabilization phase. When the physician determines as a result of his or her evaluation that a patient poses a threat to self or others, the duty to restrain that patient is heightened. This increased duty is illustrated in a recent Wisconsin case.[6] A patient with a known history of mental illness was brought to the emergency department by her sister, who had witnessed an acute episode of bizarre behavior. This behavior continued while the patient was in the emergency department, and she was placed in chest and four-point soft restraints. The emergency physician considered her to be acutely psychotic and requested an evaluation by a psychiatrist. Prior to the time the psychiatrist arrived, the patient escaped and left the hospital. Shortly thereafter, she was killed when she ran in front of an automobile. The court found that the hospital failed to exercise ordinary care to periodically monitor or to sufficiently restrain the patient until completion of her examination.

A dissenting opinion in the case recognized the difficulty emergency personnel have in balancing the need for treatment with the rights of the patient. Wisconsin law prohibited involuntary detention of a person suspected of mental illness who had not committed a crime unless there was "substantial probability of physical harm" to either the patient or other persons. This particular patient had apparently been "able to live in the community without significant threat to either her well-being or the safety of those with whom she had contact." The dissenting judge stated that "the majority in effect holds that there are circumstances where hospital personnel must violate the law in order to be free from negligence. This is clearly against public policy. It also places hospital personnel in a no-win situation. They must choose between the Scylla of tort liability for failure to detain and the Charybdis of tort liability for unwarranted detention."

In a case personally communicated to one author (DTA), an inebriated middle-aged man was admitted to the emergency department on self-referral, requesting treatment for a headache. He was noted to have slurred speech, he wandered from room to room in the emergency department, and he appeared somewhat incoherent. Nevertheless, he was neither restrained nor supervised. He angrily announced that because he was not being treated according to his expectations, he would leave the emergency department and did so. Several hours later, he was found dead next to a downed power line under circumstances that suggested he had attempted to urinate by leaning against the pole and had voided on the power line, resulting in death by electrocution. The health facility paid the tort claim, which alleged that staff had been negligent in their duty to properly assess and restrain a patient suffering an organic brain syndrome as a result of alcohol intoxication.

Whether or not a patient has been adequately supervised while in an emergency department has been held to require expert medical testimony. The mere fact that a patient escapes from the department does not prove negligent supervision. Such was the finding in *Tucker v. Metropolitan Government of Nashville and Davidson County*,[34] which involved a patient brought to an emergency department by the Nashville police while the patient was in a catatonic state. Although not restrained, the patient remained motionless for 3 to 4 hours while the staff made arrangements to transfer him to the Veterans Administration Hospital. Without warning, the patient suddenly bolted from the emergency department. An hour and a half later, he was brought back to the same emergency department after being struck by an automobile, but he was dead on arrival. The court stated that determining the standard for patient supervision under such circumstances required expert medical evidence, and it was not within the knowledge of ordinary lay persons. Because the plaintiff had not provided such expert testimony, judgment was in favor of the physician.

Even though restraint and supervision of a patient may be indicated, the carrying out of those duties may be negligently performed, resulting in injury to the patient or other persons.[17] Although a search of the medicolegal literature yielded no cases in an emergency department wherein a patient committed suicide while restrained by a Pose belt and not under direct supervision of staff, a number of such cases involved hospitalized patients; therefore, the risk is present. Taliaffero[32] has provided some practical guidance for dealing with potentially violent patients based on her experience in the Emergency Department of the San Francisco General Hospital. She points out that such clues as tattoos on a patient that convey a relationship to a violent organization or suggest hostility are important to note, although they may be totally innocent. At the very least, such a patient should be initially approached with caution. Rice and Moore[29] have also provided the emergency department physician and staff with practical and legally sufficient guidelines for restraining the violent patient. Their discussion includes the use of chemical as well as physical restraints. Although they note that the neuroleptic malignant syndrome has been described after a single dose of haloperidol, the appearance of this syndrome in a patient with no prior history should not yield the finding of negligence in use of the drug. Inappropriate diagnosis and management of the syndrome should it arise, however, could be a cause for a negligence claim. Clinton et al[9] performed a clinical study of the use of haloperidol in the emergency setting, concluding that it was "safe and efficacious . . . for use with disruptive patients in the emergency setting."

Other medications used in the treatment or stabilization of patients with psychiatric disorders have the potential to cause harm. It is recommended, for example, that patients treated with benzodiazepines for anxiety be observed for several hours to ensure that they do not experience a disinhibition reaction. Such a reaction is a paradoxic response to the usually sedating properties of benzodiazepines and can result in aggressive and violent behavior. Dangerously additive sedation may result when sedating drugs are given to a patient not suspected of abusing or overdosing with similar drugs.

Painful or life-threatening acute dystonias may follow parenteral use of neuroleptics in the emergency department. Staff should be aware of such effects and prepare to manage them. Patients may also present to the emergency department with dystonic reactions from legitimate as well as illegitimate use of oral neuroleptics. Although drug abusers may not be forthcoming with history about their use of neuroleptics, the emergency physician is under a duty to consider neuroleptic abuse in the differential diagnosis of acute dystonia. Patient denial should be confronted in a manner indicating that accurate history is important to proper medical care.

Claims have been brought against emergency department physicians who negligently misdiagnosed the often extremely unpleasant neuroleptic side effect of akathisia, believing that the patient was suffering acute anxiety or psychotic agitation. The wrong diagnosis in this circumstance may lead the physician to administer an additional dose of the offending medication, prolonging the akathisia. The seriousness of such an error is reflected in the fact that some patients have attempted suicide because of the excruciatingly unpleasant nature of akathisia.

Psychiatric patients who are being treated with monoamine oxidase inhibitors (MAOIs) may seek treatment at the emergency department for a variety of conditions for which, were the patients not using MAOIs, sympathomimetic medications would be indicated. Prescribing or recommending sympathomimetic medications for an upper respiratory condition, for example, or using lidocaine with epinephrine for local anesthesia in a patient on MAOIs can precipitate a hypertensive crisis. Effects can range from headache and tremulousness to stroke, myocardial infarction, and death. The emergency medicine physician would likely be held accountable if the current medication history of the patient were ignored or if the physician was not aware of the serious drug interaction.

It is not the occurrence of untoward effects that results in a successful suit for negligence. It is the failure to anticipate those effects, inform the patient about their likelihood, or manage them should they occur.

ISSUES INVOLVED IN THE DISPOSITION PHASE

The issue of release of information to a variety of agencies and persons presents again at the disposition phase and has been covered in the section dealing with evaluation. It should be noted, however, that proper transfer of a patient to another facility requires that procedures be in place to ensure proper and adequate conveyance of professional information to a subsequent treating facility under appropriate conditions of confidentiality.

A patient admitted to the emergency department, evaluated, and stabilized or given emergency treatment always requires a discharge or disposition plan, even though such a plan may be extremely simple and pragmatic compared with discharge planning conducted on hospitalized inpatients. A patient who has been evaluated and is considered competent and not a danger to self or others may simply choose to leave the emergency department with no further care or follow-up. If further care or follow-up was determined to be in the patient's best interests, such a plan should be entered into the medical record with a note that the patient appeared competent and refused further care. Careful documentation of the patient's actual or recommended disposition is as important as documentation of the chief complaint, the evaluation, and the interventions conducted, if any.

The most cogent goal of disposition planning is the protection of the patient from self and the protection of third parties from a potentially violent patient, even though the majority of patients suffering psychiatric disorders are not violent and do no harm. The majority of violence against others is perpetrated by sane persons. However, the public fear of mental illness, combined with the bizarre nature of violence when it does occur in a mentally disordered person, reinforce the expectation that medical personnel assess a patient's violent propensity and take necessary steps to preclude violence. Such a duty is supported in general by the courts despite ample evidence that the prediction of violent acts has an extremely low level of reliability. Even psychiatric physicians are unable to reliably predict dangerous behavior.[29]

Decisions with regard to disposition following the emergency department visit are the ones that most commonly bring the psychiatric patient, his or her family, or third parties into the legal arena with the emergency physician. Judgments made with regard to the need for hospitalization of potentially violent or suicidal patients, and the disclosure of confidential information to third parties about such patients, are the subjects of the majority of legal disputes. Gerson and Bassuk[16] have concluded that "behavior, affects and thoughts that are indicative of dangerousness—the likelihood of harming oneself or others—are perhaps the most influential class of symptoms in emergency dispositional decision-making." They caution, however, that because dangerousness is a chief legal condition for involuntary commitment, judgments that a patient is dangerous may "reflect legal justifications rather than determinants of the decision to hospitalize."[16]

Involvement of physicians in the involuntary commitment process has resulted in actions alleging civil rights violations.[18, 19, 30] Under chapter 42 of the United States Civil Code, section 1983, a private person can be held liable if, acting "under color of state law," he or she deprives the complaining party of rights guaranteed under the Constitution and laws of the United States. Such an infringement is referred to as a "constitutional tort." There is no immunity to constitutional torts even though government-employed physicians are often granted statutory immunity from ordinary tort liability when participating in the commitment process. Depriving persons of their liberty interests is reserved to the state. The United States Supreme Court has held, for example, that there is a compelling state interest in preventing violence that endangers other persons or property. Protecting the public safety and health may justify state action overriding an individual citizen's liberty interests. The state ordinarily acts through legally appointed agents ("state actors") in pursuing constitutionally proper goals, with due process. A state actor is understood to be acting under the color of state law.

A complex legal test must be met for a private person to be declared a "state actor" who is subject to a constitutional tort action, a test that is rarely met. Moreover, acting under color of state law is not the same as acting in accordance with the law. The state authorizes physicians to participate in the involuntary commitment process without making them official state agents.

Judgments that are subsequently proven to have been made in error do not necessarily subject a physician to legal liability. A Louisiana court[4] recently found that an emergency physician and his consulting psychiatrist were not negligent in allowing a patient with a history of previous suicide attempts to be released to his family's care even though the patient committed suicide the next day. The patient had been hospitalized twice in the preceding 3 months for suicide attempts. On the day of his last emergency department visit, he had fallen down a flight of stairs and complained of rib pain. His mother stated that she thought he was suicidal and requested he be hospitalized. The patient denied to the evaluating physician that he was suicidal and refused to voluntarily commit himself for psychiatric hospitalization. He related that he was "upset because he could not communicate with his family and that every time he said something adverse, his family wanted him hospitalized." The emergency physician did not find the patient's behavior to be abnormal at the time, or his mood to be depressed. The physician concluded that involuntary hospitalization would be counterproductive. A consulting psychiatrist agreed with this assessment and arranged to see the patient the following morning. The court considered that this disposition represented a reasonable treatment plan under the circumstances despite the ultimate outcome.

In other cases, however, courts have held physicians liable for negligent release of patients who committed violent acts, against themselves or others, weeks or months following the release.

Because more cases are lodged against physicians for negligent disposition of a harmful patient than for false imprisonment or assault and battery, the emergency physician should be cautious in circumstances in which a clearly mentally disordered patient has a history of dangerous behavior, appears impulsive, and is unpredictable. It is always preferable to have consultation in these cases but not always practical.

A tragic and fortunately unusual case occurred in Florida.[26] A young man was brought to an emergency department by a relative and friends, who gave the history that he had been acting strangely and may have taken LSD. The emergency department's facility did not have testing procedures to ascertain what, if any, drug had been consumed by the patient. The emergency department staff explained the circumstances to the persons accompanying the patient and advised them to seek care at another hospital, which had the necessary testing facilities. On route to the other hospital, the patient jumped out of the automobile, "ran berserk through an apartment building and fatally stabbed" a third party. The wife of the victim filed suit for wrongful death against the hospital, alleging that he had been negligently released. A jury found in favor of the wife. But a judge, based on extensive documentation by the emergency department, found that the patient demonstrated no abnormal behavior while in the emergency department. Holding that the patient's behavior was an unforeseeable and independent intervening act, the judge reversed the jury's decision and ruled in favor of the hospital. The finding was upheld on appeal. In effect, the actions of the emergency department were held not to be the proximate cause of the victim's death. Had the evidence suggested that the patient acted in a strange or mentally disturbed manner while in the emergency department, it is likely that the judgment of the jury in favor of the plaintiff would have been sustained by the trial judge. In this case, excellent documentation was crucial to the outcome.

If it appears to the emergency department physician that a patient is mentally ill but does not meet the "dangerous" requirement for involuntary commitment, efforts should be made to have the patient voluntarily sign into an appropriate facility for medical treatment. All such efforts should be carefully documented in the record, as should the basis for the conclusion that the patient is not dangerous. If the patient refuses to come into the hospital and subsequently is involved in a suicide or third-party violence, the record will lend considerable support to defense of any lawsuit.

Like the difficulty in predicting violent behavior, predicting a patient's suicide is extremely difficult. It is not difficult, however, to judge a patient's risk of suicide, using generally accepted risk factors. This is true even if there is professional dispute over the practical value of risk factor assessment in prediction of suicide. It at least shows that the emergency department physician was aware of accepted risk factors and evaluated the patient for those factors.[20] Certainly, if a mentally disordered patient demonstrates the majority of risk factors, yet is carelessly released into the community and commits suicide, the emergency physician will likely be found negligent. However, in view of countervailing values, such as "individual freedom" and "the least restrictive alternative for care," the emergency department physician who carefully considers risk factors and who implements reasonable risk factor reduction techniques should not be held liable should such a patient later commit suicide.

CONCLUSION

Although the emergency department physician and staff appear to be at a low medicolegal occurrence risk when involved in the evaluation, treatment, and disposition of persons suffering psychiatric illness, they are at a substantial per-occurrence payout risk. Clearly, the majority of that risk involves the assessment of a patient's propensity for suicide or violence to third parties. Nevertheless, there are potential medicolegal risks that occur at every phase of involvement with a psychiatric patient, which can be controlled reasonably well by the knowledgeable and atten tive physician. Although risk management has been viewed as protecting the financial resources of institutions and professionals, when done well the interests of the patient and third parties are also served.

References

1. American College of Emergency Physicians: Emergency Care Guidelines (revised). Ann Emerg Med 15:486–490, 1986
2. American College of Legal Medicine: Legal Medicine: Legal Dynamics of Medical Encounters, ed 2. St. Louis, Mosby–Year Book, 1991, p 321
3. Appleton W: Legal aspects of emergency medicine. In Tintinalli J: Emergency Medicine: A Comprehensive Study Guide. New York, McGraw-Hill, 1988, p 983
4. Bates v. Denney, 563 So. 2d 298 (1990)
5. Boisaubin EV, Dresser R: Informed consent in emergency care: Illusion and reform. Ann Emerg Med 16:62–67, 1987
6. Boles v. Milwaukee County, 443 N.W. 2d 679 (1989)
7. Brewer RA, Jones JS: Reporting elder abuse: Limitations of statutes. Ann Emerg Med 18:1217, 1989
8. Clark-Daniels CL, Daniels RS, Baumhover LA: Abuse and neglect of the elderly: Are emergency department personnel aware of mandatory reporting laws? Ann Emerg Med 19:970, 1990
9. Clinton JE, Sterner S, Stelmachers Z, et al: Haloperidol for sedation of disruptive emergency patients. Ann Emerg Med 16:319–332, 1987
10. Cruzan v. Director, Missouri Dept of Health, 497 US 261 (1990)
11. Dubin WR, Weiss KJ: Handbook of Psychiatric Emergencies. Springhouse, PA, Spring-house, 1991
12. Dubin WR, Weiss KJ, Zeccardi JA: Organic brain syndrome: The psychiatric imposter. JAMA 249:60–62, 1983
13. Emergency Medical Treatment and Active Labor Act of 1986, 42 USC s1395 et seq (1988)
14. Fiscina SF: Medical Law for the Attending Physician: A Case-oriented Analysis. Car-bondale, IL, Southern Illinois University Press, 1982, p 443
15. Fish v. Regents of the Univ of Calif., 54 Cal. Rptr. 656 (1966)
16. Gerson S, Bassuk E: Psychiatric Emergencies: An overview. Am J Psychiatry 137:1–11, 1980
17. Griglak MJ, Bucci RL: Medicolegal management of the organically impaired patient in the emergency department. Ann Emerg Med 18:1217–1221, 1989
18. Harvey v. Harvey, 949 F2d 1127 (1992)
19. Heimberg SA: Status of the emergency room psychotherapist: Privacy rights. 30 UCLA L. Rev. 1316 (August 1983)
20. Hofmann DP, Dubovsky SL: Depression and suicide assessment. Emerg Med Clin North Am 9:107–121, 1991
21. In re C.M.P., 604 A. 2d 712 (1992)
22. Karcz A, Holbrook J, Auerbach BS, et al: Preventability of malpractice claims in emer-gency medicine: A closed claims study. Ann Emerg Med 19:865–873, 1990
23. Lavoie FW, Carter GL, Danzl DF, et al: Emergency department violence in United States teaching hospitals. Ann Emerg Med 17:1227–1233, 1988
24. Maben v. Rankin et al, 10 Cal. Rptr. 353 (1961)
25. Mayer D: Refusal of care and discharging "difficult" patients from the emergency department. Ann Emerg Med 19:1436–1446, 1990
26. Nance v. James Archer Smith Hosp, 329 So. 2d 377 (1976)
27. Parham v. J.R., 442 US 584 (1979)

28. Pinkney DS: Doctors don't know all suicide risk factors. American Medical News, April 20, 1992, p 11
29. Rice MM, Moore GP: Management of the violent patient: Therapeutic and legal considerations. Emerg Med Clin North Am 9:13–30, 1991
30. Rubenstein v. Benedictine Hospital, 770 Fed. Supp. 396 (1992)
31. Summers WK, Rund DA, Levin ML: Psychiatric illness in a general urban emergency room: Daytime versus nighttime populations. J Clin Psychiatry 40:340–343, 1979
32. Taliaffero EH: Coping with the violent patient. Emerg Med May 15, 1992, pp 155–164
33. Torres v. City of NY, 408 N.Y. 2d 330 (1978)
34. Tucker v. Metropolitan Govt of Nashville and Davidson County, 686 S.W. 2d 87 (1984)
35. Zun L, Gold I: A survey of the form of the mental status examination administered by emergency physicians. Ann Emerg Med 15:916–922, 1986

Address reprint requests to

David T. Armitage, MD, JD
Department of Legal Medicine
Armed Forces Institute of Pathology
Washington, DC 20306-6000

0733–8627/93 $0.00 + .20

THE EMERGENCY DEPARTMENT MEDICAL RECORD

James E. George, MD, JD, FACEP,

Emergency physicians long to be relieved of the suffocating load of medical record documentation in the emergency department. Emergency nurses feel likewise. More and more persons seem to have more and more information that needs to be charted.

Emergency physicians yearn for the technology to dictate their medical records as quickly as they speak, have them transcribed and edited to perfection within minutes after dictation, and have all of this available at modest, if any, cost. Unfortunately, dictation technology does not yet have the emergency physician at this point of comfort and convenience, especially in high-volume emergency department settings.

Why all of this obsession with medical record documentation? Not many years ago, hospital emergency department record keeping requirements were minimal. In fact, little more was necessary than to record the patient's name and date to document that the patient had been treated in the emergency department.

However, an ever-widening net of regulatory requirements is increasing the medical record documentation pressures on the emergency physician and hospital. "Big brother" is indeed watching everything emergency physicians do, as for all physicians in the house of medicine. One organization overseeing emergency physicians is the Professional Review Organization (PRO). The PRO monitors the quality and appropriateness of medical care for recipients of federally funded programs such as Medicare. The primary tool for accomplishing this PRO review is to review medical records. Therefore, the treating physician must have

---

From Emergency Physician Associates; the Law Firm of George, Korin, Quattrone & Blumberg; and the Department of Emergency Medicine, Underwood-Memorial Hospital, Woodbury, New Jersey

---

appropriate medical records so that any questions by the reviewer are answered on the face of the medical record. The emergency physician should accomplish this level of documentation to avoid intense scrutiny by the PRO, because PRO reviews can be time-consuming for the emergency physician.

The Joint Commission on Accreditation of Healthcare Organizations (JCAHO) has always had detailed requirements for emergency department medical records, which can be found in the 1992 edition of the *Accreditation Manual for Hospitals, Emergency Services* (pp 25–26).

In addition to these requirements, each state has its own statutes, rules, and regulations governing health care and medical record keeping in particular. New Jersey, for example, recently amended its Licensing Standards for Hospitals, which became effective on July 1, 1990. Subchapter 12 of the standards deals with the emergency department. Specific requirements are laid out for the emergency department medical record under 8:43G-12.7(O). The New Jersey regulations also lay down stipulations regarding the emergency department registration log [8:43G-12.7(j)].

The insurance industry has exerted great pressure upon the emergency physician to document more in the emergency department record, to determine whether and to what extent an event is covered under a policy. Blue Cross, HMOs, workers' compensation, no-fault automobile, and other insurance programs have all contributed to the need for more information from the hospital medical record.

A most recent development with a significant impact on medical record documentation and reimbursement is the change in Medicare reimbursement methodology for all physicians, including emergency physicians. These changes were officially endorsed by the Health Care Financing Administration (HCFA) on November 25, 1991. The HCFA changes were brought about by the Consolidated Omnibus Budget Reconciliation Act (COBRA) of 1990, which set forth a new Medicare physician fee schedule to be phased in over 5 years, beginning January 1, 1992, and becoming fully effective in 1996. These rules include new definitions for emergency department visit codes developed by the American Medical Association's CPT-4 Editorial Panel. The CPT-4 provides for five levels of service that apply to emergency department patient visits. These levels of service, more particularly levels 4 and 5 (Codes 99284 and 99285), will require more detailed medical record documentation.

This is a very great challenge for emergency physicians in busy emergency departments that do not have effective medical record transcription mechanisms. Unfortunately, such mechanisms will likely result in increased costs to hospitals and emergency physicians and, therefore, to patients, and they may also result in increased delays for treatment in the emergency department. It is doubtful that federal legislators anticipated these effects when they implemented the new rules. In fact, as with many rules and regulations before them, these new HCFA changes are unlikely to increase the quality of emergency department care. Certainly, the changes will not increase the efficiency or shorten the delivery time of medical care in the emergency department setting. Unfortunately, regulatory "progress" has the inevitable side effect of increased costs, increased aggravation, and no increase in the quality of the care rendered. In fact, the "subjective quality" of interactive time between the emergency physician and the patient may decrease as a result of these increased documentation requirements.

One very good reason for completely documenting all patient encounters in the emergency department is the need for outside agencies to utilize the medical record for their own purposes. The local prosecutor, the Division of Youth and Family Services (DYFS), or even the physician's attorney, may, after appropriate procedural review by an administrative agency or court, obtain these records. The physician's chart may be important in a case involving child abuse or driving while intoxicated. Therefore, emergency physicians should document as clearly and accurately as they can.

THE HISTORY

A very important part of the emergency department record is the history portion. From this portion the emergency physician obtains an overview of why the patient is in the emergency department. A number of different participants contribute to the history portion. The first persons to document emergency department history are the triage nurse and registration clerk. The patient tells them why he or she has come to the emergency department.

Next, the emergency nurse records the patient's vital signs, takes a history, and performs a physical assessment. This nursing history is recorded at an appropriate place on the record. Failure to clarify the patient's history as taken by the emergency department clerk or the emergency nurse can result in liability for the emergency physician. Thus, clarification of the patient history must be a prime concern for the emergency physician.

Case: Baldwin v. Knight

An interesting case demonstrating the need for historical clarification is Baldwin v. Knight. In this case, an ambiguously worded history taken by the emergency nurse contributed to a faulty diagnosis by the emergency physician.

Mr. Claude Baldwin was struck in the calf with a piece of wire that was thrown by his lawnmower while he was cutting the grass. He sustained a laceration of his right calf and was taken to the emergency department for treatment. He was first interviewed by an emergency nurse who recorded that "the patient has a puncture type wound obtained when mowing grass from a broken bottle."

When the emergency physician read the history, he assumed that the patient simply cut his leg on broken glass while he was mowing the lawn. The physician indicated that there was nothing in the history to indicate a flying object had caused the laceration. As a result, the emergency physician sutured the wound without obtaining a roentgenogram to see if the leg contained a foreign body. Later, it was discovered that the patient had a wire imbedded in his leg. The emergency physician was sued for negligence in not obtaining an x-ray film.

Even though the court believed that the emergency physician should have been alerted to the possibility of a foreign object imbedded in the patient's leg when he read the history taken by the emergency nurse, one can see how an ambiguous statement could mislead the physician. During a busy day in the emergency department, one might overlook the multiple meanings that the phrasing of the emergency department patient's history may contain.

The emergency physician and emergency nurse should both note from this example that the history should be stated clearly and concisely. When there is ambiguity, the patient should be asked to clarify. Often a patient's description of the onset of his or her symptoms or of an injury can be extremely vague. In this case, questions should be asked to clarify any ambiguity, and the emergency department record should be modified to reflect the patient's statements.

Above all, it is dangerous to assume anything in the emergency department. The emergency physician should *always* ask the patient or family or both to explain why they are in the emergency department at that moment and what is it that concerns them.

FORENSIC EVENTS

Certain forensic medical events also require careful emergency department record keeping as essential in accomplishing justice. These events include such frequent occurrences as battered children, rape, and intoxicated motorists.

Finally, in addition to the importance of reimbursement, the emergency physician should be attentive to the requirements of emergency department medical record documentation because of the constant threat of medical malpractice litigation. The emergency department record is critical to a successful malpractice defense. It is the first, best, and sometimes only possibility for the emergency physician to withstand the attack of a malpractice lawsuit.

This litigation reality was driven home in the *ACEP Foresight* (April 1988):

You frequently hear that the chart can either be a friend or an enemy in court. This is absolutely true. A chart that reflects that thorough care was given can be a great ally in preventing unnecessary litigation, as well as being your primary defense when confronted with an actual suit. Few, if any, of us are blessed with a memory that can retain over a period of years all the details of each patient encounter. The child with the sore throat, after a year or so, blends in with the hundreds of other children with similar problems, and the individual details cannot be accurately recalled. Even in the rare case where the details are recalled, it is hard to get anyone else—and this includes jurors—to believe that you actually remember that patient clearly. In the litigation process, evidence other than the patient's record will be presented, but in court, the record is considered a more reliable source of information. As a result, we must prepare charts that truly reflect our actions. You are not expected to write volumes on each patient, for it is physically and mechanically impossible to do so in an active emergency department. But pertinent and valuable information must, without exception, be noted. As better charting habits are developed, it becomes a very simple and almost routine matter.

To a certain degree, better habits should become simpler and more routine as we perform actions over and over again. However, the emergency physician never knows which emergency department patient will be the one to bring a medical malpractice action. Thus, better chart documentation will increase the odds of having a more defensible emergency department record when it is necessary.

DOCUMENTATION SHORTFALLS

Many medical record complaints are cited by defense attorneys in medical malpractice cases. Among these common documentation problems are illegibility, incompleteness, failure of the physician to review the record and comment, physician/nurse conflicts, and tampering with the medical record.

Legibility has been a classic medical record problem for physicians. At a minimum, physicians should be able to read their own handwriting. Failure here would substantially erode their credibility before the judge and jury, particularly if the physicians cannot read what they allegedly are relying on in their own defense.

Illegible medical records not only damage emergency physicians' ability to validate themselves but also have an adverse effect on the credibility of other physicians and health care providers, who allegedly read the medical record and acted upon it. Imagine a jury's reaction when, on the witness stand, a subsequent treating emergency physician admits that he or she cannot read the prior treating emergency physician's emergency department medical record information. The presumption will then be made that he or she was unable to read it when initially confronted by the emergency department record in the course of treating the patient in the emergency department.

Incompleteness is another serious medical record problem for physicians, including emergency physicians. Some emergency physicians pride themselves on their ability to write the shortest, most meaningful histories and physical and treatment notes. Unfortunately, an adequate malpractice defense usually goes to the emergency physician who has written too much rather than too little.

Entries made by other health professionals, especially emergency nurses, provide valuable and necessary information for proper patient treatment. The emergency physician must review all provider notes, especially the emergency nursing notes. Inconsistent notations can communicate a confusing picture of patient care. Similarly, inaccuracy will be avoided if the physician carefully reviews the chart prior to signing transcribed notations and summaries to make certain that the information is correct.

Emotional comments and extraneous remarks have no place on any patient medical records. Recently, patients have been given greater access to their medical records, and they likely will read any derogatory or humorous comments made about them. Ill-chosen words by the emergency physician may precipitate a malpractice suit or make it less defensible. Also, complaints and criticisms by other health professionals in the medical record can frequently result in a lawsuit being filed and even increase the amount of damages awarded.

Alterations to the medical records should be made with extreme care. Errors and oversights will occur from time to time. However, alterations, erasures, and the "squeezing in" of additional comments can complicate matters and possibly discredit the physician and the emergency department record. Corrections should not be made to appear as if someone is trying to conceal something. Credibility is a key factor in any litigation, and an altered record frequently destroys the emergency physician's credibility.

When changes are absolutely necessary to correct inaccuracies in the emergency department record, one simple line should be drawn through the entry, accompanied by the emergency physician's initials and date of the change. The original entry must remain legible. At the next available spot in the emergency department record, a new note, dated and signed, should be written to explain the need for the correction. If it is necessary to record more information, a supplemental page, clearly indicated as a late entry, should be recorded.

Above all, an emergency physician should never attempt to delete information or alter existing documents once legal action has been initiated. Any alterations to the record that do not conform to the preceding suggestions may be interpreted as a deliberate "cover-up." The ultimate form of altered medical records is destruction, which occurred in the following case.

Case: Carr v. St. Paul Fire & Marine Insurance Company

This case was commenced by the wife of the decedent, Carlos Carr, to recover damages for alleged negligence on the part of the hospital and its employees in the treatment and failure to treat the decedent, who was received into the emergency department of the hospital on the evening of January 8, 1972. Mr. Carr's wife filed this lawsuit on May 20, 1972, and alleged that because of hospital and emergency department negligence, Mr. Carr was permitted to return to his home, where he died before or about midnight, January 8, 1972, after leaving the hospital.

After many delays, the case was tried before a jury on October 21, 1974. The jury returned a verdict in favor of the plaintiff. It awarded $35,000 in damages to Mrs. Carr and $40,000 for the benefit of the decedent's minor children. The defendant moved for a judgment notwithstanding the verdict, or, in the alternative, for a new trial. It was upon these motions, which were denied by the Trial Court, that the case was appealed by the defendant.

The court's opinion reviewed the general principles regarding the standard of care required of hospitals and concluded that a hospital is required to provide that degree of care and attention to its patients as circumstances may require. The court then proceeded to review the evidence presented in the case.

The evidence clearly disclosed that, before going to the hospital in the early evening of January 8, 1972, Mr. Carr called the hospital to ascertain if a doctor was present and was advised that a doctor was available. On this date, the emergency department personnel consisted of one licensed practical nurse (LPN) and two orderlies.

After arrival in the emergency department, Mr. Carr's vital signs were taken, including his blood pressure, heart rate, temperature, and respirations. These were taken by one of the orderlies and conveyed to the other orderly for inclusion in the emergency department medical record. The nurse was not in the room when the orderlies were taking the vital signs.

She conferred for a short time with the orderlies and, in accordance with Mr. Carr's wishes, telephoned his family physician, who was out of the city until the following Monday. The nurse testified that she offered to call the doctor on call from the hospital, but Mr. Carr said he preferred to wait until his own doctor returned.

However, the plaintiff testified that she and Mr. Carr demanded that any available doctor be called, but that the nurse failed to call anyone after she was unable to reach the family physician. Mrs. Carr further testified that the nurse was aware of Mr. Carr's physical condition and of the fact that he had severe abdominal pains and vomiting as well as a history of diabetes.

The nurse and the orderlies knew the decedent was in pain and in need of relief, but none was afforded. Mr. and Mrs. Carr were permitted to leave the hospital unexamined by a physician. After the Carrs returned to their home, Mr. Carr's pains grew worse. They again called the hospital, and an ambulance was sent to return them to the hospital. The testimony did not disclose the exact time of Mr. Carr's return to the hospital. The coroner, who had been called to the hospital by an undetermined party, testified that Mr. Carr had not been dead an hour before he saw him, and that his body was still warm.

The emergency department personnel testified that the decedent's vital signs were normal, but they also testified that the record of the examination of the vital signs was destroyed that night and was not seen by anyone other than the two orderlies, the nurse, and possibly the coroner. No explanation was given as to why the record was destroyed or as to what the orderlies and nurse considered normal vital signs.

A question of fact was raised by the testimony of the plaintiff, the orderlies, and the nurse. This question of fact about exactly what occurred, along with other questions, was submitted to the jury for its decision. The defendant contended that the court erred in allowing testimony as to a change in hospital procedure subsequent to the death of Mr. Carr. The defense objection was based on evidence that disclosed that the emergency department employees destroyed the emergency department record after Mr. Carr died. The defense contended that the testimony should not have been admitted because it implied that the hospital changed its procedure as a result of the incident after Mr. Carr died.

In response to this contention, the court said that it did not know why the record was destroyed. However, the court did say:

The plaintiff was greatly hampered in proving just what was done by the employees and what their examination disclosed, and the jury had a right to consider the effect that such destruction had in determining the actual facts. It seems highly unreasonable that the findings of the physical condition of a person examined by the emergency room employees would be destroyed. . . . No one knows the effect that such action had on the jury, but the jury certainly had a right to infer that the record, had it been retained, would have shown that a medical emergency existed and that a doctor should have been called and that more attention should have been given (to Mr. Carr) than was given.

Thus, the court sustained the jury's verdict in favor of the plaintiff and overruled the defendant's motions for a judgment or a new trial. The obvious lesson from the Carr case is that the emergency department staff should not attempt to alter the emergency department record by destroying it.

The discovery of an alteration in a medical record may lead to a settlement of the case owing to loss of credibility for the defense. In addition, where records are deliberately changed, the jury might award punitive damages for which the emergency physician, not his or her insurance company, will be liable. In most states public policy prohibits insuring oneself for punitive damages. The physician must pay punitive damages out of personal assets. Bankruptcy law may not provide shelter either. Although prior judgments are dischargeable in bankruptcy, damages for intentional acts, including punitive damages, may be nondischargeable. Also, intentional alteration of medical records may result in a physician's loss or suspension of licensure. This would in turn be reported to the National Practitioner Data Bank, with long-lasting consequences.

Finally, there is a duty to adequately inquire into the patient's past medical history, as illustrated by the following case.

Case: Mulligan v. Wetchler

This New York case involved a patient transfer from one hospital to another, with failure to communicate between the two institutions.

Mr. Mulligan developed abdominal pain and was taken to Jewish Memorial Hospital by ambulance. He was examined by a physician and told that he might have appendicitis but could not be admitted to Jewish Memorial for lack of beds. He was thereafter transferred to city-owned Fordham Hospital, where he was also examined by a physician, who was advised of the patient's transfer from Jewish Memorial Hospital. The second treating physician made no inquiry as to the diagnosis of the patient's condition made at Jewish Memorial Hospital.

After a limited physical examination, the Fordham Hospital physician prescribed a sedative, a stomach soothant, and an enema and discharged the patient. No laboratory or other diagnostic studies were performed. Several hours later, Mr. Mulligan was seen at home by a physician, who diagnosed appendicitis. The patient was hospitalized at Bellevue Hospital and operated on for a perforated appendix. He survived the surgery but died on the 11th postoperative day from complications.

At the trial it was the unchallenged testimony of the plaintiff's expert witness that it was a radical departure from accepted standards of practice not to have ascertained the reason for the transfer from Jewish Memorial Hospital to Fordham Hospital and the diagnosis made at Jewish Memorial Hospital. On appeal, the Appellate Court concluded that the Trial Court had properly submitted to the jury the question of whether the Fordham Hospital physician had departed from accepted medical practice in his handling of the case. The jury's conclusion was affirmed that Mr. Mulligan's illness would not have been fatal if the information from Jewish Memorial Hospital had been obtained.

The thrust of the Mulligan case was that the duty to inquire rested upon the second receiving hospital. This is not entirely true today with the advent of COBRA rules and regulations. Clearly, under the COBRA regulations, the responsibility for an appropriate, safe, and effective transfer of a patient rests with the first receiving hospital and not the second receiving hospital. In fact, it is the responsibility of the first receiving hospital to make certain that an appropriate physician at the second receiving hospital has agreed to accept the patient and has a bed available in which to admit the patient at the second receiving hospital. All appropriate medical record and test result copies must also accompany the patient to the second receiving hospital. Needless to say, it is much less likely that the outcome in the Mulligan case would have been the same today with the advent of the COBRA regulations.

DISCHARGE INSTRUCTIONS

As noted at the beginning of this article, the JCAHO and various state laws and regulations require that patients be given written instruction sheets upon their discharge from the emergency department. Just as there is no perfect emergency department medical record, so too is there no perfect discharge instruction sheet. Medical records and instruction sheets are only as good as the professionals who use them.

Case: Discharge Instruction Sheet

An interesting case dealing with head injury instruction sheets was tried in San Francisco in 1973. A 12-year-old boy was struck in the head during a fight and was taken to the hospital emergency department where he was examined and x-rayed by an intern. While in the emergency department, the patient was pale, sleepy, and diaphoretic. It was noted that he also experienced a drop in pulse from 62 to 48.

Although the radiographs were negative, the intern recommended admission. After examination and consultation by a staff pediatrician, the decision was made to discharge the patient for observation at home. Although a head injury sheet was ordered for the father, he never received appropriate instructions.

The patient was sent home despite signs of deteriorating neurologic status. The patient was returned later that evening with an acute extradural hematoma. Emergency surgery resulted in normal intelligence but total paralysis except for eye movement, which was the patient's only means of communication. The jury awarded damages of $4 million against the hospital and pediatrician.

The value and function of the head injury instruction sheet in this case would have been more fully appreciated if it had been given and if the patient had not had neurologic signs and symptoms at the time of discharge. However, this was not the case.

These facts show how important it is for the emergency physician and emergency nurse to work with the instruction sheets. Emergency physicians and nurses must provide appropriate discharge instructions to patients and their family. Finally, it is important for the patient or legal guardian to evidence by their signature that they have received instructions and the discharge instruction sheet.

Dr W. Richard Dukala, author of the chapter on the Emergency Department Medical Record in ACEP's *Emergency Medicine Risk Management* (1991) states:

> Discharge instructions are a vital and integral element of the emergency department medical record. Many claims succeed against emergency physicians because the plaintiff's lawyers are able to demonstrate that the physician failed to provide discharge instructions to patients that clearly told them when, and under what circumstances, follow-up care was needed. . . .
>
> There are two general types of follow-up instructions—mandated and as needed follow-up. Mandated follow-up is the easiest type to prescribe because it makes all the decisions for the patient. The patient is given a specific day or time when the mandated follow-up is to occur. If the emergency physician feels it necessary and appropriate, the follow-up physician can be contacted in advance to insure that the prescribed follow-up will occur. . . .
>
> As needed follow-up is the more difficult of the two types to prescribe because it always requires the patient to make certain judgments. In this regard, disease/injury processes can progress in four ways. The disease/injury symptoms can persist, improve, worsen, or new symptoms can develop. If each of these four options is addressed by as needed follow-up instructions, safe instructions can be anticipated.

CONFIDENTIALITY

Patients seek care in the emergency department for any number of reasons. Perhaps the most common is that their complaint becomes acute at a time when their personal physician is unavailable. Other times, the patient is away from home, or suffers from a sudden catastrophic event such as a gunshot wound, requiring the resources of the emergency department. Sometimes, however, the patient comes to the emergency department because he or she seeks care for a condition that he does not wish his family or personal physician to become aware of. Respecting the patient's right to confidentiality is of primary importance.

State laws protect the rights of patients who reasonably expect that information they give to a treating physician will remain confidential. For example, Chapter 110, Article VII, section 8-802 of *Smith-Hurd Illinois Annotated Statutes* provides for the general nondisclosure of privileged information by physicians. If the information was acquired in attending any patient in a professional character, necessary to enable him or her professionally to serve the patient, it is protected under this statute. Title 71, Chapter 6, section 1690.108 of *Purdon's Pennsylvania Statutes* provides that all records pertaining to the treatment of drug or alcohol abuse may be released only on the request of a patient, except in emergency medical situations. Any other disclosure without the patient's consent requires a showing of good cause in court. A physician who treated a patient in the emergency department for a heroin overdose with Narcan, and then communicated this information to an unauthorized person, would be in violation of this type of statute. Such violations could lead to civil liability, criminal penalties, and even credentialing or licensure sanctions.

Cases: Confidentiality

United States v. Eide is an interesting case involving this type of disclosure. The defendant was a patient at a Veterans Administration Medical Center who sought treatment for substance abuse. The court found that he could not later have the information he gave used against him in a criminal proceeding. To do so would violate the congressional policy of allowing confidentiality of these records so as to encourage substance abusers to come forward and seek treatment for their addictions. In Commissioner of Social Services of the City of New York v. David R.S., the court held that federal confidentiality provided to records of substance abuse treatment could not be denied simply because the patient first sought other services provided by a health care provider.

A Connecticut case reveals how strong the governmental policy is in favor of patient confidentiality. In Connecticut State Medical Society v. Commission on Hospitals and Health Care, a now repealed information gathering scheme in Connecticut required various items of patient information, including ZIP & FOUR codes. It was proven that these codes could, and do, in several instances identify only a single postal patron. The Connecticut Supreme Court ordered the ZIP & FOUR codes eliminated from the information gathering system because they could impermissibly identify the patients about whom the data were collected.

DISCLOSURE

In some clearly defined instances the public interest in disclosure of harmful information outweighs the policy in favor of confidentiality. The duty to disclose in these instances is typically defined by state statute. For example, in New Jersey, Title 9, section 6-8.16 of *New Jersey Statutes Annotated* provides that "[a]ny physician examining or treating any child . . . is empowered to take said child into protective custody when the child has suffered serious physical injury . . . and the most probable inference from the medical and factual information supplied, is that the said injury or injuries were inflicted upon the child by another person by other than accidental means, and the person suspected of inflicting, or permitting to be inflicted, the said injury upon the child, is a person into whose custody the child would normally be returned." When a child is taken into custody pursuant to this statute, section 6-8.17 provides that "[t]he physician . . . taking a child into such protective custody shall immediately report his action to the . . . Division of Youth and Family Services." When such a report is made, section 6-8.20 provides that the physician making the report "shall have immunity from any civil or criminal liability that might otherwise be imposed. Many other states' statutes impose similar reporting and immunity requirements [see, for example, *Michigan Statutes Annotated* section 25.248(3)].

Certainly, most would agree that the benefits that accrue from the reporting of suspected child abuse outweigh the costs associated with that type of disclosure. However, another type of information is currently sought more and more often: HIV status. It is strongly recommended that testing for HIV in the emergency department is inappropriate and should not be done for three reasons; (1) The inability of providing appropriate pre- and post-HIV test counseling in the emergency department makes HIV testing inappropriate in the emergency department setting. (2) Even in a moderately busy emergency department, the inordinate time and resource commitment needed to provide appropriate contact counseling is typically unavailable. (3) The problem of following up for false-positive/negative test results is unmanageable with typical emergency department resources.

The problems associated with disclosure of HIV test results are multitudinous. Primary among these is violation of the patient's right to privacy. HIV testing is a Pandora's box that should not be opened in the emergency department. If the patient's HIV status should become otherwise known to the emergency physician, that information should be safeguarded. Unless a specific statutory or court-ordered authority is presented to the emergency physician, the confidentiality of a patient's HIV status should remain inviolate.

TELEPHONE ADVICE/INSTRUCTIONS

Often, a patient will telephone the emergency department seeking medical advice. If the phone call is unsolicited and made by a patient with whom there is no physician-patient relationship, the only advice that should be given is for the patient to come to the emergency department. No treatment advice should be given in these circumstances. If possible, record the caller's name, the reason for the call, and the fact that the caller was told to come to the emergency department. If any question about the conversation arises later, this information will prove invaluable.

If a patient is waiting in the emergency department for routine laboratory results and expresses a desire to leave prior to the return of the results, inconvenience can be minimized and the outcome maximized by discharging the patient with explicit instructions to call at a specified time for the results, with the caveat that, should the results be abnormal, the patient must return to the emergency department for further evaluation. This type of instruction must be explicitly documented on the chart. Additionally, provisions should be made to contact the patient from the emergency department if he or she fails to call for the results within a reasonable period of time.

RECORDSMANSHIP

"Recordsmanship" is a term used to describe competent emergency physician record keeping in a fashion that communicates with clinical accuracy, along with the common-sense understanding that the emergency department record may be read aloud on another day in an open courtroom. The following are some random observations about the art and science of record keeping.

1. *Inquire about the patient's occupation.* In the case of hand injuries, it is important to know whether the injured extremity is the dominant one. The higher the stakes for the patient, the more important it is to have an appropriate consultant examine the patient early on.

2. *Review the nursing notes.* Emergency nurses spend considerable time taking emergency patient histories and conducting physical assessments, in addition to taking vital signs. The emergency physician should review all of the emergency nurse's notes with special attention to "red flag" words such as "lethargy" and so on.

3. *Note vital signs.* The emergency physician should review the patient's vital signs as well as subsequent vital signs if they have been taken. Evidence of hypertension should be noted and the patient referred for appropriate follow-up as soon as possible. Repeat blood pressures should be taken to show evidence of the patient becoming more normotensive during his or her stay in the emergency department.

4. *Take a detailed history and perform an appropriate physical examination.* The emergency physician should embellish or clarify the emergency nurse's history if appropriate. The emergency physician should perform an appropriate physical examination and document pertinent positive as well as negative findings. Dr. Bukata makes some comments about the commonly used abbreviation PERRLA: "When asked by a patient's attorney what the "A" means and whether "accommodation" was specifically tested, the unwary emergency physician who uses this abbreviation may appear to the jury to have documented something not actually done. The attorney can then suggest that perhaps other parts of the record are equally untrue.

5. *Never use demeaning terms to describe the patient.* There is no place on any medical record for derogatory terms, which are unprofessional and inconsiderate and may later haunt the emergency physician or nurse.

6. *Make the patient disposition consistent with the diagnosis.* If the diagnosis is "possible appendicitis" or "possible coronary insufficiency," it is not appropriate to discharge the patient. If the emergency physician is prepared to discharge the patient and is not seriously considering the preceding diagnoses, then more appropriate discharge diagnoses might include "abdominal pain of unknown etiology" or "noncardiac chest pain of unknown etiology."

7. *Document significant laboratory, radiographic, and electrocardiographic (EKG) abnormalities.* The emergency physician should make some explanatory comment next to such tests to give the reader of the

emergency department record a reasonable impression of what was in the emergency physician's mind at the time he or she examined the patient. For example, if EKGs have been compared with previously recorded EKGs in the patient's prior medical records, a note identifying this comparison should be made, such as "no significant change compared with EKG 1 year ago."

8. *Try to get a "last look" at the emergency department record.* Dr. Bukata observes: "Being the last individual to make chart entries allows the emergency physician the opportunity to scan all the notes of the other documenters and to be aware of everything that has been recorded. Special efforts should be made to identify charting inconsistencies or other potentially problematic areas that may indicate internal conflict in the record." Finally, it is important for the emergency physician to indicate the patient's condition at the time of discharge. It is not advisable to discharge patients home who are in worse condition at the time of discharge than when they arrived in the emergency department. Ideally, the emergency department patient feels better at the time of discharge, and this level of improvement should be so noted.

CONCLUSION

Unfortunately, more and more time is being spent by the emergency physician on the preparation and documentation of the emergency department medical record, and this will continue in the foreseeable future. The emergency physician must maintain a high level of commitment both to the practice of quality emergency medicine and to the practice of quality emergency department record charting. Dr. Bukata notes:

Generating the medical record is an acquired skill born of the basic understanding that a legal record is being created that must serve the care providers as well as the patient. When the medical record and discharge instructions are viewed as primarily legal documents, created to detail the assessment and care of a patient along with recommended follow-up, all the other functions of the medical record will be well served. It is essential that all who are authorized to make entries into a patient's chart understand the potential importance of the legal record they are creating, the need for carefully thought-out entries, the responsibility to chart appropriately and the potential consequences of their actions.

Therefore, emergency physicians should invest their time and effort in creating the best possible emergency department records. This wise investment should produce valuable returns. Remember that the best malpractice insurance available is an emergency department record prepared so that it is legally capable of standing on its own.

References

1. Baldwin v. Knight, 569 S.W. 2d 450 (1978)
2. Cal. Super. Ct., San Francisco, CA., Docket No. 624337

3. Carr v. St. Paul Fire & Marine Insurance Company, 384 F.Supp. 821 (1974), decided on November 19, 1974, by the U.S. District Court, Fayetteville, Arkansas
4. Commissioner of Social Services of the City of New York v. David R.S., 451 N.Y.S. 2d 1 (1982)
5. Connecticut State Medical Society v. Commission on Hospitals and Health Care, 223 Conn. 450 (1992)
6. Emergency Medicine Risk Management, Dallas, American College of Emergency Physicians (1991)
7. Mulligan v. Wetchler, 39 A.D.2d 102 (1972)
8. United States v. Eide, 875 F.2d 1429 (9th. Cir. 1989)

Address reprint requests to

James George, MD, JD
307 South Evergreen Avenue
Woodbury, NJ 08096

MEDICAL-LEGAL ISSUES 0733–8627/93 $0.00 + .20

RISK MANAGEMENT AND HIGH-RISK ISSUES IN EMERGENCY MEDICINE

Gregory L. Henry, MD, FACEP

The term *risk management* has become one of the buzz words of the 1990s corporate communities. No where is this truer than in the practice of medicine. Risk management becomes intertwined with the concept of quality assurance, and lines between various disciplines are easily blurred. But overriding principles and precise usage of terms aid everyone in understanding the real issues involved. Practitioners of the healing arts should never forget that the only real risk is to the life and wellbeing of the patient, and that risk management should really mean controlling the variables with regard to medical practice so as to maximize the patient's chances of a satisfactory outcome. To view risk management as any more or any less is to remove it from the traditional duties placed upon physicians from the time of Galen. Doing what is in the true best interest of the patient is generally in the short-term and long-term best interests of the health care professionals and the institutions they represent.

WHAT IS RISK MANAGEMENT?

From a purely historical perspective, medical risk management has had an almost Machiavellian connotation. Images of large institutional agencies conspiring to protect the assets of health care institutions come to mind. Traditionally, risk managers have used incident reports, patient

From the Department of Emergency Medicine, Beyer Hospital; Section of Emergency Medicine, University of Michigan; and Emergency Physicians Medical Group, Ann Arbor, Michigan complaints, and reported poor outcomes as the impetus for them to begin to "manage risk." In its more traditional forms, risk management is reactive and not proactive. Up to this time, it has been the division of the hospital where "bad outcomes" and "bad practice" were mitigated, if not repaired, on an after-the-fact basis. The risk was always viewed as the risk to the assets of the institution and not to the life of the patient. In the past, it was the rare institution that combined its risk management and quality assurance functions in such a way that poor specific outcomes triggered true changes in the systematic care of future patients. It was an ever-rarer occurrence for risk management personnel to have significant input and influence into creating the quality assurance standards that would prevent poor outcomes in the future.[9]

The newer trends in risk management, however, take a decidedly different view of risk and risk avoidance. The intelligent risk manager knows that his or her job is truly proactive, not reactive. The circle of policy formation includes input from risk management on a regular basis. More than ever, risk managers now analyze the actual causes of adverse outcomes and employ system thinking to help solve the problem. Before risk can be approached in any meaningful way, several concepts must be internalized if success is to be found. The number one plank in the platform of risk management is that good things happen only when they are planned; bad things can happen all by themselves.[9] Institutions have spent entirely too much time ensuring that the latest bit of equipment is present (whether its value has been proved or not) and not enough time actually analyzing the physical sojourn of the patient through the maze that is the typical health care institution of the 1990s. Studying this sojourn through the medical system from the patient's perspective and from the perspective of the provider is key to understanding where things go wrong.

The second major tenet of risk management is actually taken from the quality assurance literature, that is, to emphasize the fact that 85% of the problems are based in the system and not in the incompetent or malevolent actions of workers themselves.[4] Very few health care workers want anything for the patient but the patient's rapid return to a healthy state. But all our systems fail to properly inform us. Precious little time is spent in coordinating the activities of the various departments through which a patient will pass. Miscommunications between the emergency department and radiology, poor follow-up by outside on-call physicians, failure to properly pass information between the nurses and physicians—these are the types of system failures that frequently characterize risk management disasters in the health care system of the 1990s.

The reasons for such system failures are multiple. No longer does a patient go to a small office and see one physician who provides the examination, performs the laboratory and radiographic tests, prescribes the medication, and also functions in the role of monitor of progress and of follow-up care. Through superspecialization, seemingly every technical aspect of health care is performed by a different individual. Such individuals frequently perform their jobs well but out of context to the overall needs of the patient. The headlong race for technologic superiority and efficiency frequently leave the only person who matters—the patient—in a bewildering haze. Everyone believes it is someone else's job to oversee, coordinate, and justify his or her role to the patient as the patient is pushed along through the health care system. The lack of any type of coordinated US primary care policy continues to increase the likelihood that the patient will never have any type of in-depth discussion of why certain health care procedures are being performed or what their role is in assuring that patients have received maximum benefit from the system.

Joining the issues of start-to-finish planning for each aspect of a health care encounter allows for a conceptual model to analyze both the system's successes and failures. Entirely too much time is spent looking for the "bad apple" employee related to a specific poor outcome. Time needs to be spent in analyzing our successes, our good outcomes, to see what we did right, and then duplicating good behavior: time should not only be spent punishing bad behavior.[4] The ultimate reason why the risk management department does and should exist is to serve as the early-warning radar system for the hospital's policies, procedures, and actual functioning. Risk management should detect those areas where the system has not yet been refined in integrating medical care. It is risk management's duty to alert the highest levels of organizational structure about such problems. The intelligent and humane provision of health care as viewed by our patients is our only reason for existence. If US health care, which is now the largest and most expensive industry in the world, cannot provide such humane and integrated care, its reasons for existence in its current form must be challenged. The only way we can know that we are indeed providing such care is through the feedback loop provided by risk management.

The only valid test of an institution's commitment to truly improving their system is the resource base that is allocated to such improvement. It takes both time and effort to study our systems and improve them. It takes a serious intellectual and financial commitment for a health care provider to realize that almost all systems can and should be both monitored and continuously improved. Lastly, it takes the human touch. It is a willingness to not merely study averages and percentages, but to look at every human being who enters the system as our final examination in medical school and to recognize their outcome, regardless of the magnitude of the problem, as a reflection on the level to which we have performed our functions. The concept of zero defects, which has become the watchword in all manufacturing industries, must now become the credo of health care institutions. We must move to the point where any patient unhappiness with regard to our service should be considered unacceptable.

Understanding the variability in all human systems, however, each health care worker must be trained to handle complaints about the system on line. Every member of the health care team must be trained in understanding the patients' wants and desires and proper conflict resolution when those goals cannot be met. Often, the most satisfied patients are those who have had some type of minor problem in the system that, once brought to the attention of the health care personnel, has been properly and satisfactorily resolved with the understanding that surprise and disappointment on the part of the patient are the key elements in risk management. The first step is risk avoidance.

No one method or system avoids risk in all emergency departments, but the principal elements of a risk management format can be summarized in the following manner[8]:

1. Patients come to health care institutions anxious, afraid, and in a somewhat diminished capacity to understand everything that is happening to them. Health care workers should make a strong effort to understand and reassure patients.
2. Every health care worker is a risk manager. They manage the risk by doing what is necessary to see that the patient's needs are met.
3. When it is apparent that a patient's needs have not been met, any member of the health care team has not only the right but also the obligation to bring such concerns to the health care worker in charge of the care or the administrator in charge of that area to report that there is a potential risk situation if intervention is not forthcoming.
4. Continuous communication with the patient, no matter what the outcome or the circumstances, is the best way to show care and concern by the worker and the staff. Whenever conflict is identified, rapid action by both the health care worker and the institution to correct the situation are always in the best interests of the patient and the health care providers.
5. Whenever conflicts between the patient and the health care providers cannot be resolved simply on site, a structured, organized system, which will not only respond to that patient's particular problem but will also analyze the system reasons for that problem, is necessary in preventing future such episodes.

High-Risk Behaviors and Issues

Although any interaction between a patient and the health care system may result in litigation, certain situations clearly lend themselves to system failures. From a cursory review of some 1800 cases of emergency medicine malpractice (G. Henry and N. Little, malpractice litigation review), two observations can be made: (1) In 3% to 5% of such cases, there is no discernible pattern. There was an outcome that could not be predicted or militated against before the fact. Disease is infinitely variable, and some cases, the best of hands, will have a poor outcome. (2) In approximately 95% of the rest, however, the failure in either medical decision making or system logic is evident. Such cases can and should have been avoided by proper communications and actions. Such system failures are common to most emergency departments and constitute the vast majority of risk situations.

Change of Shift

The troublesome period when one physician is coming on shift and another is leaving is often regarded by experienced emergency physicians, risk managers, and attorneys in the malpractice field as an extremely dangerous time for both the health care provider and the patient. A casual passing of the baton from one physician or group of nurses to the next can allow the patient to "fall between the cracks." The oncoming physician often feels confident that the patient has been properly worked up, and the patient is frequently given a "diagnosis" prior to his or her assumption of the case. The patient is frequently not properly re-evaluated prior to a decision being made or time of discharge. One emergency physician may have asked the second physician coming on shift to merely check a laboratory test and roentgenogram, and, if normal, the patient can be discharged. This sort of thinking is dangerous. The results of any one roentgenogram or laboratory determination—without being integrated into the entire picture of the history, physical, and discharge situation of the patient—rarely allow one to make such a monumental decision. Change of shift should be viewed as starting anew, and such times should not result in a lower standard of care for the patient. If, for any reason, a physician cannot properly complete the work-up of a patient and such responsibility must be transferred to another physician, a proper and orderly transfer of responsibility and liability must take place. The physician leaving shift must dictate a note as to the condition at the time of leaving and the fact that the responsibility has been transferred to a specific physician. Similarly, the physician coming on must write his or her own note discussing the condition of the patient and the program that will ensue. The physician discharging the patient should be considered the physician of record and the physician responsible for the discharge program and entering the patient into the health care system.

Similarly, nursing has, within its role, the same responsibilities as do physicians. Nurses who are going off shift or leaving for break and who are responsible for the management of a specific patient should ensure that the patient's care has been specifically transferred to another nurse, who will ensure that the observation program and any treatments or studies will be completed. The litigation history of emergency medicine contains many stories of patients forgotten in rooms, forgotten in the x-ray department, or left in the waiting room because of an inadequate transfer of responsibilities. The transfer of responsibility at the change of shift should be a formal and orderly process between health care personnel and should include the patient and family. The patient and family should have no doubt as to who is in charge of the patient's care and who will direct further therapy and plan the discharge program.

Return Visits and Transfers

Patients who return to the emergency department with unscheduled visits, instead of being viewed as potential risk situations, are often treated as medical criminals. Interrogation by medical and clerical staff often sounds more like a police round-up than a medical re-evaluation. Health care personnel have a tendency to view such return patients as "doctor shopping" or having some underlying psychological problem, when in fact nothing could be farther from the truth. Careful studies have been done looking at return visits, and at least 75% of the time the patients were poorly instructed, the disease process took an unexpected turn, or the initial diagnosis was wrong. This, combined with the fact that getting into the health care "nonsystem," which is often through private physicians' offices, can be extremely difficult for many patients. Such inability to access the regular health care system should be viewed as a legitimate reason for returning to the emergency department[10] (G. Henry and N. Little, review of 1800 emergency medicine malpractice cases).

Transfers from other institutions have in common with second visits the one thing that gives a false sense of security to the members of the health care team and can represent a true impediment to rapid resolution of their problems: Such patients already have a "diagnosis." Once a diagnosis is made in medicine, frequently all intelligent thought stops. Health care personnel have a tendency to assume as correct the original diagnosis for which the patient was seen on the first visit or the original problems identified at the first hospital prior to transfer. But all experienced emergency personnel realize that transfers from another institution must be viewed as totally new patients. The conservative action for the emergency physician is to work up transferred and second-visit patients as if they were totally new. Physicians should not assume that a patient has remained totally stable during transfer or that a disease entity has not progressed since previous visits.[5,6] Such patients often arrive entirely different than "advertised," and it is no defense for the receiving institution to say that they have relied upon the first institution's evaluation or the initial evaluation on return visits. It is proper for a physician to refer to previous histories and physical examinations performed and to be aware of previous diagnoses. It is also important for the physician to realize that an independent history and physical at that moment in time should form the basis of a current clinical impression. When a return visit presents, it is often a good idea to have a different physician review the patient. Sometimes a fresh perspective can avoid intellectual traps.

A final rule, one that more and more emergency physicians are beginning to follow, is that when a patient presents for the third time, admission should be strongly considered. It is always troublesome when a patient presents continuously to an emergency department. Such patients may have an ongoing medical problem that may not be clear to the provider or the patient. The mere fact that the patient has presented three times to a health care provider should indicate that either the patient's true diagnosis has not been recognized or the patient clearly does not understand the nature of the illness and the course of the disease.[10] In any event, such multiple interactions without progress toward a successful resolution should make the concerned health care professional eager to properly resolve the problem.

Private Patients in the Emergency Department

An important concept in both philosophy and law is patient ownership. Doctors must understand that they do not "own" patients; in fact, patients "own" doctors. The doctor, and indeed the entire health care team, is the retained agent and servant of the patient.[10] Patients can change health care institutions and physicians anytime they so choose. Whenever patients present to the emergency department, they become, by the very act of their appearing, the patient of the emergency physician for at least this visit and this particular problem with which they present. The emergency physician has more than a duty; he or she has an absolute obligation to be aware of any and all patients who are in the department and their status at any time. The emergency nursing personnel have a similar duty to evaluate patients expeditiously and to keep the emergency physician informed of patients who are waiting to be seen, particularly those whose situations may be critical. The COBRA (Consolidated Omnibus Budget Reconciliation Act) law clearly states that each patient who presents must be evaluated to see if an emergency exists.[3] There is no exemption in the law that says patients do not have to be seen if they have "their own doctor" coming to see them.

The usual sticking point in all of these problems is who gets to charge for services. This should be the least important aspect in analyzing such cases. The hospital needs to go on record—and this needs to be conveyed to the medical staff at all levels—that patients presenting to the emergency department will be evaluated, and, if necessary, intervention will take place prior to the arrival of private physicians. The private attending physician has no right to jeopardize the health care institution and the emergency department personnel for ego satisfaction.

Private patients in the emergency department should be viewed as any other patients. They should be properly triaged and examined, and therapy should be started if they are in an urgent or emergent condition. There is no problem with properly transferring care to a private physician when he or she arrives, and such transfer of responsibility should be properly noted.

It should be the policy of the emergency department and the institution that patients waiting in the department for their personal physician will be evaluated to determine whether an emergency condition exists. For sake of convenience and for political purposes, the hospital may elect to provide an area where private attending physicians may meet their patients for nonemergent conditions. Such an area should be away from the emergency department and should not be governed or included in those areas covered by the federal COBRA statutes.

On-Call Physicians

The Joint Commission on Accreditation of Healthcare Organizations (JCAHO) has classified emergency departments into four levels of care.[14]

Hospitals functioning at levels I and II are required to have on-call lists for physician specialists. On-call specialists should be viewed as more than just physicians available to come to the emergency department. Hospitals are essentially required to enter patients for at least their immediate problem into the health care system. The hospital, and the medical staff by extension, has a direct duty and obligation to care for emergent patients who have presented to the emergency department. A physician who appears on the on-call panel in a hospital emergency department plays an essential role in the functioning of the health care system. When such physicians do not respond to calls to the emergency department or refuse to carry out follow-up care on patients seen in the emergency department, and when the hospital and the emergency physician are forced to send the patient to another institution, potential violations of COBRA abound.[3] The issue of transferring or "dumping" patients and economic screening of patients is one of which the federal government is well aware. The COBRA laws were an attempt to cajole and channel hospital and medical staff energies in the direction that would provide greatest protection for the patients and yet leave the private practice of medicine intact. As physicians fail to live up to their obligations with regard to the on-call process, it should not be surprising that the federal government will move to mandate such care.[3] If such systems cannot be organized in a cooperative venture between the hospital and the administration, further federal action will unquestionably move to secure such benefits for the citizens of the United States.

Several key points of the on-call panel must be emphasized. First, the on-call list is the responsibility of the hospital, not the emergency physician. It is incumbent upon hospital administrations to secure the services of physicians and to ensure proper entry of patients into the health care system.[17] Second, care delayed is care denied. When on-call physicians are not available within a reasonable period of time and patients suffer harm secondary to such lack of care, the institution and the system are equally culpable. Third, the practice of having consultant physicians screen potential patients by inquiring about their financial status or ability to pay should be considered not only ethically immoral but legally prohibited under the federal COBRA/OBRA laws.[3] Finally, continuity of care and outpatient follow-up of emergency patients are paramount issues. Health care facility on-call panels must serve not only to come to the hospital to see patients but also to accept patients for outpatient management of care for at least the acute illness for which they are referred.

Against Medical Advice

Patients who present to the emergency department and refuse to follow carefully considered medical advice should be considered "high risk." Such patients have essentially announced that they do not respect or trust the professional judgments of the emergency personnel involved.

Such actions frequently provoke less than empathetic responses from the medical staff, who take such patient responses as insults. Against-medical-advice situations call into play two divergently opposed concepts in law: the concept of a patient's freedom versus the health care worker's duty to protect.[12]

The patient's rights to self-determination are unquestioned.[20] A patient of adult years and sound mind has the right to refuse any medical care offered. This virtually always runs counter to the entire question of communication and properly informed decision making. Clearly, patients can always claim that they did not understand what was being presented by the health care personnel and, therefore, were prevented from making a proper decision in their own best interests. Informed refusal is more often a matter of opinion than fact. It is, therefore, essential that the charting on such cases recognizes the major pitfalls in advance. First, a patient or the family may claim that the refusal was uninformed because of diminished mental capacity. The first duty of the emergency staff is to properly document the mental status of the patient to properly make the decision to refuse care. Patients who are encephalopathic clearly lack capacity; therefore, the substitute judgment of the health care professionals involved or family members may be perfectly appropriate. If, however, patients are awake and alert, can carry on reasonable conversation and discuss the problems at hand, and have the mental ability to act in their own self-interests, they usually meet the test for competency to exercise judgments on their own behalf.

Second, in informed refusal cases, it is often claimed that the hospital personnel did not inform the patient in a manner that they could understand. It is important to inform and document that the patient was told in perfectly clear terms of the desire of the health care professionals and the fact that such discussion was held in lay terms that the patient could easily understand. Euphemisms should not be used. If the medical staff is afraid of sudden death, then the term "death" should be used. If they are afraid that injury to a limb might result in amputation, then use of terms that clearly indicate that the limb may need to be removed should not only be used but also recorded on the chart.

A third question in refusal of care concerns alternative forms of treatment. Patients need to be properly informed if alternative modes of treatment would solve the problem, and they should be given opportunities to use such modes of therapy. When acceptable alternatives are not available, this also needs to be properly documented.

Fourth, involvement of family is crucial. Should the patient die as a result of noncooperation with the health care system, it is the patient's relatives through the estate who will bring action against the medical professionals involved. Any and all family or friends who are with the patient when they come to the hospital must be aware of the patient's refusal. Hard-driving executives who may wish to deny their own chest pain are usually brought into more realistic thinking when they must deny care in front of their family. Should the patient expressly forbid the medical staff from speaking to family or friends, such forbiddance must also be carefully documented. It is reasonable to inform the family that you have been denied the option to speak to them by the patient. This clearly makes the family understand that the patient, not the physician, is refusing to discuss the patient's refusal to cooperate with the plans laid out by the health care personnel.

Finally, and least important, is the patient's signature. The signature line on the chart is no replacement for a properly documented record. Many times patients who leave against medical advice do so in a hostile atmosphere and refuse to sign. The fact that the patient refused to sign should also be noted. The myth has long been perpetuated that if a signature is present, the patient has waived his or her rights and has relieved the health care personnel of legal responsibility. This is clearly not the case. Documentation of against-medical-advice requires the previously listed four parts to assist in a legal verdict in favor of the doctor. A signature is not a substitute for a legal process, and the signature and the legal process must be accompanied by proper documentation if such situations are to be adjudicated in favor of the health care team.

Against-medical-advice should be a relatively rare occurrence. Most skilled health care professionals can convince patients to follow their advice. When a specific physician has a large number of against-medical-advice cases, this usually represents a doctor-patient communication problem. The attitude with which a physician approaches a patient in an against-medical-advice mode is critical to success. A "take it or leave it" ultimatum frequently results in noncompliance by the patient. Such situations should not be confrontational. When one is tempted to fight fire with fire, it is always better to remember that the fire department has had much better luck with water.

Left Before Examination

The patient who leaves before examination (LBE) or without being seen (LWBS) constitutes a much different medicolegal problem than the patient who leaves against medical advice. As previously stated, patients who leave against medical advice virtually always do so because of a doctor-patient communication problem. In the LBE situation, the doctor was not even given the opportunity to form a doctor-patient bond. Large numbers of LBE patients are invariably system problems and represent prolonged waiting time. Rates of lawsuits regarding emergency medicine go up almost exponentially after a patient has been at the hospital and waiting more than 2 hours (G. Henry and N. Little, review of 1800 emergency medicine malpractice cases). It is very difficult for patients to wait more than 2 hours to have their perceived emergency evaluated. Hostility grows, and hostility is the basis for miscommunication and lawsuits. Substantial or rising LBE rates should prompt a systems review to determine exactly why the patient flow is inadequate. Long waits for laboratory and radiology tests, difficulty in freeing beds owing to inadequate or poor admissions procedures, or delays in obtaining needed consultations should all be reviewed to determine why patient flow is inadequate to meet the patient demands.

In-House Emergencies

The emergency physician in smaller institutions, either through medical staff policy or contractual agreements, is occasionally involved with patients who are doing poorly on the medical and surgical floors. These in-house emergencies vary from cardiopulmonary arrest situations to assessing patients who have fallen out of bed to pronouncing patients dead. All such situations, however, have the potential for medicolegal problems. Whenever the emergency physician is called out of the emergency department, he or she is no longer able to provide immediate care to those who may burst through the doors. To the child with an airway obstruction, to the patient in cardiac arrest, to the patient with a tension pneumothorax, the absence of the emergency physician may spell disaster. Therefore, leaving the emergency department should be an infrequent event and one that is prompted by true medical necessity. It is wise for the emergency physician to not guarantee in any contract that he or she will answer in-house emergencies. The physician is, by such action, guaranteeing to be in two places at once. The emergency physician should agree to respond to in-house emergencies as would any other physician in the hospital when hearing the STAT call for a physician. Part of the test of a "Good Samaritan" action is that it is performed outside the usual practice setting of the physician and that the physician has not established a duty to provide such service. A contractual link might obviate a physician's eventual Good Samaritan defense. In keeping with the Good Samaritan idea, it is also wise for the emergency physician to not be paid per patient for responding in such events. Direct payment for medical services on a prearranged basis may also obviate a Good Samaritan defense.[16]

Provision for care of in-house patients is the responsibility of the hospital and not exclusively the function of the emergency physician. If the emergency physician is to be involved in the management of non–emergency department patients, then a set policy should be developed in conjunction with the medical executive committee and adopted by the board of directors or trustees.[13]

Finally, it is not the role of emergency physicians to solve all problems of the hospital merely because they are available 24 hours per day. Should a patient become ill on the floor, hospital rules and regulations should clearly delineate the responsibility for the primary attending physician to evaluate his or her patient. If indeed the primary physician cannot attend the patient for some reason, such patients can be brought to the emergency department, where the emergency physician has proper facilities and equipment and is not forced to leave the site of primary obligation.

Residents in the Emergency Department

Residents in the emergency department are often treated under two mythical concepts that seem to predominate in house staff training in the

United States: (1) the young doctors will learn by their mistakes, and (2) if they are not ready now to see patients on their own, how can we "graduate" them from the program? At the outset, the initial premise of learning by mistakes is unsound educationally and morally. No one wants pilots to learn by their mistakes as they land their 747 without supervision. Educational theory would dictate that the only thing learned from mistakes is how to make mistakes. The great advantage of emergency medicine is that each patient can be supervised in an on-line, real-time manner by an attending physician who can help the resident work through the decision process and intervene when the situation requires. No hospitals give "a training discount" reduction in the patient's bill because they have been seen by a resident in an unsupervised manner. The resident is a physician in training. The Residency Review Committee and Council on Graduate Medical Education have laid out time frames in which the physician is to function in a supervised manner. Supervision changes as the sophistication of a resident changes. However, overall responsibility for every patient in the emergency department is borne by the attending physician.[15] It is a cowardly act for an attending physician to ever blame the outcome of a case on the resident that he or she is supervising. Residents should be concurrently monitored and actively supervised while in the department.

A second point that needs to be emphasized is that the specialty of the residents should be considered unimportant. A resident rotating through the emergency department from a specialty other than Emergency Medicine should be supervised in the same manner as an Emergency Medicine resident and actually should be considered to be less familiar with emergency department policies and procedures. It should be noted that retrospective review of charts, although useful as a teaching tool, is no substitute for on-line, hands-on evaluation of the patients and the care being given by the residents.[15] Billing for residents' services that are not directly supervised by the physician doing the billing should be considered an extremely high-risk activity. The attestation statements signed by physicians who sign up with various insurance companies generally state that they will charge for only those services that they personally render or supervise. Supervision from a distance is considered no supervision at all. The federal government and many states are actively pursuing physicians under a doctrine of fraud when they have rendered a bill for services in which they have not been directly involved.

Residents frequently believe that, because their malpractice coverage is paid for by the institution and they are covered under a doctrine of *respondeat superior*, they are immune from the ravages of law suits. In fact, they may be sued individually, they may be forced to participate in any trial situation that arises, and they are not exempt from being reported to the National Practitioner Databank.[21]

An extremely touchy and often volatile situation involves off-service residents who are called down from the floors to evaluate patients in the emergency department. These physicians are still residents and are responsible to the physician in charge. It is often said by attending physicians on medicine and surgery services that their residents can function without reference to the emergency physicians and that they are essentially functioning "as their agents." Such physicians are rarely willing, however, to sign statements that they will assume all responsibility, pay all costs, and have all reported losses against their name in the databank. The emergency physician bears the liability of patients in the department until they have been properly transferred to another attending physician. The resident, no matter how advanced or from what service, cannot relieve the emergency physician from his or her responsibility to act in the best interests of the patient. Disputes on how a patient should be handled should not be conducted between the emergency physician and the off-service resident, but between the emergency physician and the physician in charge of that resident. All dispute resolutions should be between parties of equal power and who will bear equal responsibility. The resident should be considered a nonentity in such discussions.

The patient has a right to know who is providing and supervising any care received. Also, the patient or the family must know who constitutes the house staff and who are the attending physicians who have ultimate responsibility for the care.

Telephone Orders from Private Physicians

Outside physicians frequently do not appreciate the extent of liability that the hospital and emergency physicians may incur when a patient is treated without being examined by the emergency physician. Physicians may see a patient in their office and wish them to have a medication or treatment that is not conveniently available in their outpatient setting. As a result, such patients are frequently sent to emergency departments, and telephone orders are given to emergency personnel. This practice should be discouraged and eliminated whenever possible. There is no section of the hospital as tightly regulated by federal law as the emergency department.[7] There is no exemption in the COBRA/OBRA statutes that makes an exception for patients being sent from outside physicians' offices or patients who show up and receive "standard therapy," having not recently been re-evaluated. Although this practice is ubiquitous, it is considered to be anachronistic and dangerous. The federal law requires that every patient who presents to the emergency department to be seen must receive a medical examination. Nowhere does it indicate that patients may be seen without such an evaluation. Should the hospital wish to run an outpatient clinic for the convenience of their own physicians, then such a clinic should be set up separately from the emergency department, and strict criteria should be laid out as to what can and cannot be done without concomitant physician evaluation.[3] There is no reason to jeopardize emergency physician medicolegally for what amounts to a public relations activity of the hospital with its medical staff.

Similar situations exist with regard to requests for medical staff, particularly screeners and gatekeepers from health maintenance organizations (HMOs) for the emergency physician to just take a "quick look" at a patient. Medicolegally, there is no such thing. When the emergency physician has agreed to see anyone to determine whether an emergency exists, a doctor-patient relationship is properly established. Such a visit needs to be properly memorialized with correct charts and records. Again, there is no exemption in the OBRA or COBRA statutes that says that if a patient is being looked at for an HMO or a preferred provider organization (PPO), the usual duties incumbent upon the emergency physician are waived.[3]

Telephone Advice

Many health care personnel are not aware that a doctor or institution to patient relationship can be established with the telephone. It is not necessary that a patient physically present to the emergency department for such a relationship to be legally binding. As soon as the patient requests medical advice and the health care professional is willing to give that advice, a doctor-patient relationship has been established. In general, the rule for the emergency department should be "we do not give telephone advice." Numerous studies have documented the poor quality of telephone advice, and common sense dictates that without a patient being present, the most important clues to correct diagnosis and treatment, i.e., the presence of a live human being in front of you, are gone.[19] It is both acceptable and advised that patients be told in a polite and caring manner that the emergency department is open 24 hours per day and that they would be happy to properly evaluate them for an illness. Even seemingly innocent questions such as "What is the dose of Tylenol for a 2-year-old child?" can be the basis of establishing a doctor-patient interaction. No patient asks a casual question. Individuals seek advice from emergency departments in the hope of doing something with that information. It is always better to actually have seen the patient before entering into discussions that are potentially dangerous. In certain situations initial first-aid advice can or should be given with the instruction to come immediately to the hospital. If a patient calls to report uncontrolled bleeding, it is reasonable to tell them to apply direct pressure and come immediately to the emergency department. Likewise, if a patient has gotten a chemical in the eye, it might be perfectly appropriate to tell that patient to rinse the eye quickly with clear water and come immediately to the emergency department. In no circumstance, however, should advice be given that does not directly state that the patient needs to be seen and evaluated before any type of medical diagnosis or specific treatment can be given. Telephone advice reiterates that adage that you get exactly what you pay for.

PRACTICAL TIPS ON MANAGING EMERGENCY MEDICINE RISK

Having dealt with some of the larger philosophic issues involved with emergency medicine risk management, we believe it is worthwhile to turn to a more microlevel and recognize that risk is either created or avoided one patient at a time. The emergency physicians and emergency nurses must realize that they are the best risk management tools in the hospital. It is an intensely personal decision by each patient and his or her family to bring action against a health care professional and a health care organization. Such simple, nonscientific factors as "they like you" can mean the difference between a lawsuit and a patient who is still your friend despite the outcome.[1] Emergency medicine is, by its very nature, in the "bad outcome" business. We tend to see people not at their best but at their worst. Emergency departments are the place where families receive the news of their child's death, of their permanent paralysis, or of other incurable lifetime disabilities. No patient in the emergency department is truly prepared for the news that we bring, and the old concept of slaying the messenger still exists.

An American social and political maxim in this, the last half of the 20th century, is that no one is truly responsible for anything. Should any evil befall a person or a family, someone must be to blame, and someone must pay besides themselves. These factors, along with the general impersonalization and technologic isolation of modern medicine, have made physicians an ideal target for all failings. The corridors of the great health care institutions—like our schools, our prisons, and our gigantic workplaces—have become humanistically sterile and devoid of perceptible caring. Health care is never delivered in the aggregate; it is delivered one patient at a time. The degree to which the physician and health care team can individualize and personalize health care will determine its ability to prophylactically manage risk. Showing the patient and the family that the health care providers are truly the advocates of the patient's well-being will go farther than anything else to prevent the hostility and disappointment that frequently is dissipated only through legal channels.

It is often said that perception is the only reality. The patient's perception of the care they received is influenced by each aspect of the surroundings. Health care institutions that wish to reduce risk should begin by sampling the product. Physical access into the system—i.e., parking, help moving sick patients into the emergency department, and general surroundings—should all be user friendly. It should be embarrassing for a family member to struggle to get a sick patient out of a vehicle and hospital personnel not be available to lend a hand. Such an introductory attitude sets the tone for a relationship that is adversarial as opposed to therapeutic. Hospital emergency departments that have all the atmosphere of a 1950s bus depot also convey an atmosphere of institutional mediocrity.

It is well documented that patients are strongly influenced by how the health professionals appear. Clean uniforms with proper name tags and other markers of identification are essential. Patients should know from whom they are receiving their care and to whom they can go to voice problems. The usual rules of human interaction and polite social discourse often seem to be suspended in emergency departments. Physicians no longer shake hands with their patients and identify themselves.

Physicians almost treat other family members who are present as invisible instead of recognizing their presence and understanding their role in the system.[1] It is the wise physician who makes friends with the patient and the family.

The patient's first impression of the health care provider is formed much like his or her impression of the institution itself. If an ill-kept unclean emergency department sets the tone for a poor view of the department, an unkempt or inappropriately dressed physician immediately sets the impression of nonprofessionalism. Patients of all socioeconomic ranks have an amazingly similar view of how physicians and nurses should be dressed. This so-called doctor camouflage is an important element in setting the tone for the doctor-patient interaction. Patients are willing to expose the most intimate details of their lives not because of who we are personally but because we represent a profession with a code of ethics and an oath of devotion to the patient and the patient's problems. It is mandatory that the patient believe in the provider.[2] Any hint that information obtained would be used for purposes other than the advancement of the patient would certainly shut down all communications.

The two most prevalent complaints of patients who have been to an emergency department are (1) that they waited too long, and (2) that the doctor never "told them anything." Both of these factors lead to a frustration that creates an atmosphere for hostility. It is appropriate for a physician and other members of the health care team to apologize to a patient for any delay in being seen. In truth, most health care professionals would like to see every patient immediately. The recognition that no one wants to wait and that the patient's time is just as valuable as the physician's time tends to reduce hostility. When most patients receive apologies for such waits, they generally say that they understand that the emergency department is a busy place. Recognizing the situation more than any specific corrective action is important in changing patient perception.

With regard to the second major complaint—"the physician never told me anything"—the corrective actions are obvious. The moment of discharge for a patient is indeed the moment of truth for the entire health care system. The emergency physician and other health care personnel must make certain that the patient understands the discharge instructions and the diagnosis that has been given them.[3] The wisest physicians ask the patients to repeat the discharge instructions. Second, any other problems or situations should be sought at that time. Very practical matters—such as where a patient is to go, how they are to eat, can they obtain the medication, do they need a note for work, and so on—are the real-life issues with which patients must deal when they are discharged from the emergency department. The emergency physician should not believe that patients innately understand how they are to function outside the walls of the institution. Directly asking patients and their families how these everyday matters will be taken care of shows human concern, and on a practical level it allows the physician to analyze the therapeutic milieu that the patient must enter. Finally, the physician should ask the patient if there are any other specific issues requiring assistance. All patients enter an emergency department with a specific program in mind. They have specific ideas of what will or will not be accomplished and very set notions of desired outcomes. It is impossible to serve the wants and needs of the patient without specifically asking what he or she would like. It is amazing that the almost draconian, automaton-like attitudes that have been passed on from one generation of physician to another seem to legitimize a noncaring attitude in those very people we have sworn to care for in the best traditions of Galen. There is no better risk management strategy than to be certain that at the time of discharge patients and family are comfortable with the diagnosis, the health care program is advocated, and they have the ability to carry out such a program in their daily lives.

An estimated one half of law suits in emergency medicine are related in some way to either the discharge instructions given to patients or the discharge program they are given or the inability to enter patients into a coordinated health care system (G. Henry and N. Little, review of 1800 emergency medicine malpractice cases). Virtually all cases of meningitis, missed fractures, abdominal pain, and wounds relate to how patients are instructed and how they view their own role in the follow-up care.

The principal weapon of any physician in the risk management wars is attitude. The physician who is secure and happy in his or her work tends to convey that attitude to the patients and the staff. Attitude, as with anything of importance, begins at the top. Nurses and ancillary health care personnel, as well as clerical personnel, often pick up the tone in the behavior from the physician on duty. Physicians who are exceedingly kind to the staff and the patients often find such attitudes infectious. This attitude should be expressed not only to patients but also to all members of the health care team. Petty bickering and accusations between health care workers are often perceived by patients as criticism of the quality of care and form a nidus for their mistrust. The attitude of the professional should be one that extends toward the entire patient. Merely going through mindless technical hoops and making certain that the process has taken place is no substitute for outcome, and the physician who can judge outcomes separate from process in the interest of the patient has nothing to fear from the legal system.

References

1. Adamsen TE, Tscham JM, et al: Physician communication skills and malpractice claims: A complex relationship. West J Med 150:356–360, 1989
2. Cerkin DC, MacCornack FA: Patient evaluations of low back pain care from family physicians and chiropractors. West J Med 150:351–355, 1989
3. Consolidated Omnibus Budget Reconcilation Act of 1985, Section 9121, Examination and Treatment for Emergency Medical Condition and Women in Active Labor, 1876
4. Demming W: Out of Crisis. Cambridge, MIT Publications, 1986
5. Dunn J: Patient transfers. In Henry G (ed): Emergency Medicine Risk Management:

Comprehensive Review. Dallas, American College of Emergency Physicians, 1991, pp 321–329

6. Goldman P: Discharge to private physician's office. *In* Henry G (ed): Emergency Medicine Risk Management: Comprehensive Review. Dallas, American College of Emergency Physicians, 1991, pp 297–299

7. Goldman P: Telephone orders from private physicians. *In* Henry G (ed): Emergency Medicine Risk Management: Comprehensive Review. Dallas, American College of Emergency Physicians, 1991, pp 291–295

8. Henry G: Patient expectations. *In* Henry G (ed): Emergency Medicine Risk Management: Comprehensive Review. Dallas, American College of Emergency Physicians, 1991, pp 5–10

9. Henry G: Philosophy of risk management. *In* Henry G (ed): Emergency Medicine Risk Management: Comprehensive Review. Dallas, American College of Emergency Physicians, 1991, pp 1–3

10. Henry G: Specific high-risk medicolegal issues. *In* Henry G (ed): Emergency Medicine Risk Management: Comprehensive Review. Dallas, American College of Emergency Physicians, 1991, pp 409–414

11. Hill H: Discharge and follow-up instructions. *In* Henry G (ed): Emergency Medicine Risk Management: Comprehensive Review. Dallas, American College of Emergency Physicians, 1991, pp 309–313

12. Hill H: Leaving against medical advice. *In* Henry G (ed): Emergency Medicine Risk Management: Comprehensive Review. Dallas, American College of Emergency Physicians, 1991, pp 315–319

13. *Jackson v. Rowe,* Alaska Supreme Court, Oct. 16, 1987, 742 P2d, 1376

14. Joint Commission on Accreditation of Healthcare Organizations: Accreditation Manual for Hospitals, 1990

15. O'Riordan W: House staff. *In* Henry G (ed): Emergency Medicine Risk Management: Comprehensive Review. Dallas, American College of Emergency Physicians, 1991, pp 261–265

16. O'Riordan W: In-house emergencies. *In* Henry G (ed): Emergency Medicine Risk Management: Comprehensive Review. Dallas, American College of Emergency Physicians, 1991, pp 253–259

17. O'Riordan W: On-call lists. *In* Henry G (ed): Emergency Medicine Risk Management: Comprehensive Review. Dallas, American College of Emergency Physicians, 1991, pp 275–281

18. Pierce, Kellerney, et al: Bounces. Ann Emerg Med 19:752–757, 1990

19. Verdile V: Emergency department telephone advice. Ann Emerg Med 18:278–282, 1989

20. Wener R: Emergency consent. J Ky Med Assoc 10:458–462, 472, 1981 (reproduction of *Schloendorff v. Society of New York Hospitals*)

21. 42 U.S.C. 111d(a) HR Rep. No. 903, 99th Congress, 2nd Session 9

Address reprint requests to

Gregory L. Henry, MD, FACEP
2000 Green Road, Suite 300
Ann Arbor, MI 48105–1571

THE NATIONAL PRACTITIONER DATA BANK

An Overview for the Emergency Physician

Richard L. Granville, MD, JD,
and Frank T. Flannery, MD, JD, LTC, MC, USA

INTRODUCTION AND HISTORY OF THE NATIONAL PRACTITIONER DATA BANK

In 1986 the US Congress enacted the Health Care Quality Improvement Act, Title IV of Public Law 99-660. Part A of the Act concerned encouraging and supporting professional review activities of physicians and dentists. The Act offered immunity to professional review societies of hospital and other health care entities, and persons serving on or otherwise assisting such bodies. Professional review actions had to be taken in the reasonable belief that the action would further the quality of medical care and provide due process safeguards for the health care provider.[10]

Part B of the Act established the National Practitioner Data Bank (NPDB). During subcommittee hearings for the House of Representatives in 1986, concern was expressed about the ability of physicians and other health care providers to conceal substandard prior practice in one state and then move to another state and practice without disclosure of prior negligent practice.[11] The US Congress concluded that the increasing occurrence of medical malpractice and the need to improve the quality of medical care represented nationwide problems. There was also a need to prevent incompetent practitioners from moving state-to-state without discovery of prior incidents of substandard performance.[17] The NPDB was established, therefore, to improve the health care practitioner cre-

From the Department of Legal Medicine, Armed Forces Institute of Pathology, Washington, DC

dentials review process by making information available. Professional organizations such as hospitals and health maintenance organizations (HMOs) may access the NPDB concerning prior malpractice payments and adverse credentials actions taken against physicians, dentists, and other health care practitioners by licensing authorities, hospitals, and other health care entities and professional societies. The Data Bank is meant to be another resource to assist licensing boards, hospitals, and other health care entities in reviewing the credentials of physicians and other health care providers who seek privileges at their facility. Significantly, it is not intended to replace or supplant existing credentials checks.

The NPDB is administered by the Bureau of Health Professions, Health Resources and Services Administration, US Department of Health and Human Services. It officially began operations on September 1, 1990, after lengthy discussion with many medical societies and other interested parties. A 5-year, $15.9 million contract to operate the Data Bank, located in Camarillo, California, was awarded to the UNISYS Corporation.

Emergency physicians should be familiar with the various rules for reporting to the Data Bank and for requesting information from it. The impact of the NPDB on practicing emergency physicians can be significant, because as licensed health care practitioners they are subject to being reported to the Data Bank. This article will help explain the regulations surrounding the operation of the NPDB.

This brief description of the regulations pertains to private-sector practitioners, hospitals, and other entities. Federal agencies such as the Department of Defense, Department of Veterans Affairs, and the Public Health Service are participating with the Department of Health and Human Services under separate Memoranda of Understanding with different provisions that will not be covered in this article.

REPORTING DATA TO THE NATIONAL PRACTITIONER DATA BANK

The Act states that any entity (insurance company, self-insured hospital, and so on) or individual (self-insured group, physician or dentist, and so on) that makes a payment on behalf of any licensed health care practitioner resulting from a claim or judgment for medical malpractice must report specific data to the NPDB and to the appropriate state licensing board(s).[18] Specific information about the entity, the practitioner, and the payment is reported to the NPDB. At the present time, any payment made on behalf of a licensed health care practitioner must be reported to the NPDB. There has been discussion concerning whether a certain monetary threshold should be used in deciding whether a payment is reported. Proponents of the use of thresholds, such as the American Medical Association, which has supported a $30,000 threshold, agree that small payments may reflect nuisance settlements and do not always imply substandard medical care. The elimination of smaller payments below $30,000 or below $50,000 would eliminate a large portion of the administrative burden of transferring this information. Those who argue against a reporting threshold state that certain specialties presumably associated with higher payments (e.g., Neurosurgery, OB/GYN) would be overrepresented in the Data Bank. Other specialties such as Dentistry, with lower payments for malpractice actions, might almost be eliminated from the Data Bank.[8] The Secretary of the Department of Health and Human Services in 1992 endorsed a $30,000 threshold.[16] The US Congress is now reviewing the issue of the use of a threshold amount below which no report would be made.

The Act further states that an entity, which submits such information concerning malpractice information, must do so within 30 days from the date payment is made.[3] The group of licensed health care practitioners includes licensed, registered, or certified practitioners.[2] Therefore, for example, paramedics, nurses, respiratory therapists, and emergency medical technicians (EMTs) can be named in the Data Bank if they are licensed, registered, or certified by a state.

The payment must be made for the benefit of a physician, dentist, or other licensed or authorized health care practitioner for the individual to be reported to the Data Bank. Payment made on behalf of a clinic or hospital is not reportable. Also, the waiver of a debt or a bill is not a reportable event. An actual exchange of money must be involved to trigger reporting. There must also have been a written complaint or claim demanding payment for damages, naming as a defendant the practitioner in his or her personal or corporate capacity. The use of a "personal corporation" on a payment cannot avoid a report to the NPDB, and if multiple practitioners are involved, then a separate report for each is required.[12]

Official actions taken by boards of medical examiners also must be reported to the NPDB. Any disciplinary action based on reasons related to the physician's professional competence or professional conduct is to be reported, and the Board must submit such information within 30 days of the date the licensure action was taken.[20]

Hospitals and other health care entities *must* report adverse clinical privilege actions taken against a physician's privileges, and this group includes doctors of medicine, osteopathy, and dentistry. The definition of health care entity will be discussed in the next section. It is permissive or optional in the case of other health care practitioners. Professional review actions must be based on the physician's professional competence or conduct that would adversely affect the health or welfare of patients. The actions also must result in denial, revocation, suspension, limitation, or reduction of the clinical privileges of a physician for a period of longer than 30 days. Additionally, each hospital or health care entity must report the acceptance of the surrender or restriction of clinical privileges by a physician while under investigation by the hospital or health care entity, relating to possible incompetence or improper professional conduct. This also applies if the surrender of privileges occurs in return for not conducting such an investigation or proceeding. Reports must be made to the appropriate State Board of Medical Examiners within 15 days from the date the final adverse action was taken by the governing body. The state board then has another 15 days to report this information to the NPDB.[4] Reports are not made prior to hearings that are part of the due process for the individual health care practitioner. If there is an internal administrative appeal preceding final action, this also is not reportable until the conclusion of an appeal. A supplemental report can be made when an action, which was earlier reported, is subsequently modified or vacated after an appeal by the health care practitioner.

Another issue relates to the initial granting of clinical privileges to practitioners. A denial of an initial request for privileges or the granting of limited privileges, based on a professional review action relating to professional competence or conduct, would be reported. There are certain adverse clinical privilege actions that are not to be reported to the NPDB. These include suspension of a physician's privileges for failure to complete medical records on time, if patient care was not compromised; denial of clinical privileges because of the lack of a need for a physician's services; and suspension or denial of privileges because of the failure to maintain a specified level of professional liability insurance. Of interest to emergency physicians is that the lapse of Advanced Cardiac Life Support certification resulting in a reduction or nonrenewal of clinical privileges also is not reported.[14]

Professional societies of physicians that engage in professional review activity, with a formal peer review process, for the purpose of furthering quality health care must report adverse membership actions to the NPDB. Such actions again must be based on an assessment of the physician's professional competence or conduct that either affected or could affect the health and welfare of patients. Reporting is mandatory for physicians and dentists and permissive for other health care providers. The professional society must report within 15 days of the date the action was taken to the appropriate state medical or dental board. The Board then has 15 days to transmit the information to the NPDB.[15]

OBTAINING INFORMATION FROM THE NATIONAL PRACTITIONER DATA BANK

Clearly, in the Health Care Quality Improvement Act there are very strict rules concerning the obtaining of information from the NPDB. Hospitals *must,* when they screen applicants for medical staff appointment or granting of clinical privileges, request information from the NPDB concerning the health care practitioner. Additionally, hospitals *must* obtain information from the Data Bank every 2 years for dentists, physicians, and other health care practitioners on the medical staff or those who are granted clinical privileges. Additionally, hospitals *may* at other times obtain information from the Data Bank when it is appropriate.[23] Health care entities that provide health care and that engage in professional review activity, through a formal peer review process for the purpose of furthering quality health care, also may request information from the NPDB, but they also must report their adverse clinical privilege actions regarding physicians to the Data Bank. An example of a qualifying health care entity would be an HMO or a prepaid medical practice or group that provides both health care services and engages in professional review activity through a formal peer review process. These entities would meet NPDB eligibility requirements, for both reporting and obtaining information.[2] In 1990, the American College of Emergency Physicians requested clarification from the Department of Health and Human Services concerning the issue of whether emergency medicine groups meet the criteria of a health care entity for the purposes of obtaining information from the NPDB, and of reporting to the NPDB any adverse clinical privilege actions against their physicians. In a response on June 8, 1990, the Director, Division of Quality Assurance and Liability Management, Bureau of Health Professions, Department of Health and Human Services, indicated that a group practice would qualify as a health care entity if it met the two criteria of *providing health care services* and of *engaging in professional review activity through a formal peer review process for the purpose of furthering quality health care.* A "formal peer review process" is further defined as the conduct of professional peer review activities through formally adopted written procedures that provide for adequate notice and an opportunity for a hearing. Group practices and emergency medicine physician groups should apply these criteria to determine whether they meet the definition of a health care entity.[7] Health care entities that meet the two criteria may request information from the NPDB when they enter into employment relationships with health care practitioners and engage in professional review activities.

State licensing boards may also request information from the NPDB, but they are not required to do so. Malpractice insurers and the general public are not authorized to request information from the NPDB. Professional societies that meet the eligibility requirements for reporting to and requesting information from the NPDB, as stated previously, may request information when they enter into membership relationships with physicians, dentists, and other health care providers or with respect to professional review activities.[5]

Practitioners may at any time ask the NPDB for the information that is maintained on them and receive the same information that an eligible requesting entity would also receive. No fee is charged to practitioners requesting information on their own files, as opposed to a specific fee for other entities that request information.[5]

In some circumstances the plaintiff's attorneys can request information from the NPDB. The attorney may obtain such information if involved with a medical malpractice action or claim against a hospital and the specific physician, dentist, or other health care practitioner on whom information is being requested. Some evidence must be submitted that demonstrates that the hospital failed to make its mandatory query of the NPDB regarding this practitioner. This must be obtained through discovery procedures in the litigation process, such as interrogatories and depositions. Information obtained from the NPDB on a practitioner can be used, with respect to the legal action or claim, only against the hospital and may not be used against the practitioner. A further disclosure or use of this information would violate the confidentiality provisions outlined subsequently, and it would subject the attorney or plaintiff or both to monetary damages up to $10,000. Defense attorneys do not have access to the NPDB, because defendants can request that information on their own behalf for actions involved in the Data Bank process.[1]

SANCTIONS

Insurance companies and other entities that make a payment in a medical malpractice case and fail to report this information to the NPDB will be subject to a civil monetary penalty of up to $10,000 for each payment involved.[19] Hospitals and health care entities that fail to report adverse professional actions against the clinical privileges of physicians or dentists, as required, can lose their peer review immunity protection under Part A of the Health Care Quality Improvement Act for a 3-year period.[22] If a state medical or dental board does not comply with Data Bank reporting requirements, another entity can be designated to perform the same services.[21]

A hospital that does not request information on a practitioner at the time of application for clinical privileges, and every 2 years thereafter, is presumed to have knowledge of any information in the NPDB. This may give a plaintiff's attorney access to information in the NPDB in a subsequent malpractice suit as stated previously.[24]

CONFIDENTIALITY OF DATA BANK INFORMATION

These sensitive medical malpractice data and adverse clinical privilege actions data must be protected by statute and by comprehensive security measures. The Act specifically provides a penalty for violation of the confidentiality provision. Information received from the NPDB is to be used only with regard to the professional review activity for the purposes as stated in the Health Care Quality Improvement Act. Any person who violates confidentiality provisions is subject to a civil penalty of up to $10,000 for each such violation. The intent is to ensure that the information provided is used solely with respect to activities in the furthering of quality health care.

Concerning the management of the Data Bank, it is essential that there be confidential receipt, disclosure, and storage of such information. The NPDB staff has undergone thorough background security investigations. The Privacy Act also protects information in the Data Bank from disclosure without the consent of the individual. Disclosure to the general public is not permitted. Information in the Data Bank is exempt from disclosure under the Freedom of Information Act, 5 U.S.C. § 52A. There are certain instances in which a hospital, for example, may disclose the information that it receives from the Data Bank to other officials who review the application of the health care practitioner. Both parties—the individuals who receive the information from the NPDB and the officials who review the applicant's paperwork—are subject to the confidentiality provisions of the Health Care Quality Improvement Act. If individual practitioners obtain information about themselves from the Data Bank, they are permitted to disclose that information to other persons as deemed appropriate.[6]

DISPUTES WITH THE DATA BANK

Disputing the accuracy of NPDB information is an important aspect of the NPDB for all practitioners. Emergency physicians and other practitioners should be aware of the procedure by which one can dispute the accuracy of information that was submitted to the NPDB, if one believes that the information reported to the NPDB is inaccurate. When data are entered into the Data Bank, each practitioner is given notice via a Practitioner Notification Document. Within 60 days the practitioner must file a dispute; the Practitioner Notification Document must be signed by the practitioner to inform the Secretary of the Department of Health and Human Services of the dispute and to request that the report be entered in a disputed status. In the event of inquiries, it will then be reported as being in a disputed status. Additionally, the practitioner should record the basis of the disagreement with the report on the Practitioner Notification Document. The practitioner should also inform the reporting entity of the disagreement, to attempt resolution of the dispute with the entity. When the reporting entity will not change a disputed report, the health care practitioner can request a review by the Secretary of the Department of Health and Human Services. The merit of the claim and the appropriateness of the health care entity review action are not reviewed. The Secretary will determine whether the information is correct. If it is incorrect, the Secretary will correct the information. If he or she determines that the information should never have been reported, the report will then be voided. If the Secretary determines that the information is accurate, then an explanation of this decision will be included with the information. Health care practitioners also will be able to add a brief statement to their file describing their view. The changes will then be made known to all prior requestors of information concerning this file, as well as the practitioners and the reporting entity.[9]

COMMENT

This brief description highlighted the basic provisions of the Health Care Quality Improvement Act that govern the operation of the NPDB. In its first year of operation, there were 15,782 malpractice reports, 1968 adverse licensure reports, 790 adverse clinical privilege reports, and 21 professional society membership reports. Additionally, 781,247 requests for information about practitioners were made to the NPDB. This amounted to more than 3000 requests per working day. The majority of the requests came from hospitals, and 80% of all hospitals made at least one request. Concerning disputes, 1829 physicians disputed information reported about them. This totaled about 10% of the 18,561 reports. Only 151 physicians proceeded to review by the Secretary of the Department of Health and Human Services.[13] It is therefore important that every physician be somewhat familiar with the various provisions of the Health Care Quality Improvement Act as they relate to the NPDB. The Data Bank can have a significant impact on the career of an emergency physician, because information on malpractice payments and adverse clinical actions is maintained within its files. It is also important that every physician be familiar with how to obtain information from the Data Bank about themselves, as well as the methods of disputing the accuracy of reported information, if it is believed that the information is inaccurate. Emergency medicine groups should obtain a copy of the *NPDB Guidebook—a Reference for Individuals and Entities Reporting to and Querying the Data Bank* from the US Department of Health and Human Services, Public Health Service, Health Resources and Services Administration. Additionally, a toll-free Data Bank telephone help line (1-800-767-6732) provides telephone service to entities and health care practitioners requesting information about the Data Bank. Both individual practitioners and emergency medicine groups must keep current about the NPDB, which should have an increasing impact on the practice of virtually every health care provider.

References

1. Attorney Requests for Data Bank Information. Rockville, MD, US Dept of Health and Human Services, Public Health Service, Health Resources and Services, Administration Bureau of Health Professions, p 39
2. 45 CFR Part 60.3 October 17, 1989
3. 45 CFR Part 60.5 October 17, 1989
4. 45 CFR Part 60.9 October 17, 1989
5. 45 CFR Part 60.11
6. Confidentiality of Data Bank Information. National Practitioner Data Bank Guidebook.
7. Cowell, Daniel, Letter June 8, 1990
8. Gianelli DM: Should it go in the bank? American Medical News Sept 21, 1992, p 1
9. Health Care Practitioners. Disputing the accuracy of Data Bank Information. National Practitioner Data Bank Guidebook. Rockville, MD, US Dept of Health and Human Services, Public Health Service, Health Resources and Services, Administration Bureau of Health Professions, pp 35–37
10. Health Care Quality Improvement Act of 1986. Pub. L. No. 99-660, Sec. 401–416, Nov. 17, 1986
11. Hearings Before the Subcommittee on Health and the Environment of the Committee on Energy and Commerce, 99th Cong. 2nd Sess. House of Representatives, July 15, 1986 (testimony of Jack Owen, Executive Vice President of the American Hospital Association)
12. Medical Malpractice Insurers. *In* National Practitioner Data Bank Guidebook. Rockville, MD, US Dept of Health and Human Services, Public Health Service, Health Resources and Services, Administration Bureau of Health Professions, p 21

13. Mullan F, et al: The National Practitioner Data Bank Report from the first year. JAMA 268:1, 1992
14. National Practitioner Data Bank. American Medical Association. Chicago, Illinois. June, 1990, pp 8–111
15. Professional Societies. National Practitioner Data Bank Guidebook. Rockville, MD, US Dept of Health and Human Services, Public Health Service, Health Resources and Services, Administration Bureau of Health Professions, pp 31–32
16. Oberman L: Dr. Sullivan backs hike in data bank reporting threshold. American Medical News. Nov 16, 1992, p 1
17. Pub. L. No. 99-660 Sec. 402, Nov. 14, 1986
18. Pub. L. No. 99-660 Sec. 421(a)
19. Pub. L. No. 99-660 Sec. 421(c)
20. Pub. L. No. 99-660 Sec. 422 and 45 CFR Part 60.5
21. Pub. L. No. 99-660 Sec. 422(b)
22. Pub. L. No. 99-660 Sec. 423(c)(1)
23. Pub. L. No. 99-660 Sec. 425(a)
24. Pub. L. No. 99-660 Sec. 425(b)

Address reprint requests to

Richard L. Granville, MD, JD
Department of Legal Medicine
Armed Forces Institute of Pathology
Washington, DC 20306–6000

FUTURE LEGAL ISSUES IN EMERGENCY MEDICINE

John D. Dunn, MD, and Thom A. Mayer, MD

It is probably a sign more of the age of the authors than any particular prescience that the topic of future legal trends in emergency medicine is presented. It also may be indicative of the aging of this specialty that the authors have grown older (we resent more and more the use of the word "old") and now we have changed our definition of elderly into what we used to think was ancient. It does provide a certain perspective, however, and we begin now to feel like physicians who practiced medicine through the 1950s, 1960s, 1970s and 1980s and saw at least three cycles of medical thought on the use of anticoagulants in myocardial infarction. We believe that we understand some trends of the past and that those trends help us to project what legal trends and what legal developments will be a part of the future.

Emergency medicine may have begun as a convenience to the attending staff, when emergency departments were "emergency rooms" with little status in the hospital, but times have changed. Emergency departments in 1990 cared for approximately 90 million patient visits, accounted for more than 25% of all admissions to hospitals across the country, and in most hospital environments accounted for significant percentages of the total hospital business. Although perhaps not as glamorous as other parts of the hospital, the emergency department is vital to hospital operations, and emergency physicians hold a very important place in the health care system.

The legal challenges facing emergency medicine are the same as they were 15 years ago with some added complications, including the following:

From the Emergency Department, Brownwood Regional Medical Center, Brownwood, Texas (JDD); and the Department of Emergency Medicine, Fairfax Hospital, Falls Church, Virginia (TAM)

1. The relationship between the health care industry and the public, particularly government, has deteriorated.
2. Congress has displayed a special interest in legislating in the area of emergency care and transfers.[33]
3. Practice parameters and practice guidelines are developing at a very fast pace, placing increased legal demands on emergency physicians.
4. There is no turning back the trend of increased litigation in this country.
5. Tort reform is unlikely to be a major benefit in the near future.
6. For emergency physicians, the cost of professional liability insurance will continue to be the most expensive overhead item.
7. The economic realities of health care in the emergency department mean more patients, less money, and wavering support from the medical staff, creating a potential for greater legal problems for emergency departments and emergency physicians.

The best way to approach dealing with future legal issues in emergency medicine is to approach them chronologically. Santayana's caveat that "those who are not aware of history are condemned to repeat it" obligates us to look at the past legal problems for emergency medicine.

THE PAST

1960s

During the 1960s any physician could buy occurrence malpractice insurance for a few hundred dollars, no matter what the specialty, and receive excellent coverage. The 1960s were a great time for physicians, and professional liability problems were not a significant factor in the practice of medicine.

1970s

The 1970s saw the boom in malpractice suits and the development of two phenomena that have left their imprint on the present—tort reform and serious professional liability concerns.

During the 1970s a significant number of states inaugurated tort reform measures that have since been demonstrated to have mixed effects. In fact, a mid-1980s General Accounting Office study on the effects of tort reform in five states showed that the net effect of tort reform was negligible.[28]

The 1970s also saw the birth of physician mutual insurance companies in response to a declining availability of professional liability insurance coverage and a reluctance by general liability insurers to continue their books of business in professional liability. The development of these "bedpan mutuals" and the attention focused on medical malpractice and professional liability problems led to professional liability becoming a continued and constant source of great physician concern.

During that same period, the American College of Emergency Physicians (ACEP), through the brokerage of I. David Gordon, developed an "endorsed" program of professional liability coverage for emergency physicians. The brokerage arrangement resulted in claims management and risk management activities that were the basis for developing a level of expertise within the specialty, best exemplified by John T. Rogers, MD. Dr. Rogers was an expert on risk management who wrote the first publication devoted to professional liability risk management for ACEP; it is still used as a standard text reference and still has important commentary about medical malpractice and risk management in emergency medicine.[29]

Another area of expertise developed through the endorsed programs was an opportunity to examine purified emergency medicine malpractice claims. Statistical analysis was done by John T. Rogers and Joseph S. Fastow, two members of ACEP who were on the insurance committee, which subsequently became the professional liability committee. The claims information and analysis resulted in the pie charts that frequently appeared in ACEP risk management information.[12] These pie charts show that dollar losses are related to a short list of clinical problems. The obvious result of all of this loss analysis was an improved risk management focus and an effort to make the specialty aware of areas of high professional liability losses for emergency physicians.

During the 1970s multihospital contract groups became a factor in professional liability and risk management for emergency medicine. Multihospital groups have the financial power and motivation to become self-insured and, as a result, expertise within the specialty was bound to develop. Moreover, if risk management and professional liability concerns affect a significant part of the overhead of emergency medicine, it would make good sense to manage those risks, and that translates into personnel efforts and expenditures.

During the late 1970s multicontract emergency medicine groups became important factors in the insurance market for emergency physicians. Multihospital groups still insure a significant percentage of all physicians practicing emergency medicine in the United States. These groups have the financial power to arrange their own insurance coverage, to take self-insured retentions, to develop their own risk management and claims management programs, and to use their market power to obtain creative new forms of professional liability coverage. Within the specialty of emergency medicine, the risk management experts have, in most cases, come from either academic backgrounds or experience in risk management for their own group practices. This has resulted in a pool of experts on risk management that has developed rapidly during the 1980s for the specialty of emergency medicine.

1980s

During the 1980s ACEP, in response to a continuing perceived malpractice problem, reformed the insurance committee as the professional liability committee, later the medical/legal committee, to deal with malpractice and other legal concerns of the membership and of the specialty. Malpractice was certainly a major focus, but there were other pertinent subjects addressed by the committee and by ACEP leadership that related to other legal issues, such as the following:

Do-not-resuscitate orders in the prehospital care setting
Medical director legal responsibility for prehospital care services
Legal aspect of practice parameters
Child abuse, elder abuse, and reporting requirements
Consent-to-treatment legal problems
Management of intoxicated, impaired, and uncooperative patients
Professional liability needs of the membership
Risk management education on high-risk cases such as chest pain, abdominal pain, febrile infants and children, wounds, and trauma
Legal aspects of transfers and the obligation to treat under federal and state laws
Position statements on management of legal problems such as phone orders,[36] phone advice,[27] and admitting orders[41]
Development of publications, educational seminars, and college resources on federal law, state law, and legal problems in emergency medicine

During the 1980s the Professional Liability Committee initiated and supervised the publication of *foresight*, devoted to risk management questions.[12] The ACEP education committee developed a Quality Assurance/Risk Management course that was presented throughout the United States as a special effort to educate members on quality assurance, risk management, and related matters. The subject matter of these courses included education on professional liability insurance, transfers, risk management problems, administrative matters relating to quality assurance and risk management, the development of practice parameters, and proper administration of the emergency department and prehospital care systems to address legal issues and effect risk reduction for emergency medicine.

As another major effort during the 1980s, ACEP, under the editorship of Greg Henry, MD, published *Risk Management in Emergency Medicine: A Comprehensive Review,* as an authoritative successor to the 1985 publication written by John Rogers. This book was published in 1990 and became one of the authoritative texts and reference books on risk management and legal matters for emergency medicine.

The 1980s also saw the development of risk retention groups, self-insurance groups, and tailor-made professional liability programs designed to address the needs of small and large emergency medicine groups. The insurance industry, recognizing the unique needs of emergency physicians and benefiting from the fact that professional liability premiums for emergency physicians were substantial, spawned independent brokers and insurance companies devoted to emergency department professional liability.

The Federal Risk Retention Act,[8] modified during the early 1980s to include purchasing groups and self-insured groups in addition to the original manufacturer's and product liability insurance, resulted in programs and insurance packages becoming available to emergency physicians, increased in number and kind. At the same time, more multihospital contract groups developed multimillion-dollar operations that allowed them to self-insure and to develop their own risk retention groups, tailor-made for their group professional liability needs. Contract physicians working with these groups looked to the groups not only for payment for their services but also for professional liability insurance.

During the 1980s, hospitals increased their focus on the problems of emergency department apparent agency, and agency by estoppel, legal corrupts that created liability for hospitals for the actions of the emergency physicians in the department.[32] Hospitals began to require increasing professional liability coverage from emergency physicians. During that same period, the occurrence type of insurance disappeared from the marketplace. This increased the financial problems for emergency physician groups, such as the question of coverage for claims not reported during the insurance period for physicians who left the group, or in situations in which a contract was lost and the physician group left the location. "Tailor-made" insurance packages developed to include specific arrangements for insurance for a location rather than a particular physician, and to address the difficulties of small physician groups at one hospital, but also the more imposing potential problems of contract groups with multiple physicians and multiple locations.

During the 1980s an interesting insurance phenomenon developed as a direct result of all of the activities in American medicine directed toward improved risk management. Normally, insurance experts consider liability markets in terms of 3- to 5-year cycles of hard markets and then soft markets. (In a hard market insurance capacity is limited and the cost of premiums float up. A soft market is a phenomenon in the insurance industry that occurs when capacity and aggressive selling tend to soften prices and either maintain them at former levels or even produce reductions in prices of premiums.) There was a hard market during the 1970s as a result of a number of major liability insurance companies experiencing bad financial trends in professional liability and exiting the market in many states. Many of the previously active professional liability insurers stopped insuring physicians altogether, which created, in many areas of the United States, a crisis in availability and higher prices.

In the late 1970s and early 1980s, premiums increased dramatically and physicians were suddenly paying thousands of dollars rather than hundreds of dollars for their malpractice premiums. At the same time, the same professional liability insurers, on the basis of projected trends, stated that the price of malpractice insurance would increase into the foreseeable future. However, through the 1980s, a soft, not a hard, cycle continued, and prices have remained soft, or stable, until today.

There may be good reasons as to why the "soft" market persisted

As previously mentioned, the endorsed program of ACEP produced a wealth of claims information for a period of approximately 8 years from the mid 1970s until the mid 1980s, when the endorsed program was unendorsed. During that period, 55 million emergency department visits were insured in the endorsed program, and the closed claims information showed that $29 million was paid on approximately 1700 claims. A quick analysis shows that the losses were in the range of fifty cents per visit during the 1976 through 1984 period.

Premium prices have remained relatively competitive and constant since the mid 1980s because there has been no dramatic increase in claims or losses, as compared with the late 1970s early 1980s experience of the endorsed program. In the early 1980s professional liability premiums were probably overpriced, and as a result the soft market is nothing more than a maintenance of premium prices in the face of the flattening curve of malpractice losses. In fact, the trends have remained relatively stable through the late 1980s and to the present, with a slight increase in rate of claims and evidence of an increasing tendency of juries to award multimillion-dollar verdicts. No trends have developed to indicate that a hard market is on the horizon, but time will tell. Also, the general health of the insurance industry can be affected outside of the professional liability environment.

Actuarial science in the insurance industry in underwriting is inexact at best. Exquisite formulas are designed to project what in some cases is a "best guess." Also, loss trends in many cases are not as important as the insurance company's experience in investments. Close analysis of the insurance crisis in the late 1970s leads many experts to suggest that bad investments during the 1970s had more to do with the hard market and an increase in premium prices than did the actual loss experience. The experience of the ACEP-endorsed insurers during the late 1970s and early 1980s did not reflect catastrophic losses from professional liability claims.

The soft market of the 1980s was a result of a combination of the following factors: (1) a steadily improving economy that did not compromise insurance company investments; (2) a perception that professional liability litigation was a burden on society and a certain backlash from the community keeping litigation and judgments down; (3) the development of multiple sources of professional liability insurance operating in the same market, which tended to soften prices and increase capacity; and (4) the development of risk management programs throughout the medical community intended to reduce unnecessary losses and improve professional liability experience for physicians in general. In the case of ACEP and emergency medicine in particular, these authors have seen a dramatic improvement in record keeping, general administration, and quality assurance–risk management in the emergency department, which cannot help but improve the experience of emergency physicians in the area of professional liability losses.

THE 1990S AND BEYOND

The ACEP medical legal committee is the successor to the professional liability committee and continues to promote and develop educational programs in risk management. *foresight* has now matured, and in the last 2 years it has become not only an informative publication but also a continuing medical education (CME) source, with credits provided to those who are interested in completing the CME materials. A reference publication was published for the members of ACEP, addressing legal issues related to contracts and management of emergency departments.[34] The ACEP education committee developed an "academy" approach to seminars on administrative risk management and quality assurance matters, which has enjoyed great success as a successor to the quality assurance, risk management seminars of the late 1980s and early 1990s. State chapters and the national chapter have continued to provide excellent educational and support services for the membership in the area of quality assurance and risk management. The annual ACEP Scientific Assembly continues to provide an in-depth program on administrative matters, which includes risk management as a major focus. ACEP's annual strategic plan continues to focus on the professional liability needs of the membership, and a significant effort continues, particularly in the practice management division of the College.

Insurance

Some suggest that a hard market may be developing. The experience of California after the enactment of MICRA,[24] a comprehensive tort reform proposal that included caps on recovery and periodic payments for catastrophic losses, showed that stability in California was a characteristic of the market. However, the early 1990s have shown some trends toward increasing size of jury awards and judgments,[1] which may increase the cost of professional liability coverage.

The physicians' mutual insurance industry has stabilized in most states; in fact, physician mutuals in some states are branching out into other states to increase their market share and their financial viability. These experiments involve some risk, and a bad investment market may ultimately also contribute to a hardened market in professional liability. Most specialist insurers live or die by the professional liability market, and as a result they are sensitive to changes in loss experience. Whenever the investment market returns dip, we can expect an increase in premiums and a tightening of underwriting criteria. During the late 1970s and the early 1980s joint underwriting authorities and high-risk pools became a significant factor in states such as New York, and at one point many of them were considered to be technically insolvent. They have worked themselves out of these problems, sometimes at the expense of the physicians insured, by increasing premiums, and the insurance marketplace now appears to be relatively stable and in much better condition than it was in the late 1970s, when Aetna, St. Paul, and many other large insurers were pulling out of some states and the physician mutuals had not been developed to replace that capacity.

MEDICAL DOCUMENTATION AND PRACTICE TRENDS

The Armed Forces Institute of Pathology (AFIP), financed by a Robert Wood Johnson Grant, under Flannery and Granville (the physicians who ran the program), studied emergency department record keeping and evaluated its adequacy based upon a survey of emergency physicians and what they expected to see in the medical record. Taking the top 10 historical items considered important by emergency physicians in the survey, the AFIP studied medical records from busy community hospitals and found less than 60% compliance with suggested acceptable record keeping requirements. The authors in their administrative work have reviewed thousands of emergency department records and find a wide range of quality in emergency department records.

Whenever a nationally recognized lecturer in emergency medicine–risk management asks the audience to raise their hand if they dictate records, the result is usually that less than 25% of the audience have dictated records. Just the problem of a lack of dictated records in the emergency department increases the difficulties of adequate documentation. Under no circumstances will a handwritten record be as thorough and complete as a dictated record, because of space and time limitations. As a result, medical records in emergency departments vary significantly in their quality. ACEP has promoted the use of the dictated record,[6] and most experts advocate it an excellent risk management tool. However, experts on both sides of a case will continue to scrutinize charts, looking for omissions of documentation that show, in retrospect, whether the physician did an adequate evaluation. This medical record dilemma will continue to represent a significant barrier to risk management in emergency medicine through the 1990s.

STANDARD OF CARE DISPUTES

The Massachusetts Chapter of ACEP has been doing an in-depth study on malpractice and risk management, focusing on standards of care and documentation. In addition to tracking charts on the question of practice patterns, the studies have also demonstrated that in emergency medicine malpractice there is a phenomenon called the "trigger diagnosis." Briefly, the "trigger diagnosis" is a diagnosis that is often associated with a missed diagnosis—for example, the patient who is discharged home with bronchitis when, in fact, the diagnosis should have been cardiac disease, or the patient who is diagnosed as having gastroenteritis, when the diagnosis should have been appendicitis or meningitis. In analyzing these "trigger diagnosis" cases, Massachusetts

ACEP proposed documentation and evaluation guidelines to help reduce risks for emergency physicians. Most of these recommendations center on the idea that a complete evaluation and good documentation leave the impression on the medical record of a conscientious and thorough evaluation, so that even a missed diagnosis can be defensible.[15]

Holbrook also has found that a number of standards of care should be redefined and re-evaluated if we hope to define "emergency medicine" as it exists in the real world versus how we would like it to be practiced. The concept put forward is the "normative" versus the real standard of care. The normative standard of care is that to which we all aspire and that we achieve on occasion with ideal circumstances and the ideal physician. The classic example would be the complete neurologic examination by the emergency physician. However, the real standard of care is something practiced by reasonable and prudent physicians, and that is another matter altogether. For example, Dr. Holbrook analyzed the examinations of physicians for patients who present with headache and found that funduscopic examination was done in less than 10% of the charts reviewed (J. Holbrook, personal communication). Obviously, such a significant deviation between what we say we do and what we actually do creates an excellent opportunity for the critical plaintiff's expert, either from emergency medicine or another specialty, and it also obligates the specialty of emergency medicine to address what really happens in the emergency department when a patient arrives at 7 P.M. on a Friday night in a crush of emergency department traffic.

Legislative Changes

Despite the fact that the medical community continues to push for tort reform, few tort reform measures will make a major impact on professional liability. Periodic payments (small payments over a period of time, rather than one large lump payment) can improve the financial picture for professional liability insurance, but most of the other tort reform measures have little, if any, effect on the big picture.

Most states have constitutional guarantees to access the courts. These guarantees will have to be modified if administrative remedies are to be created for medical malpractice. The state of Utah and possibly some other states within the next few years will be looking at the American Medical Association (AMA) proposal on arbitration[25] for medical malpractice and attempting pilot studies on the benefits. At this time the outcome of the studies are not known, but most physicians agree that juries are not qualified to review complex medical cases. On the other hand, it may be better from the defense point of view to have juries rather than medical experts, who might be more harsh in their criticism of the quality of care provided in a case. A classic example of tort reform gone awry was the Florida proposal that losers pay the opposing attorney's fees. In the Florida experience, the net result was that losing, solvent defendants were responsible for the additional cost of lawyer's fees, but insolvent or judgment proof plaintiffs did not pay the defendant's attorney's fees. Thus, the attempt to penalize persons for inappropriate litigation only resulted in costing defendants. Another, more recent Florida change to require proof of gross negligence in emergency medicine malpractice cases has had more beneficial effects.[10] Previous malpractice reform proposals that have been in effect include the following:

1. *Caps on nonmonetary damages such as pain and suffering.* These caps have survived some challenges but have been ruled unconstitutional in many states.[20]
2. *Elimination of joint and several liability.* This legal concept allows defendants to be liable for other defendants' damages if those other defendants are insolvent or uninsured. In states in which "joint and several" exists, very few legislative efforts have been successful in eliminating the concept, but some legislation[37] has created limits on sharing of the total judgment depending upon percentage of liability.
3. *Statutes of limitations.* These limits of time to sue from the time of incident vary widely from state to state, but they have had beneficial effects in many states and have withstood constitutional challenge most of the time. Exceptions to these limitations were placed in cases involving minors[31] or in states in which "discovery" allowed a delay in the law suit if the victim of malpractice could not discover the negligence within the statute of limitations.[39]
4. *Panels and arbitration.* In some states (e.g., Virginia, Louisiana, Indiana) panels have survived, and losers who insist on going to trial may be liable for attorneys' costs.
5. *Limitations on qualifying of experts.* These generally have been subject to federal rules of civil procedures, with few exceptions.[3]
6. *Patient compensation funds.* Some states still have patient compensation funds that essentially provide money out of a state fund for judgments in excess of a particular limit.[19] These compensation funds are usually attached to legislation limiting recovery or other tort reform measures.
7. *Brain damage funds.* Brain damage funds have been developed to address the question of the catastrophic birth injury.[11] Usually these measures have been motivated by decreasing availability of obstetric services and a public interest in guaranteeing that availability.

Overall, these kinds of tort reform measures have limited impact and benefit on the medical professional liability environment. They do address, in some cases, important issues, but they are in place in very few states, with limited benefit. We do not believe that the climate of the 1990s will create any appreciable tort reform benefit. Mandatory arbitration or administrative law–type remedies or both will be attempted in the 1990s, and their success or lack of it, as well as a perception of an ongoing professional liability crisis, may move the federal government to overcome its inertia and the likely internal resistance of legislatures and government dominated by attorneys.

Practice Parameters

The interest in practice parameters by the ACEP began in the late 1980s and continues. The ACEP standards committee, chaired by Harris Graves, MD, produced the first parameter on nontraumatic adult chest pain[5] and followed this with a series of practice parameters addressing question such as blunt trauma, seizures, febrile infants and children, extremity trauma, and other basic practice issues for emergency physicians. ACEP continues to be represented on the AMA's Practice Parameters Forum and to participate in the discussions of the AMA and the medical specialty society practice parameter groups along with the Agency for Health Care Policy and Research, the federal branch of the Department of Health and Human Services, which is organized to promote patient outcomes research and practice guidelines and parameters.

It is difficult to project the impact of practice parameter development on professional liability litigation. In the past, malpractice litigation always involved an attempt to identify what acceptable standards of care would be, but those acceptable standards were outlined by the medical experts engaged to provide testimony in the case. Pilot projects and developments in many states would suggest that practice parameters may become a real factor in professional liability litigation in the 1990s. For example, in the state of Maine, obstetric and emergency care practice guidelines have been developed and are being used as proof of proper practice in the defense of professional liability claims.[21] Many states, including Florida and Texas, have adopted practice parameters in proposed legislation and in regulatory matters.[9] In Massachusetts, the Industrial Accident Board is using practice parameters to measure appropriations of care for back injuries and conditions such as carpal tunnel syndrome.[22] In many states, new health care reform proposals have suggested that practice parameters may be the only way to create uniformly acceptable patterns of practice. These proposals cite "small area analysis" medical literature to demonstrate wide variances in practice in various parts of the United States.[17] The proposals attempt to improve appropriateness of care in some cases, and they are intended to avoid unnecessary and expensive approaches to medical problems.

Practice parameters are mushrooming. These are being produced by various groups including specialty societies, the Rand Corporation, the Agency for Health Care Policy and Research, and other sources. Patient outcome research teams (PORTS) have been funded by the Agency for Health Care Policy and Research, at $5 million apiece, to do literature searches and original research on patient outcomes in areas of clinical importance. The result of all of this activity is that, as of 1992, more than 1000 practice parameters were included in the AMA's practice parameter catalogue,[35] and the Agency for Health Care Policy and Research plans dozens of practice parameters in all areas of practice over the next few years.

Examples of this activity are numerous. The American Academy of Otolaryngology–Head and Neck Surgery has published practice parameters on all of the major surgeries done by physicians in their specialty. The American College of Cardiology has published practice parameters on the management of angioplasty, coronary artery bypass surgery, and other important clinical entities in the practice of cardiology.

Not surprisingly, the taxonomy of practice parameters has become very confused. For example, the practice parameters catalogue from the AMA includes monographs, extended comprehensive texts, and other sources of information that most physicians would not consider to be a "practice parameter." The development of these parameters could very easily outstrip the ability of American physicians to assimilate the parameters. Under those circumstances, the legal implications are obvious—a plaintiff's attorney being familiar with the practice parameter that a defendant physician was unaware of.

A series of essays and articles have recently appeared on the question of practice parameters in an effort to control variances in practice across the United States.[7] These articles suggest that practice guidelines will result in pressures on physicians to comply with suggested parameters for the benefit of the patient and to control dramatically increasing health care costs. The effect on professional liability exposure for emergency physicians is unpredictable. The applicability of practice parameters to the emergency department certainly must be weighed against the limitations of emergency department resources and time, but the suggestion is that compliance with practice parameters in the future will become a significant part of improving risk management efforts in the emergency department.

RESEARCH IN MEDICAL MALPRACTICE

A recent analysis by Harvard reviewers of the New York state hospital discharges shows that more malpractice incidents occurred than claims were filed.[2] A close analysis of this study leaves some questions with regard to methodology. For example, sentinel events were screened by nonphysicians and then a three-physician panel, with one of the physicians a supervisor, was asked to determine whether malpractice occurred. If there was a disagreement between two physicians, then a third physician had the deciding vote.

Given that the principles of malpractice require that a respectable minority of physicians still represent a legally acceptable standard of care, it is difficult to understand how the Harvard screening and "deciding vote" analysis measured the incidence of malpractice.

Congressional voices will continue to be heard on the question of whether there is widespread malpractice. The AMA, in its analysis of the Harvard research, emphasized that these medical incidents occurred at a rate of only about 1% of hospitilizations. The question is whether these compensable events were, in fact, compensable, given the methodology.

The American Society of Anesthesiologists (ASA) report on the problem of blinding physician reviewers to outcomes illustrates the problem. In their study, the ASA took 50 closed claims involving anesthesia and asked experts to review the cases for negligence, with arbitrary changes in the outcome of the case. The patient's chart was presented to two reviewers, with variances in outcome. In one case the patient would have a terrible outcome with death or permanent disability, in the other case a reviewer would review the same care, and the patient would be given an arbitrary minor problem or temporary disability. The study found that reviewer judgments of malpractice were varied by 30% toward malpractice if a bad outcome was known.[4]

Physicians by instinct assume that good care results in good outcomes and bad care results in bad outcomes. If physician reviewers can be prejudiced by a bad outcome, a study such as the Harvard study with known outcomes demonstrates a flawed methodology that is difficult to address. Given the fact that the Harvard study screened out cases with bad outcomes and sentinel events for analysis, variances in medical care that would otherwise be considered unimportant developed more importance, possibly because of the known adverse event.

In the world of bad outcomes, the attention of emergency physicians is readily drawn to the research; the best is on the management of emergency department chest pain. This research shows that, even under rigid protocols, 4% of myocardial infarctions or unstable angina are missed, reflecting the inaccuracies of medicine and the uncertainties of the history, physical, and the electrocardiogram.[18]

The research on febrile infants and children undoubtedly gives emergency physicians some valued pointers on clinical evaluation. Given the rarity of sepsis, meningitis, and other catastrophic illnesses in the pediatric age group, and given that most of these conditions develop against the background of frequent febrile illnesses, there is always a retrospectoscopic analysis of the clinical evaluation, which is prejudiced by the bad outcome in a medical malpractice case. The question of Peter Rosen, MD, must be raised: "What is an acceptable error rate in the emergency department?"[30]

However, refined actuarial analysis showing the kinds of losses that emergency physicians have in medical malpractice cases undoubtedly allow us to entertain the hope that we can continue to reduce our risk. Some hospitals have developed chest pain monitoring units and observation units to reduce the possibility of discharging home a patient with a myocardial infarction or unstable angina.[14] Some hospitals are very conservative in discharging adult patients with nontraumatic chest pain, but the chest pain study group shows that one third to one half of all nontrauma chest pain patients are discharged from the emergency department.[18] Because their work also suggests that 4% of the myocardial infarctions are discharged home, a rough statistical analysis can show the following hypothetical.

If 90 million patients presented to emergency departments across the nation and 5% of those are adult patients with nontraumatic chest pain, then, based upon the experience of the Chest Pain Study Group, 4.5 million adult chest pain patient visits occur and approximately 2,250,000 patients would be discharged. Approximately 2,250,000 patients would then be admitted, and because most emergency departments experience a 25% confirmed rate of myocardial infarction or unstable angina, 560,000 cases would be identified. That means that if everyone is as competent as the Chest Pain Study Group, then across the nation every year about 22,000 patients (0.025% of all visits) with myocardial infarctions or unstable angina are discharged inappropriately from the emergency department. So for every 10,000 emergency department visits, 2.5 myocardial infarctions or unstable ischemia patients might be discharged home by even the best physicians every year. Does that answer the question about acceptable error rates? Unfortunately, the question in the mind of jurors, attorneys, and nonphysicians is: If a taxi driver knows when he takes the chest pain patient to the emergency department that it may be his heart, how could a physician miss such an obvious diagnosis?

Future of Tort Reform

The AMA proposes comprehensive tort reform measures and an arbitration system that is dependent upon experts and eliminates juries as a factor.[25] Given recent research, emergency physicians should not be prepared to commit to an expert review, which can be just as flawed as the reviews done by the experts from the ASA.[4] Even experts are swayed by bad patient outcomes. How this will develop in the 1990s cannot be predicted, but tort reform efforts can go only so far. There still must be a focus on defense of acceptable "error" cases.

In the case of febrile infants, research has demonstrated that physicians are 95% sensitive and equally specific on identifying which febrile infant is sick on the basis of observation factors.[23] The Yale Observation Scale is simple. The use of objective observations should be a legitimate defense when later the patient's condition deteriorates. Certain "acceptable errors" must be considered in malpractice cases resulting from bad outcomes.

These catastrophic cases—the executive that goes home to have his myocardial infarction and the child who is taken home and develops meningitis—require our continued attention. In these difficult cases clinical judgment based upon clinical evaluation is being assessed. There is rarely a magical test. In the future the challenge will still be trying to match up jury and society expectations with the limitations of medicine. It is not easy to defend a malpractice case when the plaintiff is in a wheelchair and requires 24-hour medical care or is deceased.

More than one third of all malpractice cases in emergency medicine involve death or permanent serious disability.[38] Therefore, the defense of emergency medicine cases is more difficult for the following reasons: (1) limited time and resources in the emergency department; (2) a lack of any kind of guaranteed follow-up or good physician-patient relationship; (3) unreasonable society expectations of perfection; (4) pressure from medical staff and hospitals to avoid inappropriate admissions; (5) the difficulties of defense when the plaintiff is seriously injured or dead; and (6) rising standard of care expectations generated by the specialty of emergency medicine, and by our colleagues in medicine outside of emergency medicine.

Expert Witnesses

All medical malpractice cases require experts for both sides. In the current malpractice climate, there is no such thing as the "conspiracy of silence." Numerous physicians are available to do expert witness review and testimony on emergency medicine cases. One of the big challenges facing emergency physicians is that physicians in all specialties consider themselves to be experts in their specialty on the care of emergency cases. For example, emergency physicians are frequently condemned by general surgeons, pediatricians, infectious disease specialists, and other specialists who claim a knowledge of a standard of care for the emergency physician. The basis of their claim is that they "moonlighted" in emergency departments when they were residents, or they occasionally see a patient in the emergency department.

The hypercritical outside expert sometimes is exceeded by the hypercritical emergency physician who accepts nothing but perfect results and who is critical of anything less than a three-page emergency department report detailing a complete history and physical. A joke in emergency medicine malpractice is the expectation according to the plaintiff's expert that any patient in the emergency department should receive a "complete and thorough history and physical." Presuming that an emergency physician could do a complete and thorough physical examination acceptable to a specialist in another area, eventually the problem of time and appropriate use of resources must be addressed.

Emergency medicine is a triage specialty, but unfortunately in courtrooms across the United States, experts may allege it to be a critical care specialty. In addition, if one looks at the malpractice litigation brought against emergency physicians, it usually involves patients that the physician judged could be discharged from the emergency department. Therefore, we are dealing with a question of missed diagnosis or delayed diagnosis as a major factor in emergency medicine malpractice. Naturally, the medical documentation in a case in which the physician determines that the patient has no serious problems is going to be less compulsive than when the patient is critically ill and is admitted to the hospital. Emergency medicine, in its risk management efforts, must look at the importance of improved documentation on any patient discharged from the emergency department, particularly those who present with the major risk management complaints—nontraumatic chest pain in the adult, abdominal pain in all age groups, febrile infants and children, and wounds and extremity trauma. Obviously, many other patients who are discharged may be potential malpractice claims, such as the patient with altered sensorium, the patient with a vague neurologic complaint, or the patient with vague and nonspecific complaints that are ultimately the prodrome of a disease that a week later is much easier to diagnosis. Given that emergency physicians see patients in a very small window of time, it is important to focus on medical documentation in the emergency department record that demonstrates a reasonably thorough examination and creates a defensible chart.

Emergency physicians have many responsibilities and must manage many conflicting demands. One of the most serious and problematic developments in emergency medicine malpractice litigation is the propensity for academic emergency physicians to present an ideal rather than practical standard of care. Expectations that a history and physical should be on par with a specialist's such as the vascular surgeon in peripheral vascular problems, or the neurologist if the patient has a neurologic problem, or even the internist if the patient has multiple vague and difficult-to-evaluate complaints, is unrealistic. Emergency physicians are extremely adept at managing crisis and triage, but the limitations of the emergency department will continue to create conflicts between experts on the acceptable standard of care. We return to the question of what is "acceptable error."

In California, a specific civil procedure law prohibits experts from appearing against emergency physicians unless they can demonstrate full-time practice of emergency medicine and extensive experience.[3] That is not a rule in any other state. As a result, there are outside experts who are willing to evaluate emergency medicine cases and be witnesses. There is also a problem of experts with specialty training and experience in other areas who believe they really understand the standard of care for a practicing emergency physician.

Undoubtedly, more and more experts will be ready to testify against physicians in all specialties, but emergency medicine is particularly vulnerable to the medical elite element who cannot or will not understand the limits of emergency medicine.

The Harvard malpractice study group proposes that a no-fault professional liability insurance programs would be the best solution to the inefficiencies of the current tort system.[40] Although the current tort system is ponderous and expensive, and legitimately injured persons receive only 25% to 50% of the monies expended, a no-fault approach to medical malpractice is an administrative nightmare. Given the fact that eventually 100% of all patients die and there may always be an expert ready to say that a little better care would have prevented that death, the question could be raised whether everyone would have a claim for death in or out of the hospital. Recent research by the Rand Corporation[16] condemning the quality of rural hospitals shows the prejudice of health care researchers in outcomes research. Given the 100% mortality of the American population and the 100% accuracy of the retrospectoscope, a no-fault medical malpractice plan might remove the stress and the scars of medical malpractice litigation, but it would open public coffers to an unending demand for compensation. Obviously, the Harvard researchers have not looked at the disaster of workers' compensation programs across the country,[13] or they would have hesitated to suggest that no-fault was the answer. Already uncomfortable with the Harvard methodology, emergency physicians may be equally uncomfortable with their proposed solution.

FUTURE LEGAL TRENDS

Our view is that little tort reform will be accomplished by the end of the 1990s, and our predictions follow:

1. Malpractice insurance costs should remain relatively stable if the American economy does not decline.
2. Trends show an increasing importance for emergency departments in the evaluation of adult nontraumatic chest pain. Recent loss runs show that this is an increasingly important part of emergency physician losses.[26]
3. Malpractice arrangements and programs for multihospital contract groups will stabilize as the specialty ages. New arrangements for insurance will come from some trends toward decentralization of emergency medicine contract management.
4. Hospitals will continue to demand extremely high professional liability coverage from their emergency physicians.
5. Emergency medicine will continue to suffer from the lack of availability of appropriate insurance packages from the mainstream insurance companies.
6. Problems with the standard of care and defense of emergency medicine cases will increase because of standard of care problems within the specialty and between emergency medicine and other specialties.
7. Patient visit volumes in emergency departments will increase, increasing the risk that the critically ill and critically injured will get less attention as the emergency department becomes the last and increasingly inappropriately used resource for primary care.
8. Emergency physicians will continue to struggle with appropriateness of care criteria in the face of increased volume and demand.
9. The specialty will gain strength and stature within the hospital environment and within the health care systems by virtue of its major contributions to the total health care system.
10. Continuous quality improvement activities by emergency departments will address many of the problems aggravating liability exposures for emergency physicians.
11. ACEP will continue to provide educational and member resources in the area of legal research, risk management, and other activities related to improving the risk management experience for emergency medicine.
12. Multihospital groups will continue to play a major role in professional liability matters for emergency physicians.
13. Some physician mutuals and some mainstream insurance companies may offer better packages for emergency physicians to obtain the business.

14. There will be no major tort reform during the 1990s. There will be major restructuring of health care, resulting in increased pressure on emergency departments and an increased potential for emergency medicine professional liability litigation.

During the 1990s emergency medicine will increase in stature and influence because of the major contributions it makes to the total health care system. As the specialty ages, the influence of its individual members will increase at the medical staff, local, and state levels. Management expertise of emergency physicians and their position within the hospital environment will lead to involvement in areas outside the emergency department and contributions to the hospital separate from emergency care. All of these changes and trends will affect the legal environment for emergency physicians, increasing the interest of emergency medicine in legal and regulatory activities. Professional liability litigation will continue to be a major source of stress and financial expense for emergency physicians in the future.

References

1. Boczo G: Liability rates likely to inch up during 1993. American Medical News, Jan 11, 1993, p 3
2. Brennan TA, Leape LL, Laird NM, et al: Incidence of adverse events and negligence in hospitalized patients. N Engl J Med 324:370–376, 1991
3. California Health and Safety Code 1799.01
4. Caplan RA, Posner KL, Cheney FW: Effect of outcome on physician judgements of appropriateness of care. JAMA 265:1957–1960, 1990
5. Clinical Policy for Management of Adult Patients Presenting with a Chief Complaint of Chest Pain with no History of Trauma. American College of Emergency Physicians, Dallas, 1990
6. Dictation/Transcriptions of Records. Position Summaries, ed 8. Dallas, American College of Emergency Medicine, 1992, p 26
7. Eddy DM: Clinical decision making: From theory to practice. (A Series). JAMA 1990-1991
8. Federal Risk Retention Act, 15 U.S.C.A. 3901–3906
9. The Florida Health Plan, Florida Laws, Chapter 92-33, Sec 408.02, (1992)
10. Florida Statutes 768.13. West 1992
11. Florida Statutes 766.301-316 West 1992
12. Foresight Series. American College of Emergency Physicians, Dallas, 1986 to present
13. Gashill M: Workers Compensation: Trouble for employers, workers, hospitals. Health Texas 44:19, 1989
14. Jancin B: Programs to reduce CCU admissions showing success. Family Practice News, Jan 15, 1993, p 6
15. Karcy A, Holbrook J, Auerbach B, et al: Preventability of malpractice claims in Emergency Medicine: A closed claims study. Ann Emerg Med 19:865–873, 1990
16. Kueler EB, Rubenstein LV, Kahn KL, et al: Hospital characteristics and quality of care. JAMA 268:1709–1714, 1992
17. Leape L, Park RE, Solomon DH, et al: Relation between surgeons' practice volumes and geographic variations in the rate of carotid endarterectomy. N Engl J Med 321:653–657, 1989
18. Lee TH, Rowan GW, Weisberg RN, et al: Clinical characteristics and natural history of patients with acute myocardial infarction sent home from the emergency room. Am J Cardiol 60:219–224, 1987
19. Louisiana Patient Compensation Fund. La. R.S. 40:1299.44 West 1992

20. Lucas v. United States, 757 S.W. 2d 687 (Tex 1988)
21. Maine Liability Demonstration Project. Maine Laws, Chapter 24, Sec. 2971–2978, 1989
22. Massachusetts Workers' Compensation Law, Chapter 398 of the Acts of 1991, [St. 1991, Chapter 398, Section 53]
23. McCarthy PL, Lembo RM, Baron MA, et al: Predictive value of abnormal physical examination findings in ill-appearing and well-appearing febrile children. Pediatrics 76:167–171, 1985
24. (MICRA) California Statutes 1975 Ex Sess 1975–1976 Chapters 1 and 2, pp 3949–4007
25. Model Medical Liability and Patient Protection Act American Medical Association, Chicago, 1989
26. Personal review of multiple loss runs, 1990–1992
27. Providing Telephone Advice from the Emergency Department. Position Summaries, ed 8. Dallas, American College of Emergency Physicians, 1990, p 33
28. Report to the Congressional Requesters, Medical Malpractice (A Series). United States General Accounting Office, Gaathersberg, MD, 1986
29. Rogers JT: Risk Management in Emergency Medicine. Dallas, American College of Emergency Physicians, 1985
30. Rosen P (ed): Emergency Medicine: Concepts and Clinical Practice, eds 1–3. St Louis, CV Mosby, 1983, 1988, 1992
31. Sax v. Votteler, 648 S.W. 2d 661 (Texas 1983)
32. Smith v. Baptist Memorial Hospital System, 720 S.W. 2d 618 Tex. App. San Antonio, 1986 ref. n.r.e.
33. Social Security Act, sections 1866, 1867, 42 USC 1395 dd
34. Strauss RW: Contracts: A Practical Guide for the Emergency Physician. Dallas, American College of Emergency Physicians, 1990
35. Swartout J: Directory of Practice Parameters. Chicago, American Medical Association, 1992
36. Telephone Orders in the Emergency Department. Position Summaries, ed 8. Dallas, American College of Emergency Physicians, 1989, p 34
37. Tex. Civ. Proc. and Rem. Code. Section 33.013
38. Trautlein H, Lambert RL, Miller J: Malpractice in the Emergency Department—review of 200 cases. Ann Emerg Med 13:709–711, 1984
39. Tsai v. Wells 725 S.W. 2d 271 Tex. App. Corpus Christi 1986 Ref. n.r.e.
40. Weiler PC, Newhouse JP, Hiatt HH: Proposal for medical liability reform. JAMA 267:2355–2358, 1992
41. Writing Admissions Orders. Position Summaries, ed 8. Dallas, American College of Emergency Physicians, 1990, p 18

Address reprint requests to

John D. Dunn, MD
Brownwood Regional Medical Center
1501 Burnet Drive
Brownwood, TX 76801

CUMULATIVE INDEX 1993

Volume 11

February   ADVANCES IN TRAUMA, pages 1–271
May   HEMATOLOGIC/ONCOLOGIC EMERGENCIES, pages 273–555
August   THE HAND IN EMERGENCY MEDICINE, pages 557–818
November   MEDICAL-LEGAL ISSUES, pages 819–984

Note: Page numbers of article and issue titles are in **boldface** type

Abbreviated informed consent, 836
Abbreviated injury scale (AIS), 17–18
Abdomen, cancer of, in children, 522–523
    examination of, in blunt trauma patient,
        107–108
    limitations in trauma setting, 39
Abdominal trauma, blunt. See *Blunt
    abdominal trauma.*
    in intoxicated patient, 228
    pediatric, 199–200
        computed tomography in, 200
    penetrating. See *Penetrating abdominal
        trauma.*
Abscess, of the hand, fascial space
        infection, 611
    paronychia, 606–607
Abuse, of child. See *Abused child; Child/
    children, abuse of.*
    of elderly. See *Elderly, abuse of.*
Abused child, 847–848
    temporary protective custody for, 849
Acanthosis nigricans, 279, 280
ACEP. See *American College of Physicians
    (ACEP).*
Acetabular fractures, 154
    acetabulum anatomy, 154
    classification, 155, 156, 157
    radiographic diagnosis of, 154–155
    treatment of, 155–157
Acetabulum, anatomy of, 154
    fractures of. See *Acetabular fractures.*
Acquired ichthyosis, 279–280, 281
Acquired immunodeficiency syndrome
        (AIDS), hemophilia treatment causing,
        353–355
    patients fearful of contracting, treatment
        dilemma posed by, 540

Acquired neutropenia, 505
    autoimmune, 506
    chronic benign, 506–507
    chronic idiopathic, 507
    drug-induced, 505–506
    metabolic and nutritional, 506
Acrolentiginous melanoma, 295
Actinomycin D, pharmacology and
        toxicology of, 440
Actuarial analysis, insurance companies
        and, 938
    risk reduction and, 945–946
Acute lymphocytic leukemia (ALL), 504
Acute myelogenous leukemia (AML), 498–
        499
Acyclovir, 616–617
    in treatment of febrile neutropenic pa-
        tient, 511–512
Adamantinoma, radiologic manifestations
        of, 330–331
ADH (antidiuretic syndrome). See
        *Syndrome of inappropriate antidiuretic
        hormone (SIADH).*
Adhesions, following extensor tendon
        repair, 648
    following flexor tendon repair, 634
Advanced life support (ALS), 1–2
Advice/instructions, on discharge from
        Emergency Department. See *Discharge
        instructions.*
    for follow-up, 898
    via telephone. See *Telephone advice/in-
        structions.*
Against-medical-advice, high-risk patient
        actions, 912–914
AIDS. See *Acquired immunodeficiency
        syndrome (AIDS).*

Air embolism, following transfusion
therapy, 398
Air medical services, in prehospital care, 9–
10
Airway management, **53–57**
controversies, combative trauma patient,
paralysis versus rapid tranquilization, 56–57
nasotracheal versus oral endotracheal
intubation, 55
neuromuscular blocking agents, 54–55
oral intubation in cervical spine injury,
53–54
surgical and percutaneous techniques,
56
in head trauma patient, 168–169
in intoxicated patient, 227, 230–231
in multiple trauma patient, 34
pediatric, equipment needs, 193
equipment sizes, 194
rapid sequence induction and intubation, 195
recommendations, 57
Airway obstruction, cancer-associated,
lower, 423–424
upper, 421–422
AIS. See *Abbreviated injury scale (AIS)*.
Akathisia, neuroleptic side effect of,
misdiagnosis, 882
Alcohol, and trauma, **225–234**
Alcoholic patient, medicolegal
considerations, 233–234
rehabilitation or referral of, 232–233
screening questions to recognize, 233
Alcohol intoxication, in trauma patient,
acute, initial evaluation, 226
deaths related to, epidemiology, 225–226
pathophysiology of, abdominal effects,
228
airway/anesthesia, 230–231
and alcohol withdrawal, 232
bone effects, 229
cardiac affects, 227
central nervous system effects, 229–230
cervical spine precautions, 231
hematologic/hemostatic effects, 228–
229
hypothermia, 229
immune system effects, 229
metabolic effects, 231
psychiatric effects, 231
pulmonary effects, 227
response to hemorrhage, 227
Alcoholism, epidemiology, 225–226
in thrombocytopenia differential diagnosis, 450
Alcohol-related deaths, epidemiology, 225–
226
Alcohol withdrawal, 232

Alkylating agents, pharmacology and
toxicology of, cisplatin, 437
cyclophosphamide, 435–436
melphalan, 436–437
ALL. See *Acute lymphocytic leukemia (ALL)*.
Allen's test, in hand trauma evaluation, 594
Allergic reaction, causing eosinophilia, 502
to transfusion, 395
All-terrain vehicle (ATV), successful injury
control strategies with, 259
Alport syndrome, in thrombocytopenia
differential diagnosis, 450
ALS. See *Advanced life support (ALS)*.
Alterations, to medical records, destruction
as form of, 894–896
discovery of, 896
making, 894
Alternative therapy, availability for high-
risk patient, 913
Ambulance service, historical origins, 1
Amelanotic melanoma, 295
Ameloblastoma, radiologic manifestations
of, 330–331
American College of Physicians (ACEP),
endorsed liability coverage program,
935, 938
guidelines for care of psychiatric patients, 870
medical control issues and, 853–855
American Medical Association (AMA),
arbitration proposals, 941–942
practice parameters forum, 943
tort reform proposals, 946
American Society of Anesthesiologists
(ASA), practice parameters report, 945
Aminoglycosides, in treatment of febrile
neutropenic patient, 510
AML. See *Acute myelogenous leukemia
(AML)*.
Amphotericin B, in treatment of febrile
neutropenic patient, 511
Amputation(s), care of amputated part,
741–742
classification by mechanism, 745
crush and avulsion, 750
fingertip. See *Fingertip injuries, amputations*.
hemorrhage management, 740–741
incomplete, 743, 744
initial evaluation, 740
and replantations, **739–751**. See also *Re-
plantation(s)*.
tetanus and intravenous antibiotics administration, 742–743
wound cleansing and debridement, 741
Amyloidosis, 288
Analgesia, for multiple trauma patient, 41
Anaphylaxis, causing thrombocytopenia,
452

Anemia(s), of chronic disease, 485
  cobalamin and folate deficiency, 486
  hemolytic, 486–488
  inflammatory, 485
  iron deficiency, 482–484
  symptomatic, as complication of sickle
    cell anemia, 372
  thalassemia and thalassemia traits, 484–
    485
  treatment of, 488–489
Anesthesia, in intoxicated patient, 230–231
Angiomas, malignancy associated with, 279
Animal bites, to hand, infections caused by,
    615–616
  microbiology of, 604–605
Aniridia, 307
Anterior chamber, of eye, hematologic and
    oncologic diseases affecting, 305–307
Anthracyclines, pharmacology and
    toxicology of, 438–439
Antibiotic treatment, for febrile
    neutropenia patient, 508–512
  in hand burn injuries, systemic, 806
    topical, 805–806
  in hand infections, 602–605
    human and animal bite wounds, 615,
      616
  in hand nerve injury, 663
  intravenous, in amputation injury, 742–
    743
  as prophylactic measure in high-pressure
    injection injuries, to the hand, 770
Antibody screening, of blood, 383–384
Anticoagulant therapy, in disseminated
    intravascular coagulation, 474
Antidiuretic hormone (ADH),
    inappropriate secretion of. See
    *Syndrome of inappropriate antidiuretic
    hormone (SIADH).*
Antidumping statutes, 861–862
Antifibrinolytics, in disseminated
    intravascular coagulation, 474
Antimetabolites, pharmacology and
    toxicology of, cytosine arabinoside,
    435
    5-fluorouracil, 432, 434
    6-mercaptopurine and 6-thioguanine,
      434–435
    methotrexate, 431–432
Antineoplastic agents, pharmacology and
    toxicology of, actinomycin D, 440
    anthracyclines, 438–439
    bleomycin, 437–438
    mitomycin C, 439–440
Antiviral agents, in treatment of febrile
    neutropenic patient, 511–512
Anxiety, as complication of sickle cell
    anemia, 375
Aortic rupture, 88–89

evaluation of, 89–91
  radiographic signs of, 90
Aplastic anemia, in thrombocytopenia
    differential diagnosis, 450
Aplastic crisis, as complication of sickle cell
    anemia, 372
Apnea test, in brain death determination,
    42–43, 44
Arbitration, AMA proposals on, 941–942
Atasoy flap, 761–762
Attitude, of EMS providers, patient's
    perception of, 863–864
  risk management and, 921
  toward psychiatric patient, 870
ATV. See *All-terrain vehicle (ATV).*
Automobile crashes. See *Motor vehicle
    crashes.*
Autonomy, of patient, as basic medical
    value, 532
  versus beneficence, 539
Autotransfusion, 401–402
  in thoracotomy for penetrating chest
    trauma, 103
Avascular osteonecrosis, as complication of
    sickle cell anemia, 374–375
Avulsion injury(ies), amputations, 750
  middle phalanx fractures, collateral liga-
    ment, 691, 692–693
    extensor surface, 691, 692
  nail bed, 759
  pelvic fractures, anterior iliac spine, infe-
    rior, 150
    superior, 149
    coccyx, 151
    ischial tuberosity, 150
    pelvic wing fracture, 150
    sacrum, 151

Baciquent (bacitracin), in treatment of hand
    burn injuries, 805–806
Bacitracin, in treatment of hand burn
    injuries, 805–806
Bacterial infections, following transfusion
    therapy, 397–398
  in neutropenic patient, 510
Baldwin v. Knight, 891–892
Barton's fracture, distal radius, DISI and
    VISI patterns as sequelae to, 731
  dorsal rim, 711
  volar rim, 711–712
Basal cell carcinoma, of skin, 293
Basic life support (BLS), 1–2
Beneficence, as basic medical value, 532
Bennett fracture, first metacarpal, 699, 700,
    701
Benzodiazepines, use with disruptive
    patients, 881–882

Betadine (iodophor), in treatment of hand burn injuries, 805

β-lactam agents, in treatment of febrile neutropenic patient, 510

Bioethics committees, as surrogate decision-makers, 538

Biomedical ethics. See *Ethics, dilemmas in hematologic/oncologic emergencies.*

Bites, to hand, infections resulting from, 613–616

Bladder, trauma to, diagnosis of, 141
 management of, 142
 radiographic examination, 141–142
 significant forms, 140–141

Bleeding disorders. See *Hemophilia.*

Bleeding episodes, in hemophilia. See *Hemophilia, bleeding episodes.*

Bleomycin, pharmacology and toxicology of, 437–438

Blood, antibody screening and crossmatching, 383–384
 collection and storage for transfusion, 380
 red cell antigens and antibodies, 381–382
 uncrossmatched, massive transfusion and, 398–399

Blood feud, as Anglo-Saxon law, 821

Blood pressure, in pediatric patient, formula for calculating, 190
 in pregnant patient, decreased, 208–209
 normal, 209

Blood products, for transfusion therapy, cryoprecipitate, 389
 fresh frozen plasma, 388–389
 granulocyte concentrates, 388
 plasma derivatives, 389–392
 platelet concentrates, 387–388
 red cells. See *Red blood cells.*
 whole blood, 384–385

Blood substitutes, in prehospital fluid resuscitation, 63–64

Blood supply, evaluating in hand trauma, 589
 to the hand, 581
 to the wrist, 718

Blood typing, expediting for massive transfusion, 399

Blood volume, in pediatric patient, formula for calculating, 190
 in pregnant patient, 209

BLS. See *Basic life support (BLS).*

Blunt abdominal trauma, **107–119**
 diagnostic peritoneal lavage, 110–113. See also *Diagnostic peritoneal lavage.*
 imaging modalities to evaluate, computed tomography, 114–115. See also *Computed tomography (CT).*
 plain radiography, 108–109
 ultrasound, 118–119

 other, 109
 laboratory studies, 109–110
 laparoscopy to evaluate, 113–114
 laparotomy, therapeutic versus nontherapeutic, 115
 physical examination for, 107–108
 in pregnancy, evaluating maternal injury, 210–211
 suspected placental injury, 211–212
 uterine contractions, 211
 risk factors for, 107

Blunt chest trauma, **81–93**
 aortic rupture, 88–91
 diaphragm rupture, 92–93
 esophageal rupture, 91–92
 flail chest, 82–83
 myocardial contusion, 85–88
 myocardial rupture, 88
 pulmonary contusion, 83–84
 sternal fracture, 81–82
 tracheobronchial injuries, 84–85

Blunt neck injury, **71–77**. See also *Cervical spine injury.*

Boarding schools, minors requiring emergency treatment while at, 845

Bone, effect of alcohol on, 229

Bone lesions, benign versus malignant, 309
 multiple myeloma, radiological manifestations, 321–322
 "onion-skin" reaction and, 310
 radiological manifestations of, 308–312
 metastatic tumors, 312–320

"Borrowed servant," legal doctrine of, 855

Boutonniere deformity, 575, 576
 middle phalangeal fracture and, 690, 691

Bowen's disease, of skin, 293, 294

Boxer's fractures, 695

Brain death determination, 42–43
 apnea test, 42–43, 44
 consent for organ donation following, 44–45
 establishing coma etiologies, 42, 43
 maintenance therapy following, 45, 46
 neurologic examination, 43
 pediatric, 43, 44

Brain injury, diffuse, in head trauma patient, 178, 180

Breach of duty, negligence and, 828–829

Breast cancer, metastasis to the skin, 290–291

Breathing problems, cancer-associated, 424–425

Bucket handle fracture, 154

Bupivacaine, for replantation surgery, 751

Burn injuries, of the hand, assessment of, depth, 798, 799, 800
 extent, 797–798, 799
 chemical, 802
 electrical, 801

Emergency Department treatment, **797–808**
  flame, 798
  frostbite, 803, 804
  hot objects, 801
  hot tar, 802–803
  scald, 798, 800
  treatment, 803
    admission to hospital, 807
    antibiotics, 805–806
    escharotomy, 806–807
    as outpatient, 807–808
    pain management, 803–805
    wound management, 805
  in multiple trauma patients, 39
Burr hole decompression, in head trauma
  patient, 170

Call screening, 859
Camp, minors requiring emergency
  treatment while at, 845
Cancer. See also *Oncologic disease.*
  in children. See *Childhood malignancies.*
  mechanical complications of, **421–428**
    cardiovascular, 425–427
    neurologic, 427–428
    respiratory system, 421–425
  skin, common forms, 293–298
Cancer patients, edema in, 274–275
  hormone-related conditions in, 274–276
  pruritus in, 274
Candida albicans, hand infection caused by,
  602
Canterbury v. Spence, 834
Capacity, of patient for decision-making,
  536–537
Capitate fractures, 709
Capitolunate angle, in dorsal intercalary
  segment instability, 729, 730
  radiographic evaluation, 725, 726
Capnography, in prehospital care, 8
Carbon dioxide partial pressure
  (pCOS12T), normal maternal, 207–208
Carboxyhemoglobin, pulse oximetry and,
  490
Cardiac tamponade, cancer-associated,
  426–427
Cardinal line, 586–587
Cardiovascular system, and cancer-
  associated mechanical problems, 425–
  427
Cardioversion, in pregnant patient, 210
Carotenemia, 276
Carpal bones. See also *specific bones.*
  fractures. See *Carpal fractures.*
  movement, 720–721
  radiographic evaluation, 724

structure and arrangement, 565–566, 718
Carpal fractures, 703
  capitate, 709
  hamate, 708–709
  lunate, 706, 707
  pisiform, 707–708
  scaphoid, 704–705
  trapezium, 706–707
  trapezoid, 709
  triquetrum, 705–706, 708
Carpal instability patterns, 721, 727, 729–
  731
Carpometacarpal joint, injuries to, fingers,
  791–792
  thumb, 794
*Carr v. St. Paul Fire and Marine Insurance
  Company*, 894–896
Case-based ethics, 534
Casuistry, 534
Cefoperazone, in treatment of febrile
  neutropenic patient, 510–511
Ceftazidime, in treatment of febrile
  neutropenic patient, 510–511
Central nervous system, effect of alcohol
  on, 229–230
Central venous pressure line, in pregnant
  patient, 209–210
Cerebral edema, in head trauma patient,
  178, 180
Cerebral herniation, in head trauma
  patient, 180
Cerebral infarction, in head trauma patient,
  178
Cerebral perfusion pressure (CPP), in head
  trauma patient, 166
Cerebrovascular accident, as complication
  of sickle cell disease, 370–371
Cervical spine injury, evaluation in blunt
    trauma patient, cervical cross table
    lateral view, 73–74
  computed tomography, indications for,
    75–76
  flexion/extension views, 74–75
  recommendations, 76–77
  three-view versus five-view series, 74
  head and facial injuries predicting, 73
  in intoxicated patient, 231
  missed fracture, 71–73
  oral intubation, safety issues in airway
    management, 53–54
  pediatric, 196–197
Cesarean section, perimortem, delivery of
  fetus by, 219–220
Changes, to medical records. See
  Alterations, to medical records.
Chauffeur's fracture, 719
Chemical burn injury, to the hand, 802
Chemotherapeutic agents, pharmacology
  and toxicology of, **431–441**. See also
  specific drugs.

Chemotherapeutic agents *(Continued)*
  acute toxicity, 433
  alkylating agents, 435–437
  antimetabolites, 431–435
  antineoplastic agents, 437–440
  plant (vinca) alkaloids, 440–441
Chest trauma, blunt. See *Blunt chest trauma.*
  pediatric, 199
  penetrating. See *Penetrating chest trauma.*
Chest tube, placement in pregnant trauma
    patient, 208
Child/children. See also *Minor(s).*
  abuse of. See also *Abused child.*
    reporting suspicion of, 848
      physician's immunity from liability
        in, 848
  brain death determination in, 43, 44
  Jehovah's witness, management guide-
    lines, 41
  malignancies in. See *Childhood malignan-
    cies.*
  as multiple trauma patients, 38
  neglected, 848
  traumatic injury to. See *Pediatric trauma.*
Childhood malignancies, abdominal, 522–
    523
  common forms, 518
  Emergency Department presentation of,
    517–527
    beginning treatment, 517–518
    common complaints, 518
    diagnosis, aspects of making, 517
    head and neck, 518–521
    hematologic, 525–527
    mediastinal, 521
    skeletal, 524–525
Cholelithiasis, as complication of sickle cell
    anemia, 374
Choroid, hematologic and oncologic
    diseases affecting, 307–308
Chronic disease, anemia of, 485
Chronic idiopathic neutropenia (CIN), 507
Chronic myelogenous leukemia (CML),
    497–498
CIN. See *Chronic idiopathic neutropenia
    (CIN).*
Circulation, in hand trauma evaluation, 594
Circulation, respiration, abdomen, motor,
    and speech scale (CRAMS), 20, 23
Cisplatin, pharmacology and toxicology of,
    437
Civil rights violation, EMS liability issues
    and, 864
Claims prevention, medical control and,
    855
Claw deformity, 570
Clawson, Dr. J., emergency medical
    dispatch protocol, 859
Clenched fist injury, 613–614

Clostridium perfringens, hand infection
    caused by, 616
CML. See *Chronic myelogenous leukemia
    (CML).*
Coagulation disorders, accompanying
    massive transfusion, 399–400
Cobalamin anemia, 486
COBRA. See *Consolidated Omnibus Budget
    Reconciliation Act (COBRA).*
Coccyx, fracture or dislocation of, 151
Code(s), development in early
    communities, 819–821
  of Hammurabi, 820
  Justinian, 820–821
  Mosaic, 820
Codman's triangle, 310, 312
"Collar button" abscess, 611
Colles' fracture, 710–711
  DISI and VISI patterns as sequelae to,
    731
Colloid solutions, in prehospital fluid
    resuscitation, versus crystalloid
    solutions, 62
  nonprotein type, 63–64
Coma, acute, as complication of sickle cell
    disease, 371
  etiologies of, brain death determination
    and, 42, 43
Combative trauma patient, airway
    management in, paralysis versus rapid
    tranquilization, 56–57
Commitment process, 871. See also
    Involuntary commitment.
Common law, establishment of, 822–823
  professional liability under, 823
Communications, and miscommunication,
    906
  between prehospital care units and med-
    ical control, 858–859
Community care, injury control and, 260–
    261
Competence, of patient for decision-
    making, 536–537
Complaints, handling of, 907–908
  from patients, 920–921
"Compurgation," 821
Computed tomography (CT), blunt
    abdominal trauma evaluation
    complementing diagnostic peritoneal
      lavage, 117–118
    diagnostic peritoneal lavage versus,
      116–117
    scan interpretations, 115
    scanning protocols, 114–115
  evaluating blunt chest trauma. See under
    specific clinical entities.
  evaluating blunt neck injury, indications
    for, 75–76
    as secondary tool, 77

in head trauma evaluation, 170–171
clinical objectives, 171
diffuse brain injury, 178, 180
extra-axial lesions, 174–177
indications for use, patient categories, 171–173
intra-axial lesions, 177–178, 179
limitations of, 180–181
technique, 171
in pediatric patient, abdominal trauma, 200
head trauma, 197
penetrating abdominal trauma evaluation, 130
in pregnant trauma patient, 218, 219
blunt abdominal trauma evaluation, 211
Confidentiality, 532–533
of information held in National Practitioner Data Bank, 928–929
of medical record, 898–899
of psychiatric patient's disclosures, 878
Congenital melanosis, of sclera, 304–305
Congestive heart failure, following transfusion therapy, 398
Conjunctiva, hematologic and oncologic diseases affecting, 304–305
Consent, abbreviated informed, 836
background of, 833–834
COBRA and, 836
deferred, 836
emergency, 835–836
express, 834
general, 834–835
implied, 537, 834
informed. See *Informed consent.*
for minors, in an emergency, 841–842
exceptional situations, 842–843
problems, 837–838
specific situations, 843–845
in prehospital care, 856–858
problems determining, 856–857
of terminally ill patient, 857–858
problem areas in, 836–838
problem patients and, 837–838
and refusal of treatment, **833–839**
specific, 835
types of, 834–836
Consolidated Omnibus Budget Reconciliation Act (COBRA). See also *Emergency Medical Treatment and Active Labor Act (EMTALA).*
consent issues and, 836
destination diversion and transfer issues, 861–862
patient dumping violations, 912
transferred patient's medical records, 897
Consultation, physician's duty regarding, 878

Contamination, in hand trauma, 589
Contract, liability for negligence and, 824–825
Contractions, uterine, in pregnant trauma patient, 211
Contusion(s), in head trauma patient, 177–178
bifrontal hemorrhagic, 178
cerebral, 179
myocardial. See *Myocardial contusion.*
pulmonary. See *Pulmonary contusion.*
Coombs' test, 383–384
Cornea, hematologic and oncologic diseases affecting, 305–307
Corn picker injuries, to the hand, 773–774
clinical presentation, 774, 775
pathophysiology, 774, 775
treatment, 776
Cost of injury, **241–251**
age at injury, 242–243
cost analysis sources, 242
cost definitions, 242
from falls, 248
firearm incidents, 247–248
government funding to cover, 250
head and spinal cord injuries, 244–245
lifetime costs, 243–244
long-term control, 249–250
motor vehicle crashes, 245–247
payment systems, 249–250
productivity issues, 250
prospective payment systems, 251
trauma center and, 250–251
other accidents, 248
Courts, as surrogate decision-makers, 538–539
CPP. See *Cerebral perfusion pressure (CPP).*
CRAMS. See *Circulation, respiration, abdomen, motor, and speech scale (CRAMS).*
Crash survivor, death of companion. See *Death, of crash victim.*
discharge and follow-up, 47
Crash victim, death of. See *Death, of crash victim.*
survival of, discharge and follow-up, 47
Cricothyroidotomy, in airway management, 56
Cross-finger flap, 763–764
Crossmatching, of blood, 383–384
expediting for massive transfusion, 399
Crush amputations, involving the hand, 750
Cryoprecipitate, 340
in transfusion therapy, 389
Crystalloid solutions, in prehospital fluid resuscitation, colloid solutions versus, 62
hypertonic solutions, 62–63

CT. See *Computed tomography (CT)*.
Cutaneous ischemia, 288–289
Cyclophosphamide, pharmacology and
  toxicology of, 435–436
Cytomegalovirus, congenital, in
  thrombocytopenia differential
  diagnosis, 450
Cytosine arabinoside, pharmacology and
  toxicology of, 435

Damages, negligence and, 829
Data Bank. See *National Practitioner Data
  Bank (NPDB)*.
Daunorubicin, pharmacology and
  toxicology of, 438–439
Death, alcohol-related, epidemiology, 225–
  226
  brain death. See *Brain death determination*.
  of crash victim, 44–45
    delivering news of, 46
    from multiple injuries, 29, 30
    notifying family of, 45–46
    survivor discharge and follow-up, 47
    viewing body and closure, 46–47
  fetal, causes of, 213
  malpractice cases involving, 946–947
  maternal, perimortem cesarean section
    following, 219–220
Debridement, amputation wound, 741
Decision-making, consent, 537
  in emergency situation, model for, 535–
    536
  patient capacity for, evaluating, 536–537
  surrogates, 537–539. See also *Surrogate
    decision-makers*.
Decompression, burr hole, in head trauma
    patient, 170
  in treatment of high-pressure injection
    injuries to hand, 769–770
Deferred consent, 836
Delayed repair, of damaged peripheral
    nerves in the hand, 664
Deontology, 533–534
Depression, as complication of sickle cell
    anemia, 375
Desmopressin, 339, 342–343
Destination choice, and destination
    protocol flexibility, 860
  medical director determining, factors in-
    volved, 859–860
Destruction, of medical records, 894–896
Detention, of patient. See *Restraint, of
    patient*.
Detention facilities, minors requiring
    emergency treatment while at, 844
Diabetic patients, hand infections in, 604

Diagnostic peritoneal lavage (DPL),
    evaluating blunt abdominal trauma,
    110
  complications, 112–113
  versus computed tomography, 116–
    117
  computed tomography as complement
    to, 117–118
  indications, 110
  lavage fluid analysis, 112
  limitations, 113
  in pregnant patient, 210
  techniques, 110–111
  evaluating penetrating abdominal
    trauma, 129–130
  in pregnant patient, 216
  in pelvic fracture management, 158
  in penetrating chest trauma, 101–102
  positive, criteria for, 112
Diaphragm rupture, 92
  evaluation of, 92–93
  treatment of, 93
DIC. See *Disseminated intravascular
    coagulation (DIC)*.
Diffuse brain injury, in head trauma
    patient, 178, 180
Digital joints, 566
  functional anatomy, 781–784
  injuries to, carpometacarpal joint, fingers,
    791–792
    thumb, 794
  distal interphalangeal joint, 786–787
  examination, 785
  history, 784–785
  management principles, 786
  metacarpophalangeal joint, fingers,
    788–791
    thumb, 792–794
  proximal interphalangeal joint, 787–
    788
  radiographic evaluation, 785
Digital motion, extension, 575–576
  flexion, 574–575
Digital nerves, in hand, injury to, 657
  Emergency Department management,
    662–663
  operative management, 663–665
  outcome following repair, 666–667
Digits. See *Phalanx; Thumb*.
DIP. See *Distal interphalangeal joint (DIP)*.
Disability, malpractice cases involving,
    946–947
Discharge, of crash survivor, 47
Discharge instructions, law suits
    concerning, 921
  in medical record, 897–898
Discharge plan. See *Disposition plan*.
Disclosure of information, confidentiality
    issues and, 878–879

consequences of, 879
differing needs of staff to know, 879
limited, 879
from medical record, 899–900
to police and governmental agencies, 879
DISI. See *Dorsal intercalary segment instability (DISI)*.
Dislocation(s), lunate. See *Lunate dislocations*.
perilunate. See *Perilunate dislocations*.
scaphoid, 736
Dispatching, of emergency medical services. See *Emergency medical dispatching*.
Displaced transverse fractures, metacarpals, 697, 698
proximal phalanx, 683, 684
Disposition plan, and discharge instructions, 897–898
for psychiatric patient, commitment. See *Involuntary commitment*.
goal of, 883
judgments made in error, 884
legal disputes concerning, 883
negligent release, 884–885
suicide prediction, 885
Disseminated intravascular coagulation (DIC), **465–478**
clinical presentations of, 470–471
hemorrhagic manifestations, 471
thrombotic manifestations, 470–471
clinical syndromes of, 475
infectious, 476
malignancy, 477
obstetric, 476–477
snake envenomation, 477
traumatic, 476
diagnosis of, 471–472
differential diagnosis of, 472–473
hemophilia treatment causing, 353
hemostasis review, 465–468
pathophysiology of, 468–469, 470
plasmin role, 469
thrombin role, 469
thrombocytopenia as early manifestation of, 456
treatment of, 473
fibrinolytic inhibitors, 474
future therapies, 474–475
heparin therapy, 474
principles, 473
replacement therapy, 473–474
Distal interphalangeal joint (DIP), injury to, 786–787
nail bed and fingertip anatomy, 755–756
Distal radius fractures, 709
Barton's, dorsal rim, 711
volar rim, 711–712
Colles', 710–711

radioulnar joint, 713–714
Smith's, 711
styloid, 712–713
Distributive justice, as basic medical value, 532
Diversion, of prehospital patient, legislation governing, 861–862
protocols for, 860–861
and transfer relationship, 861
Doctrines. See *Legal doctrines*.
Documentation, HCA changes concerning, 890–891
regulatory requirements, 889
shortfalls in medical record, 893–897
statutes governing, 890
trends in, 940
utilization by outside agencies, 891
Do not resuscitate (DNR) orders, prehospital consent controversy over, 857–858
Dorsal intercalary segment instability (DISI), 721, 729, 731, 733
Dorsal rim fracture, radius, 711
Doxorubicin, pharmacology and toxicology of, 438–439
DPL. See *Diagnostic peritoneal lavage (DPL)*.
Drugs. See also *specific agents*.
causing secondary leukocytosis, 499–500
implicated in immune-mediated thrombocytopenia, 451–452
inducing neutropenia, 505–506
Drug therapy, for hemophiliac, 344
Drug users, intravenous, hand infections in, 602, 604
Dumping, of patients, 861
and antidumping statutes, 861–862
Duty, breach of, negligence and, 828–829
to consult with colleague, 878
extent of, negligence and, 827–828
Duverney's fracture, 150
Dysfibrinogenemia, in DIC differential diagnosis, 473
Dyskeratosis, 304
Dystrophy, sympathetic, following nerve injury in the hand, 667

Ecchymosis, metastatic neuroblastoma and, 299
Edema, in cancer patient, 274–275
cerebral, in head trauma patient, 178, 180
Educational institutions, minors requiring emergency treatment while at, 845
Eikenella corrodens, human bite wound to hand and, 615
Elderly, abuse of, 877–878
reporting, 878
as multiple trauma patients, 38–39

Electrical burn injury, of the hand, 801
Electrolyte abnormalities, massive
    transfusion and, 399–400
Emancipated minor, consent issues, 842–
    843
  refusing care, 845
Emergency, consent of minor in, 841–842
  definitions of, 841–842
  treatment for minors and, 841–842
Emergency consent, 835–836
Emergency Department, childhood
    malignancies presenting in, **517–527**
  classification by care level, 911–912
  medical record, **889–902**
  transfusion therapy in, **379–403**
Emergency medical dispatching, call
    screening and, 859
  Clawson protocol, 859
  destination and transfer issues, 859–862
  legal issues involving, 858–859
Emergency medical services (EMS),
    communications system for, 858–859
  employee claims against, 864
  and Good Samaritan legislation, 855–856
  historical origins, 1
  medical director relationship to, 853–854
  medical risk-taking activities by, 863
  perceived attitude of, 863–864
  prehospital care and. See *Prehospital care.*
  regulatory activity in, 855
  service demands versus funds available,
    863
Emergency Medical Treatment and Active
    Labor Act (EMTALA), 861–862
  noncompliant patient and, 873
Emergency medicine, documentation
    trends in, 940
  future legal issues in, **933–950**
  injury control as aspect in, **255–261**. See
    also *Injury control.*
  legal challenges facing, 933–934
  minors and, **841–850**
  psychiatry, and the law, **869–886**. See
    also *Psychiatric patient.*
  risk management and high-risk issues in,
    905–921
  and standard of care legal issues. See
    Standard of care.
Emergency rapid decision-making model,
    535–536
  algorithm for, 535
EMTALA. See *Emergency Medical Treatment
    and Active Labor Act (EMTALA).*
Endobronchial obstruction, cancer-
    associated, 423–424
Endoscopic examination. See *Laparoscopy.*
Envenomation, by snakes. See *Snake
    envenomation.*
Enzyme analysis, of peritoneal lavage fluid,
    112

Eosinopenia, etiology of, 501
Eosinophilia, 500–501
  defined, 502
  and eosinophil function, 501–502
  etiology of, 501, 502–503
  familial, 503
  tropical, 502–503
Eosinophilic granuloma, in children, 520–
    521
Epidural hematoma, in head trauma
    patient, 175, 176
Epineurial repair, of damaged peripheral
    nerves in the hand, 664–665
Epiphyseal plate injury, in children, 699,
    700, 721
Epistaxis, in hemophiliacs, 348–349
Epsilon-aminocaproic acid, 343
Equipment, for pediatric airway
    management, emergency room
    requirements, 193
  for rapid sequence induction and intuba-
    tion, 195
  sizes, 194
Erythema, gyratum repens, 280, 281
  necrolytic migratory, 284
  palmar, disease associated with, 279
Erythrocytosis, 489
Erythroderma, 277
Escharotomy, in hand burn injuries, 806–
    807
Escherichia coli infection, in neutropenic
    patient, 510
Esophageal rupture, 91
  evaluation of, 91
  treatment of, 91–92
Estrogens, in thrombocytopenia differential
    diagnosis, 450
Ethics, dilemmas in hematologic/oncologic
    emergencies, **531–543**
  applying values. See *Ethics methodology.*
  decision-making capacity of patient, 536–
    539. See also *Decision-making.*
  demanding futile care, 541–542
  patient autonomy versus beneficence,
    539
  truth-telling, 540–541
  unknown circumstances, 542–543
  values, 531–533
Ethics methodology, case-based (casuistry),
    534
  emergency rapid decision-making model,
    535–536
  rule-based (deontology), 533–534
  utilitarianism (teleology), 534
Evans's syndrome, and chronic ITP
    similarities, 453
Ewing's tumor, 310, 311–312
  in children, 524
Examination, high-risk patient leaving
    before, 914

Exophthalmos, 299–301, 302
Expert witnesses, in standard of care
    disputes, 947–949
Express consent, 834
Extensor tendon injuries, hand, **637–648**
    anatomy, 637–639
    complications, 648
    distal phalangeal fracture involving, 677,
        678
    Emergency Department evaluation, his-
        tory, 639–640
        physical examination, 640–641
    postoperative care, 647–648
    splinting, 648
    treatment principles, zone classification,
        641
        zone I, 641–642, 643
        zone II, 642
        zone III, 643–644
        zone IV, 644
        zone V, 644–645
        zone VI, 645
        zone VIII (dorsal forearm), 647
        zone VII (wrist level), 645–647
Extensor tendons, of the hand, 599
    anatomy, 570–573
    injuries to. See *Extensor tendon injuries,
        hand.*
    interosseus muscles relationship to,
        679, 680
Eye, hematologic and oncologic diseases
    affecting, anterior pole, 304–307
    exophthalmos, 299–301, 302
    eyelids and lacrimal apparatus, 301–304
    ophthalmoplegia, 300–301, 302
    posterior pole, 307–308
Eyelids, hematologic and oncologic
    diseases affecting, primary and
    metastatic involvement, 303–304
    ptosis, 301–303
Eye movements, disrupted, 300, 302

Facial injury, predicting cervical spine
    injury, 73
Factor replacement therapy, in bleeding
    disorders, 340
    desmopressin, 342–343
    epsilon-aminocaproic acid and tranex-
        amic acid, 343
    formulas for calculating, 343
    inhibitor antibody development follow-
        ing, 349, 352
Factor VIII, 340, 342
Falls, injury costs associated with, 246, 248,
    249
    rate and fatality rate by age, 249
Familial eosinophilia, 503

Family, patient's refusal of treatment and,
    913–914
    as surrogate decision-makers, 538
Fascial space infections, of the hand, 610–
    612
Fascicular repair, of damaged peripheral
    nerves in the hand, 664–665
Favism, 487
    signs and symptoms of, 488
Febrile transfusion reaction, 394–395
Federal Risk Retention Act, 937
Felons, drainage of, 608–609
Fetal death, causes of, 213
Fetal monitoring, in pregnant trauma
    patient, 212
    fetus in distress, 212–213
    suspected fetomaternal hemorrhage,
        213–216
Fetomaternal hemorrhage, 214–216
Fetus, delivery by perimortem cesarean
    section, 219–220
    in distress, 213–214
    monitoring following trauma event. See
        Fetal monitoring.
    radiation doses from CT scans, 218, 219
    viability issues, 213, 217
Fibrinolytic inhibitors, in disseminated
    intravascular coagulation, 474
Fidelity, as medical value, 533
"Finders of fact," 821
Fingers, extensor mechanism in, 572, 573
    joints of, 566
    lengths and functions of, 562–563
    motion of, extension, 575–576
        flexion, 574–575
Fingertip, anatomy, 755–757
    injuries to. See *Fingertip injuries.*
Fingertip injuries, **755–765**
    amputations, nail preservation, 764–765
        partial and complete, 760–761
        transverse, 765
    flaps and flap indications, 761–765
    subungual hematoma, 757–758
Firearms, control of injury by, Haddon
    matrix for, 257
    wounds from. See *Gunshot wounds.*
Flail chest, 82
    evaluation of, 82
    treatment of, 82–83
Flame burn injury, of the hand, 798
Flaps, for repair of fingertip injuries,
    Atasoy technique, 761–762
    choosing, 761
    cross-finger, 763–764
    H-shaped, 762, 763
    Kutler technique, 761, 762
    Moberg, 762–763
    thenar, 762, 763
    other types, 765

Flexor digitorum profundus tendon,
avulsion injury, 632–633
in hand trauma evaluation, 598
Flexor tendon injuries, hand, **621–634**
anatomy, 621–625
avulsion of profundus tendon, 632–633
classification, 629
zone I, 629
zone II ("No Man's Land"), 629–630
zone III, 630
zone IV, 630
zone V, 631
complications, 633–634
Emergency Department evaluation, history, 625
physical examination, 625–626
healing of, schools of thought regarding, 622
partial lacerations, 631–632
postoperative rehabilitation, 633–634
treatment principles, 626–627
preparation, 627
repair, 627–628
Flexor tendons, of the hand, anatomy, 573–574
injuries to. See *Flexor tendon injuries, hand.*
pulley system, 623, 624
in hand trauma evaluation, carpi radialis, 598
carpi ulnaris, 598–599
digitorum profundus, 598
digitorum superficialis, 598
palmaris longus, 599
Flexor tenosynovitis, 576
acute signs, 609–610
Fluid resuscitation, in head trauma patient, 169–170
Jehovah's witness and, guidelines for, 41
prehospital. See *Prehospital fluid resuscitation, of trauma patient.*
5-Fluorouracil, pharmacology and toxicology of, 432, 434
Flushing, skin, disease associated with, 278
Folate deficiency anemia, 486
Follow-up instructions, 898
Forearm, dorsal, extensor tendon injuries involving, 647
Forensic medical events, medical record and, 892–893
Foster home, minors requiring emergency treatment whilst in, 844
Fracture(s), and associated injury in multiple trauma patient, 36, 37
cervical spine, asymptomatic, 71–73
in hemophiliac, 345–346
metacarpal and phalangeal, **671–701**. See also *Metacarpal fractures; Phalangeal fractures.*

pelvic. See *Pelvic fractures.*
skull, head trauma patient and, 181–182
sternal, 81–82
wrist, **703–714**. See also *Carpal fractures; Distal radius fractures; Ulna fractures.*
Fresh frozen plasma, 339–340
in transfusion therapy, 388–389
Froment's sign, 596, 597
Frostbite, of the hand, 803, 804
Fungal infections, of the hand, 605
Futile care, situations addressing appropriateness of, 541–542

Gamekeeper's thumb, 793
Gangrene, in high-pressure injection injuries to the hand, 770
Gardner's syndrome, 286
Gas forming infections, of the hand, 616
Gas gangrene, of the hand, 616
Gastrointestinal bleeding, in hemophiliacs, 349
GCS. See *Glasgow coma scale (GCS).*
General consent, 834–835
Genitourinary trauma, **137–145**
confusing aspects of, 137
lower tract, bladder, 140–142
urethra, 138–140
overview, 137
pediatric, 201
physical examination, 138
upper tract, 143–145. See also *Renal trauma.*
Glasgow coma scale (GCS), 19–20, 167
defining severe head trauma, 165
Glucagonoma, 284
Good faith restraint, 876–877
Good Samaritan legislation, 855–856
in-house emergencies and, 915
prehospital care providers reliance on, 864
Graft-versus-host disease, following transfusion therapy, 395
Grand jury, origins of, 821
Granulocyte transfusion therapy, 388
Grave's disease, and chronic ITP similarities, 453
Greenstick fracture, proximal phalanx, 683, 684
Gunshot wounds, abdominal, management of, algorithmic approach, 131–133
principles, 131
costs associated with, 246, 247–248
to uterus, 217
Gutter splints, phalangeal and metacarpal fractures, 683, 686–687

Haddon matrix, for firearm injury control, 257

Hairpin splint, distal phalangeal fractures, 676

Haloperidol, use with disruptive patients, 881

Hamate fractures, 708–709

Hammurabi, Code of, 820

Hand, acute joint injuries, **781–795**
  amputations and replantations, **739–751**
  burns, Emergency Department treatment of, **797–808**. See also *Burn injuries, of the hand.*
  extensor tendon injuries of, **637–648**
  fingertip and nail bed injuries, **755–765**
  flexor tendon injuries of, **621–634**
  functional anatomy of, **557–583**
    blood supply, 581
    digital motion, 574–576
    extensor tendons, 570–573
    flexor tendons, 573–574
    intrinsic muscles, 569–570
    nerve supply, 581–583
    skeletal framework, 562–569
    skin, 557–561
    surface, 561–562, 586–588
    synovial spaces, 576–-577
    thumb, 577–581
  infections, **601–618**. See also *Infections, of the hand.*
  injured, evaluation of, **585–599**. See also *Hand trauma.*
  metacarpal and phalangeal fractures, **671–701**
  nerve injuries in, **651–667**
  sensory areas, 653
  special injuries of, **767–778**. See also *Corn picker injuries; High-pressure injection injuries; Snowblower injuries; Wringer injuries.*
  terminology, 585–586

Hand-Schuller-Christian disease, in children, 520–521

Hand trauma, anesthesia, 590
  approach to, 588
  contamination, 589
  flexor tendons. See *Flexor tendon injuries.*
  hemorrhage control, 588–589
  initial assessment and resuscitation, 588
  mechanism of injury, 589
  neurovascular and tendon function evaluation, 589, 594–599
  patient's medical history and, 589
  physical examination, circulatory status, 594
    observation, 591–593
    palpation, 593–594
    sensory and motor evaluation, 594–599
  wound inspection, 590, 591–593

HCFA. See *Health Care Financing Administration (HCFA).*

Head, cancer of, in children, 518–521
  trauma to. See *Head trauma.*

Headaches, childhood malignancies and, 519, 526

Head trauma, **165–183**
  clinical presentation, 165–168
  computed tomography scanning in, 170–173
    diffuse brain injury, 178, 180
    extra-axial lesions, 174–177
    intra-axial lesions, 177–178, 179
    limitations of, 180–181
  disposition of patient, 182
  incidence, 165
  injury costs associated with, 244–245
  lesion classification, 173–174
  magnetic resonance imaging in, 182
  management of, in hospital, 168–170
    prehospital, 168
  pathophysiology of injury, 165–166
  pediatric, 197–198
    computed tomography in, indications for, 197
  predicting cervical spine injury, 73
  severe form, 165
  skull radiography in, 181–182

Health Care Financing Administration (HCFA), emergency visit code changes, 890
  quality of care and, 890–891

Health Care Quality Improvement Act, 923. See also *National Practitioner Data Bank.*

Heart, effect of alcohol on, 227

Heart massage, perimortem cesarean section and, 220

HELLP syndrome, 455

Hemarthrosis, in hemophiliac, 345–346

Hematologic diseases, emergency situation, ethical dilemmas in. See *Ethics, dilemmas in hematologic/oncologic emergencies.*
  and oncologic diseases, visual diagnosis of, **273–332**. See also *specific diseases.*
    altered skin coloration, 279–292
    ophthalmological manifestations, 298–308
    paraneoplastic syndromes, 279–292
    radiologic manifestations, 308–331

Hematologic/hemostatic effect, of alcohol, 228–229

Hematologic malignancies, in children, 525–527

Hematoma(s), in head trauma patient, epidural, 175, 176
    intracerebral, 175, 176
    subdural, 174–175, 176

Hematoma(s) *(Continued)*
 subungual, 757–758
Hematuria, gross, as complication of sickle
  cell anemia, 372–373
 in hemophiliacs, 347
Hemoglobin, genetically engineered
  human, for prehospital fluid
  resuscitation, 66–67
Hemolytic anemias, 486–488
 categories of, 487
Hemolytic transfusion reaction,
  extravascular, 394
 intravascular, 392–394
Hemolytic-uremic syndrome (HUS), 488
 distinguishing from ITP, 452
 as variant of TTP, 454
Hemophilia, **337–356**. See also *Hemophiliac.*
 acquired, 352
 acquired immunodeficiency syndrome
  and, 353–355
 bleeding episodes, epistaxis, 348–349
  gastrointestinal, 349
  hemarthrosis and fractures, 345–346
  hematuria, 347
  intracranial, 347–348
  intramuscular, 346–347
  management of, 343–344
  retropharyngeal, 349
  skin, 345
 case example, 337
 complications of, 349, 352
 consultation and hospital admission, 349
 dental management in, 344–345
 disseminated intravascular coagulation
  and red cell hemolysis, 352–353
 factor replacement, calculation of, 343
 hemarthrosis and fractures in, 345–346
 hematuria in, 347
 hepatitis/liver dysfunction and, 355–356
 incidence and classification of, 338
 thrombosis/pulmonary hypertension
  and, 353
 treatment of, future developments, 356
  guidelines, 350–351
 von Willibrand's disease, 338–342
Hemophiliac, comprehensive care and
  home therapy for, 343–344
 dental care for, 344–345
 drug therapy for, 344
 supportive care for, 344
Hemoptysis, cancer-associated, 422–423
Hemorrhage, alcohol affecting
  physiological response to, 227
 amputation wound, 740–741
 controlling in hand trauma, 588–589
 fetomaternal, 214–216
 in hemophiliacs. See *Hemophilia, bleeding
  episodes.*
 pelvic, diagnosis and control in, 158–161

subarachnoid, in head trauma patient,
  175, 177
Heparin therapy, in disseminated
  intravascular coagulation, 474
 inducing thrombocytopenia, 455–456
Hepatitis, in hemophiliacs, 355–356
Hepatoblastoma, in children, 523
Hepatocellular carcinoma, in children, 523
Herniation, head trauma and, cerebral, 180
 transtentorial, 167
Herpes simplex virus, digits infected by,
  616–617
Herpes zoster, 290
Herpetic whitlow, of the hand, 616
High-pressure injection injuries, to the
  hand, clinical presentation, 769
 equipment causing, 767–768
 pathophysiology, 768–769
 treatment, 769–770
High-risk behaviors, management of
  patient with, 908
High-risk issues, risk management and, in
  emergency medicine, **905–921**
Hippocratic oath, 820
Histiocytosis X, in children, 520–521
HIV. See *Human immunodeficiency virus
  (HIV).*
Hodgkin's disease, conjunctival
  abnormalities in, 304
 pruritus in, 273
Hodgkin's lymphoma, in children, 526
Hormone-related conditions, in cancer
  patients, 274–276
Horner's syndrome, 301–303
Hospital admission, for hand burn injuries,
  807
Hot object burn injury, to the hand, 801
Hot tar burn injury, to the hand, 802–803
H-shaped flap, 762, 763
Human bites, to hand, infections resulting
  from, 614–615
 microbiology of, 604
Human immunodeficiency virus (HIV),
  immune-mediated thrombocytopenia
  and, 453
 testing for, confidentiality issues and, 900
  inappropriateness of, reasons for, 900
 universal precautions against, 32
HUS. See *Hemolytic-uremic syndrome (HUS).*
Hutchinson's fracture, 719
HVS. See *Hyperviscosity syndrome (HVS).*
Hypercalcemia, as complication of cancer,
  407–411
 calcium hemostasis and, 408
 clinical presentation, 408–409
 differential diagnosis, 409
 pathophysiology, 408
 treatment, 409–411
 as "good death," 542–543

Hypereosinophilic syndrome, idiopathic, 503
Hypertension, pulmonary, hemophilia treatment causing, 353
Hypertrichosis lanuginosa, 282, 283
Hyperviscosity syndrome (HVS), as complication of cancer, 412–415
    clinical presentation, 414
    pathophysiology, 413–414
    treatment, 415
Hyphema, as complication of sickle cell anemia, 373
Hypopyon, of eye, 305
Hypothermia, alcohol causing, 229
    massive transfusion and, 399
    in multiple trauma patient, 40
Hypovolemic shock, assessment of, 39–40

Ichthyosis, acquired, 279–280, 281
ICP. See *Intracranial pressure (ICP)*.
Idiopathic hypereosinophilic syndrome, 503
Idiopathic thrombocytopenic purpura (ITP), acute immune, 452–453
    chronic immune, 453
    neonatal, 451
Iliac spine, avulsion fractures of, anterior inferior, 150
    anterior superior, 149
Illegibility, of medical records, 893
Illness, initiating or mimicking a trauma event, 39
Imipenem, in treatment of febrile neutropenic patient, 511
Immobilization of hand, "safe position" for, 673, 674
Immune system, effect of alcohol on, 229
Immunity, for physicians reporting child abuse, 848
Impalements, categories of, 103–104
Impartiality test, in decision-making model, 535–536
Implied consent, 537, 834
Inappropriate remarks, in medical records, 893–894, 901
Incompatibility, interdonor, massive transfusion and, 400–401
    of transfused red cells, 392, 393
Incompetent patients, consent issues and, 837
Incompleteness, of medical records, 893
Infarction, pulmonary, as complication of sickle cell anemia, 370
Infections, of the hand, **601–618**
    bacterial, 602–605
    bites, human and animal, 613–616
    fascial space, 610–612

felons, 608–609
fungal, 605
gas forming, 616
herpetic whitlow, 616
microbiology and antibiotic use, 602–605
mycobacterial, 605
osteomyelitis, 612–613
paronychia, 606–607
patterns, 601–602
septic arthritis, 612–613
surgical treatment principles, 606
synovial space, 609–610
Infection(s), causing disseminated intravascular coagulation, 476
    causing eosinophilia, 502–503
    causing secondary leukocytosis, 499
    as complication of sickle cell anemia, 369–370
    neutropenia and, 507–508
    antibiotic therapy for febrile patient, 508–511
    preceding TTP, 454–455
Inflammation, causing secondary leukocytosis, 499
Inflammatory anemia, 485
Informed consent, 537
    abbreviated, 836
    background of, 833–834
    general consent versus, 834–835
    for release of medical information, 878–879
    therapeutic privilege and, 874
Informed refusal, 838
    high-risk patient and, 912–914
In-house emergencies, risk management in, 915
Injection injuries, to the hand, high-pressure. See *High-pressure injection injuries, to the hand.*
Injury control, **255–261**
    concepts of, 256–258
    effective strategies, 258
    emergency physician role in, 259
    community care, 260–261
    patient care, 259–260
    implementing strategies for, 258–259
    scope of the problem, 256
Injury(ies), avulsion type. See *Avulsion injury(ies).*
    burns. See *Burn injuries..*
    cost of. See *Cost of injury.*
    of the hand, extensor tendon, **637–648**
        fingertip and nail bed, **755–765**
        flexor tendon, **621–634**
        nerve damage, **651–667**
    high-pressure injection. See *High-pressure injection injuries, to the hand.*
    intraabdominal, pelvic fracture management and, 158

Injury(ies) *(Continued)*
  ligamentous wrist, **717–737**
  prevention of. See *Injury control.*
  spinal cord. See *Spinal cord injuries..*
Injury severity score (ISS), 18, 23
Innervation, sensory, assessment methods,
    594–596
Insurance companies, actuarial science in,
    938
  failing to report to NPDB, sanctions
    against, 928
  hard market and, 939
  and malpractice insurance. See *Malprac-
    tice insurance.*
  medical record documentation and, 890
  physician mutual. See *Physician mutual
    insurance companies.*
  premium increases by, 937–938
  soft market and, 938
Integrity, as medical value, 533
Interosseus muscles, palmar and dorsal,
    569–570
  relationship to extensor tendon in hand,
    679, 680
Interpersonal justifiability test, in decision-
    making model, 535–536
Interphalangeal joints, 566
  claw deformity and, 570
  fingers, distal. See *Distal interphalangeal
    joint (DIP).*
    proximal. See *Proximal interphalangeal
    joint.*
  ligamentous structures supporting, 568–
    569
  thumb, 792
Intoxicated patients, consent issues and,
    837
  evaluating, 875, 877
Intraabdominal injury, diagnosis of, pelvic
    fracture management and, 158
Intracranial hemorrhage, in hemophiliacs,
    347–348
Intracranial pressure (ICP), severe head
    trauma and, 165, 166
Intracranial tumors, in children, 519
Intravenous drug users, hand infections in,
    602, 604
Intravenous lines, in prehospital care,
    controversy over use of, 3–4
  initiation of, 4–5
  management of, 5–6
Intrinsic muscles, of the hand, 569–570
  and pulley muscles of thumb, 579–580
Intubation, in airway management, in
    cervical spine injury, safety issues,
    53–54
    nasotracheal versus oral endotracheal,
    55
    pediatric, rapid sequence induction
    and, 195

Involuntary commitment, 871
  meeting "dangerous" requirement for,
    885
  physician's involvement in, 883–884
Involuntary patient (psychiatric), 872
  minors as, 873–874
Iodophor, in treatment of hand burn
    injuries, 805
Ionizing radiation, in thrombocytopenia
    differential diagnosis, 450
Iris, metastasis of, 305
Iron deficiency anemia, 482–484
Ischemia, cutaneous, 288–289
Ischial tuberosity, avulsion fracture of, 150
ISS. See *Injury severity score (ISS).*
ITP. See *Idiopathic thrombocytopenic purpura
    (ITP).*

Jaundice, disease associated with, 276
JCAHO. See *Joint Commission on
    Accreditation of Healthcare Organizations
    (JCAHO).*
Jehovah's witness, 539–540
  as multiple trauma patient, guidelines
    for handling, 41
Johnson v. University of Chicago Hospitals,
    861
Joint Commission on Accreditation of
    Healthcare Organizations (JCAHO),
    care level classification, 911–912
  medical record requirements, 890
Joints, acute injuries, of the hand, **781–795**
  bleeding into, in hemophiliacs, 345–346
  of fingers and thumb. See *Digital joints.*
  of hand, skin crease relationship to, 558–
    559
Jury system, origins of, 821–822
Justinian Code, 820–821

Kaposi's sarcoma, 296–297
Keratoses, multiple seborrheic, 282
Kidneys, cancer and. See *Renal cell
    carcinoma.*
  failure of, in DIC differential diagnosis,
    473
  trauma to. See *Renal trauma.*
Kienbck's disease, 706, 707
Klebsiella sp. infection, in neutropenic
    patient, 510
Kleihauer-Betke test, fetomaternal
    hemorrhage detected by, 215–216
  for pregnant multiple trauma patient, 38
Kutler flap, 761, 762

Laboratory tests, for blunt abdominal trauma patient, 109–110
   peritoneal lavage fluid analysis, 112
   for multiple trauma patient, 40–41
   recording, 901–902
Lacerations, to fingertip and nail bed, distal phalanx fracture associated, 759
   with loss of skin and pulp tissue, 760
   simple and crushing, 758–759
   to flexor tendons. See *Flexor tendon injuries.*
Lacrimal apparatus, hematologic and oncologic diseases affecting, primary and metastatic involvement, 303–304
   ptosis, 301–303
Laparoscopy, penetrating abdominal trauma evaluation, 130, 132
Laparotomy, in blunt abdominal trauma evaluation, 115
   in penetrating abdominal trauma evaluation, gunshot wounds, 132, 133
   options for, 126
   stab wounds, 127–130
"Lap belt complex," 38
Law, American, emergence of negligence concept in, 825–826
   common. See *Common law.*
   emergency medicine, psychiatry, and, **869–886**. See also *Psychiatric patient.*
   introduction of, medical practice and, 819–820. See also *Medical malpractice law.*
   legal system development and, 821–822
   medical malpractice, negligence and, historical perspectives on, **819–831**
   regarding standard of care, legislative changes, 941–943
LBE (leaves before examination), 914
"Least onerous alternative" doctrine, 879
Leaves before examination (LBE), 914
Leaves without being seen (LWBS), 914
Legal counsel, interfacing with medical control and EMS providers, 857
Legal doctrines, "borrowed servant," 855
   "least onerous alternative," 879
   parens patriae, 846
   respondeat superior, 916
Legal issues, alcoholic patient and, 233–234
   concerning patient history in medical record, 891–891
   of the future, in emergency medicine, **933–950**
   involving emergency medical dispatching, 858–859
   and standard of emergency medical care. See *Standard of care.*
Legal system, development of, 821–822
Legibility, of medical records, 893
Leg ulcers, as complication of sickle cell anemia, 374

Lentigo melanoma, 295
Letterer-Siwe disease, in children, 520–521
Leukemia, acute lymphocytic, 504
   in children, 525–527
      osteoarticular lesions associated with, 524–525
   myelogenous. See *Myelogenous leukemia.*
   pruritus in, 273
   radiologic manifestations of bony abnormalities in, 322, 324
Leukemoid reaction, 499
Leukocoria, 306
Leukocytosis, acute lymphocytic leukemia and, 504
   defined, 495, 497
   eosinophilia and, 500–503
   lymphocytosis and, 503–504
   monocytosis and, 503
   neutrophilia, 497, 500
   normal leukocyte counts and, 495, 496
   primary forms, 497–499
   secondary forms, 499–500
   spurious, 500
   stress, 499
Leukopenia, acquired forms, 505–507
   neutropenia. See *Neutropenia.*
   primary form, 504–505
Liability, basis of (tort), 823–824
   under common law, 823
   for negligence, contractual basis of, 824–825
   prehospital care and, 862–864
   risk to medical control physician, 854–855
   state and local government employee exceptions, 855–856
Life- and limb-preserving therapy, unwanted, ethical dilemma presented by, 539–540
Ligamentous wrist injuries, **717–737**
   anatomy, ligamentous and functional, 718–721
      wrist bones, 717–718
   carpal instability patterns, 727, 729–731
   clinical assessment, 721–722, 723
      radiographic evaluation, 722, 724–726
   perilunate and lunate dislocations, 731–736
   range, 726
   scapholunate dissociation/rotatory subluxation of scaphoid, 726–727, 728–729
   triquetrolunate dissociation, 727
Ligaments, supporting metacarpophalangeal joint, 567
   supporting the wrist, 718–721
      injuries to. See *Ligamentous wrist injuries.*
Light touch. See *Localization test.*

Limited disclosure, 879
Liver disease, in DIC differential diagnosis, 473
Liver dysfunction, in hemophiliacs, 355–356
Living wills, prehospital consent controversy over, 857–858
Localization test, in hand trauma evaluation, 595, 658–659
Loeffler's syndrome, 502
Lower airway obstruction, cancer-associated, 423–424
Lumbrical muscles, 570, 571
Lunate dislocations, 731, 733, 735
    DISI and VISI patterns following reduction of, 733
Lunate fractures, 706, 707
Lung cancer, metastasis to the skin, 292
Lung disease, as complication of sickle cell anemia, 373
Lung(s), effect of alcohol on, 227
    metastases to, radiologic manifestations of, 326–327, 328
LWBS (leaves without being seen), 914
Lycopenemia, 276
Lymphocytosis, 503–504
Lymphomas, in children, 519–520, 526–527
Lynching, as Anglo-Saxon law, 821

Mafenide, in treatment of hand burn injuries, 805
Magnetic resonance imaging (MRI), in head trauma evaluation, 182
    in pregnant patient, 218
    for blunt abdominal trauma, 211
    confirming placental abruption, 212
Malgaigne fractures, 153
Malignancy(ies). See also *Cancer*; *Oncologic disease*.
    as cause of disseminated intravascular coagulation, 477
    causing eosinophilia, 502
    causing secondary leukocytosis, 499–500
    in childhood. See *Childhood malignancies*.
Malignant melanoma, clinical stages, 296
    of conjunctiva, 304
    incidence, morbidity and mortality of, 294–295
    prognosis, 296
    superficial spreading, signs of, 295
    types recognized, 295
Mallett fracture, 677
Malpractice. See *Medical malpractice*.
Malpractice insurance, current and future issues concerning, 940
    past issues concerning, in 1960s, 934
    in 1970s, 934–935

in 1980s, 936–938
Mannitol, administration in head trauma patient, 169–170
MAOIs. See *Monoamine oxidase inhibitors (MAOIs)*.
Massive transfusion, defined, 398
    difficulties associated with, 398–401
    and platelet loss, in thrombocytopenia differential diagnosis, 449
Mature minors, 843
    consent issues, 843
    refusing care, 845–846
May-Hegglin anomaly, in thrombocytopenia differential diagnosis, 450
Median nerve, in hand, 582–583
    functional anatomy, 652–653
    injury to, 654
        Emergency Department management, 662–663
        operative management, 663–665
    motor function testing, 653
    outcome following repair, 666
    trauma evaluation, 596
        motor function, 597, 598
Mediastinum, cancer of, in children, 521
Medical control, claims prevention, 855
    communications with prehospital care providers, 858–859
    direct versus indirect, 854
    and EMS providers, legal counsel interfacing with, 857
    legal considerations in, 853–856
    physician's liability, 854
    and quality assurance issues, 855
    risk management programs availability, 855
Medical director, prehospital patient destination and transfer issues, 859–862
    relationship to EMS system, 853–854
    relationship to prehospital care providers, 854
Medical history, of patient. See *Patient history*.
Medical malpractice, claims made by psychiatric patients, 871
    current decade issues concerning, 939
        insurance, 939–940
    first recorded case, 826
    involving minors, 849–850
    law, negligence and, historical perspectives on, **819–831**
    medical record in defense of, 892–893
    past decade review of issues concerning, in 1960s, 934
        in 1970s, 934–935
        in 1980s, 936–938
        reform proposals, 942

Medical malpractice law, early
practitioners and, 820
origin of influences on, 820–821
Medical practice, introduction of law and,
819–820
and malpractice. See *Medical malpractice.*
parameters, in standard of care disputes,
943–946
trends in, 940
Medical record, checking by physician, 902
competent record-keeping, 900–901
confidentiality of, 898–899
United States v. Eide, 899
discharge instructions, 897–898
disclosure, 899–900
Emergency Department, **889–902**
forensic events, 892–893
patient history in, 891
Baldwin v. Knight, 891–892
and recordmanship, 900–902
shortfalls in, 893–894
*Carr v. St. Paul Fire and Marine Insur-
ance Company*, 894–896
Mulligan v. Wetchler, 896–897
telephone advice/instructions recorded
in, 900
Medicare reimbursement, medical record
documentation and, 890
Medicine men, 820
Medicolegal issues. See *Legal issues.*
Melanoma, amelanotic, 295
choroidal, 307–308
malignant. See *Malignant melanoma.*
uveal, 305
vitiligo and, 277
Melanosis, 276–277
Melanuria, 277
Melphalan, pharmacology and toxicology
of, 436–437
Mental status examination, determining
patient consent and, 857
emergency physician's use of, 875
6-Mercaptopurine, pharmacology and
toxicology of, 434–435
Metabolism, effect of alcohol on, 231
Metacarpal fractures, **671–701**, 693. See also
specific fractures.
classification, 674
first metacarpal, extra-articular base and
shaft fractures, 699, 700
intra-articular base fractures, 699, 700–
701
general concepts, 671–674
second through fifth metacarpals, classification, 693
metacarpal base fractures, 698–699
metacarpal head fractures, 693–694,
695
metacarpal neck fractures, 694–697

metacarpal shaft fractures, 697–698
Metacarpals, fractures of. See *Metacarpal
fractures.*
structure and arrangement of, 565–566
Metacarpophalangeal joint, 566–567
anatomy, fingers, 783, 784
thumb, 783–784
claw deformity and, 570
injuries to, fingers, 788–791
thumb, 792–794
ligamentous structures supporting, 567
Metastasis, in children, 522–523
to eyelids and lacrimal apparatus, 303
iris, 305
to lung, 326–327, 328
osteoplastic, 313, 316
to the skin, 290–292
Methemoglobinemia, pulse oximetry and,
490
Methotrexate, pharmacology and
toxicology of, 431–432
Microaggregates, massive transfusion and,
400
Migratory thrombophlebitis, 289
Military anti-shock trousers. See *Pneumatic
anti-shock garments (PASG).*
Minor(s). See also *Child/children.*
abused. See *Abused child.*
in boarding schools, camps, and related
institutions, 845
consent for. See *Consent, for minors.*
in detention facilities, 844
emancipated, 842–843
and emergency medicine, **841–850**
as involuntary patients, 873–874
mature, 843
medical malpractice involving, 849–850
neglected, 848
presenting with adult other than parent,
844
presenting with single parent, 843–844
refusal of treatment by or on behalf of,
845–847
residing in foster home, 844
runaways, 845
treatment statutes, 843
Miscommunication, risk management and,
906
Mistriage rates, calculating, 18, 23, 25
Mitomycin C, pharmacology and
toxicology of, 439–440
Moberg flap, 762–763
Monoamine oxidase inhibitors (MAOIs),
psychiatric patient's use of, 882
Monocytosis, 503
Mosaic Code, 820
Motor function, in hand trauma evaluation,
nerves, 596–597
tendons, 597–599

Motor vehicle crashes, injury costs
associated with, 245–247
multiple trauma resulting from, death
due to, 29, 30. See also *Death, of crash
victim.*
management of. See *Multiple trauma,
management of.*
MRI. See *Magnetic resonance imaging (MRI).*
Mulligan v. Wetchler, 896–897
Multihospital contract groups, 935
Multiple myeloma, radiological
manifestations of, 321–322, 323
Multiple seborrheic keratoses, 282
Multiple trauma, management of, **29–47**
burns and, 39
in children, 38
clinical outline, 30
death of crash victim. See *Death, of crash
victim; Organ donation.*
in the elderly, 38–39
initial evaluation, 33
for Jehovah's Witness patient, 41
laboratory data, 40–41
"non-trauma" trauma and, 39
organ donation. See *Organ donation.*
physical examination, 39–40
in pregnant women, 37–38
prehospital care and organization of personnel, 30–31
resuscitation and intervention, 34–35
secondary evaluation, 35–36
sedation and analgesia, 41
in substance abusers, 39
tertiary evaluation, 36–37
trauma center organization, 29–30
vital signs, 40
Munchausen syndrome by proxy, 877
Muscle, hemorrhage in hemophiliac, 346
Mycobacterium marinum, causing hand
infections, 605
Mycosis fungoides, 297–298
Myelofibrosis, in thrombocytopenia
differential diagnosis, 450
Myelogenous leukemia, acute, 498–499
chronic, 497–498
Myeloma, multiple, radiological
manifestations of, 321–322, 323
Myelosuppressive drugs, in
thrombocytopenia differential
diagnosis, 450
Myocardial contusion, 85–86
evaluation of, 86–87
management of, 87–88
Myocardial rupture, 88

NAEMSP. See *National Association of EMS
Physicians (NAEMSP).*

Nail, function of, 757
growth rate, 757
Nail bed, anatomy, 755–757
injuries to. See *Nail bed injuries.*
Nail bed injuries, **755–765**
acute forms, distal phalanx fracture associated, 759
Kleinert classification, 758
nail bed avulsion, 759
simple and crushing lacerations, 758–
759
skin and pulp tissue loss, 760
in fingertip amputations, 764–765
subungual hematoma, 757–758
Nail bed repair, distal phalangeal fractures
and, 676, 677
Nail fold, 756
Nail matrix, 755
Nail plate, composition of, 756
Nail wall, 756
National Association of EMS Physicians
(NAEMSP), medical control issues and
definitions, 853–855
National Practitioner Data Bank (NPDB),
administration of, 924
altered records reported to, 896
an overview for the emergency physician, **923–930**
confidentiality of information held in,
928–929
disputes with, 929
history of, 923–924
organizations accessing, 924
reporting requirements for, 924–926
rules for obtaining information from,
926–928
sanctions imposed by, 928
Neck, blunt trauma to, **71–77**. See also
Cervical spine injury.
cancer of, in children, 518–521
Necrotizing fasciitis, of the hand, 616
Neglected child, 848
Negligence, alcoholic patient and, 233–234
concept of, 826–827
breach of duty, 828–829
case example, 828
damages, 829
law, medical malpractice and, historical perspectives on, **819–831**
proximate cause, 829–830
contractual basis of liability for, 824–825
defined, 826
emergence in American law, 825–826
Neisseria gonorrhoeae, hand infection caused
by, 602
Neonatal alloimmune thrombocytopenia,
451
Nephroblastoma, in children, 522
Nerve injuries, in the hand, **651–667**

Emergency Department management,
history, 662
physical examination, 662–663
radiographic evaluation, 663
referral, 663
stabilization, 663
wound care, antibiotics, and tetanus,
663
functional anatomy, 651–657
operative management, 663
epineurial versus fascicular repair,
664–665
primary versus delayed repair, 664
repair considerations, 665
outcome, complications, 667
median, radial, ulnar, and digital
nerve, 666–667
regeneration physiology, 665–666
sensory testing, 657–662
Nerve supply, evaluating in hand trauma,
589
to the hand, 581–583
to thumb, 580–581
to the wrist, 718
Neuroblastoma, in children, 522–523
radiologic manifestations of, 325–326
Neurofibromatosis, 287–288
Neuroleptic malignant syndrome, 881
Neuroleptics, use with disruptive patients,
882
Neurologic complaints, cancer-associated,
427–428
Neurologic examination, in brain death
determination, 43
Neuromas, following nerve injury in the
hand, 667
Neuromuscular blocking agents, use in
airway management, 54–55
Neuropsychiatric conditions, physician's
evaluation of, 877
Neurovascular function, evaluating in hand
trauma, 589
Neutropenia, acquired forms. See *Acquired
neutropenia.*
afebrile patient with, 507
febrile patient with, antibiotic therapy
for, 508–512
infection propensity, 507–508
primary form, 504–505
Neutrophilia, 497, 500
Ninhydrin sweat test. See *Sudomotor testing.*
Nodular melanoma, 295
Nondisplaced nonangulated fracture,
metacarpals, 695–696, 697, 698
proximal phalanx, comminuted midshaft, 683, 684
transverse midshaft, 683, 684
Non-Hodgkin's lymphoma, in children,
526–527

Nonimmune mechanisms, in
thrombocytopenia differential
diagnosis, 454–456
Nonmaleficence, as basic medical value,
532
Nonparent adult, minors presenting for
emergency treatment with, 844
"Non-trauma" trauma, in multiple trauma
patients, 39
Notification, of death, 45–46
NPDB. See *National Practitioner Data Bank
(NPDB).*
Nursing notes, in medical records, 893
physician's review of, 901
Nutritional deficiency, in
thrombocytopenia differential
diagnosis, 450

Obstetric complications, as cause of
disseminated intravascular
coagulation, 476–477
Occupations, hand infections linked to, 605
On-call physicians, risk management and,
911–912
Oncologic disease. See also *Cancer.*
in children. See *Childhood malignancies.*
emergency situation, ethical dilemmas in.
See *Ethics, dilemmas in hematologic/on-
cologic emergencies.*
hematologic diseases and, visual diagnosis of, **273–332**. See also *specific diseases.*
altered skin coloration, 276–279
common cancers of the skin, 293–298
ophthalmological manifestations, 298–
308
paraneoplastic syndromes, 279–292
radiologic manifestations, 308–331
medical complications of, **407–416**. See
also *specific conditions.*
Open book injury, 153
Ophthalmoplegia, 300, 302
Opposition movement, of thumb, 578–579
Opsite, in treatment of hand burn injuries,
805
Opsoclonus-myoclonus, in children, 523
Orange peel appearance, metastatic disease
to the skin, 292
Orbit, rhabdomyosarcoma of, 301
Ordeal, trial by, 821–822
Organ donation, from crash victim, consent
by family, 43–44
criteria for, 42
declaration of brain death, 42–43, 44
maintenance therapy and, 43–44, 45
organ recovery steps, 42
O'Riain wrinkle test. See *Sudomotor testing.*

Orthopedic trauma, alcohol as risk factor in, 229
Osseus tumors. See *Bone lesions.*
Osteoarticular lesions, associated with childhood acute leukemia, 524–525
Osteolytic lesions, radiologic manifestations of, 313, 316
Osteomyelitis, of the hand, 612–613
    bacteriology of, 602
Osteonecrosis, avascular, as complication of sickle cell anemia, 374–375
Osteoplastic metastases, radiologic manifestations of, 313, 316
Osteosarcoma, in children, 524
Outpatient treatment, of hand burn injuries, 807–808
Ovarian tumors, in children, 523
Overtriage, 16, 23, 25
Oximetry, in prehospital care, 8

Paget's disease, extramammary, 289, 290
    mammary, 289
Pain, as complication of sickle cell anemia, acute. See *Sickle cell pain crises, acute.*
    chronic, 375
    management of, in hand burn injuries, 803–805
    perception of, in hand nerve injury evaluation, 661
Palmar erythema, disease associated with, 279
Palmar hand, anatomy, 623, 624
Pancoast tumor, 329–330
Pancytopenia, and thrombocytopenia differential diagnosis, 449–450
Paralysis, versus rapid tranquilization, in combative trauma patient, 56–57
Paramedics. See *Prehospital care providers.*
Paraneoplastic syndromes, acanthosis nigricans, 279, 280
    acquired ichthyosis, 279–280, 281
    amyloidosis, 288
    Cowden's disease, 286, 287
    cutaneous ischemia, 288–289
    erythema gyratum repens, 280, 281
    Gardner's syndrome, 286
    glucagonoma, 284
    herpes zoster, 290
    hypertrichosis lanuginosa, 282, 283
    metastatic disease to the skin, 290–292
    migratory thrombophlebitis, 289
    multiple seborrheic keratoses, 282
    neurofibromatosis, 287–288
    Paget's disease (mammary and extramammary), 289, 290
    Peutz-Jeghers syndrome, 284, 285
Parasites, causing eosinophilia, 502

Parens patriae, doctrine of, 846
Parent, nonparent adult, minors presenting for emergency treatment with, 844
    refusing medical care on behalf of minor, 846
    religious freedom claims, 847
    single, minors presenting for emergency treatment with, 843–844
Paresthesia, chronic, following nerve injury in the hand, 667
Parham v. J.R., 873
"Parkland Protocol," 856

Paronychia, treatment of, 606–607
Paroxysmal nocturnal hemoglobinuria (PNH), in thrombocytopenia differential diagnosis, 450
Pasteurella multocida, hand infection caused by, 616
Patient dumping, 861, 912
Patient history, in medical record, legal issues and action, 891–891
    past, making adequate inquiry about, 896–897
Patient outcome, 945
Patient outcome research teams (PORTS), 943–944
Patient(s), care of, injury control and, 259–260
    complaints by, 920
    consent problems and, 837–838
    destination and transfer issues affecting, 859–862
    dumping of, 861, 912
    at high risk, going against medical advice, 912–914
        leaving before examination, 914
        managing visits and transfers, 909–910
        private patient in Emergency Department, 909–910
        telephone advice to, 918
    medical history of. See *Patient history.*
    perception of health care services and providers, 919–920
    psychiatric. See *Psychiatric patient.*
    restraint of. See *Restraint, of patient.*
    signature on chart, against-medical-advice and, 914
    transportation by EMS, retrospective study, 863
pCO₂. See *Carbon dioxide partial pressure (pCO₂).*
Peau d'orange appearance, metastatic disease to the skin, 292
Pediatric brain death determination, 43, 44
Pediatric trauma, **187–201**
    abdominal trauma, 199–200
    age of child, key differences related to, 190–191

airway management in, 191–192, 193–195
approach to injured child, 191
brain death determination, 43, 44
cervical spine injury, 196–197
chest trauma, 199
computed tomography in, abdominal trauma, 200
head trauma, 197
epidemiology, 187–188
head trauma, 197–198
management issues, primary survey, 191–196
secondary survey, 196–201
pelvic and genitourinary trauma, 201
prehospital care issues, 188
shock and, 192–193, 195
trauma score, 188–190
vascular access, 195–196
Pelvic fractures, **147–161**
of acetabulum. See *Acetabular fractures.*
avulsion fractures, 149–151
classification scheme, 148
double breaks in the pelvic ring, 152–154
management of, intraabdominal injury diagnosis, 158
pelvic hemorrhage, diagnosis and control of, 158–161
recommendations, 161
pediatric, 201
pelvic anatomy, 147–148
single breaks in the pelvic ring, 151–152
Pelvic hemorrhage, diagnosis and control in, 158–161
Pelvic ring fractures, double breaks, 152–154
single breaks, 151–152
Pelvic wing fracture, 150
Pelvis, anatomy of, 147–148
dislocation of, 153
fractures of. See *Pelvic fractures.*
Penetrating abdominal trauma, **125–133**
gunshot wounds, 131–133
laparotomy options, 126
management approaches, 126
organs at risk, 125–126
in pregnancy, 216–217
stab wounds, 126–131
Penetrating chest trauma, assessment and management of, 98–102
autotransfusion in, 103
central wounds, 99–100
classification of, 98–99
impalements, 103–104
peripheral wounds, 100–102
prehospital care for, 97–98
thoracotomy in, indications for, 102–104
Penetrating head trauma, 180
Pericardial effusion, cancer-associated, 426–427

Perilunate dislocations, 731, 733
DISI and VISI patterns following reduction of, 733
progression during, 732
transscaphoid, 734
Perimortem cesarean section, delivery of fetus by, 219–220
Perionychium, 755
Peripheral nerves, in the hand. See also *specific nerves.*
repairing injuries to, epineurial versus fascicular, 664–665
primary versus delayed, 664
sensory testing. See *Sensory innervation, hand injuries.*
structure, 651–652
Peritoneal cavity, diagnostic lavage. See *Diagnostic peritoneal lavage (DPL).*
violation of, gunshot wounds, 132–133
stab wounds, 128
Periumbilical lesions, metastatic, 291–292
PERRLA abbreviation, comments on, 901
Petit jury, origins of, 822
Peutz-Jeghers syndrome, 284, 285
Phalangeal fractures, **671–701**
classification, 674
distal, 674
extra-articular, 675–677
intra-articular avulsion, dorsal surface, 677–679
volar surface, 679, 680
general concepts, 671–674
middle, 679–681. See also *specific fractures.*
classification, 682
examination, 681–682
extra-articular, 686–687, 689
intra-articular, 688, 690–693
proximal, 679–681. See also *specific fractures.*
classification, 682
examination, 681–682
extra-articular, 682–683, 684–687
intra-articular, 683, 686, 688
Phalanx, amputation injuries, 748–749
fractures of. See *Phalangeal fractures.*
Pharmacology, and toxicology of chemotherapeutic agents, **431–441**
Phronesis, in case-based ethics, 534
Physical disease, masquerading as psychiatric disorders, 877
Physical examination, in blunt abdominal trauma evaluation, 107–108
genitourinary trauma, 138
in head trauma, 166–168
in trauma setting, 39–40
"Physician extenders." See *Prehospital care providers.*
Physician mutual insurance companies, 934–935

Physician mutual insurance companies
(*Continued*)
stabilization of, 939
Physicians, as surrogate decision-makers,
538
"Physician surrogates." See *Prehospital care
providers.*
PIE. See *Pulmonary infiltrate with eosinophilia
(PIE).*
Piece of pie sign, 733
"Pinch purpura," 288
Pisiform, fractures, 707–708
radiographic evaluation of, 726
Placenta, suspected injury to, following
blunt abdominal trauma, 211–212
Placental abruption, after blunt trauma,
211–212
and fetal distress, 213–214
Plant (vinca) alkaloids, pharmacology and
toxicology of, 440–441
Plasma derivatives, in transfusion therapy,
389–392
Plasmin, role in disseminated intravascular
coagulation, 469
Platelet(s), concentrates in transfusion
therapy, 387–388
function of, thrombocytopenia and, 445–
446
kinetics, 446
in thrombocytopenia differential diagnosis, defective production of, 449–451
increased destruction of, 451–456
loss of, 449
Platelet sequestration, acute syndromes, as
complication of sickle cell anemia, 372
in thrombocytopenia differential diagnosis, 449
Pneumatic anti-shock garments (PASG),
controversy over use of, 3
effect in pregnant trauma patient, 209
pelvic hemorrhage control, 159
in prehospital care, 6–7
Pneumocephalus, head trauma and, 180,
181
Pneumocystis carinii pneumonia, 511
PNH. See *Paroxysmal nocturnal
hemoglobinuria (PNH).*
Poirer, space of, 719
Polycythemia, 489
Polycythemia rubra vera (PRV), 489
pruritus in, 273
treatment of, 489
PORTS. See *Patient outcome research teams
(PORTS).*
Pose belt, for patient restraint, 881
Posttransfusion hepatitis, 396
Practice parameters, 943–946
taxonomy of, 944
Pregnancy, blood pressure in, 208–209

blood volume in, 209
cardioversion in, 210
central venous pressure in, 209–210
leukocytosis in, 500
normal maternal pCOS12T, 207–208
sickle-related complications of, 373
trauma in, **207–220**
blunt abdominal, 210–212
chest tube placement, 208
effect of military anti-shock trousers,
209
failed resuscitation and perimortem
section, 219–220
fetal monitoring, 212–216
multiple trauma, 37–38
penetrating abdominal, 216–217
radiographic evaluation, 218–219
Prehospital care, **1–11**
communications in, 858–859
concepts, air medical services, 9–10
intravenous lines, 4–6
pneumatic anti-shock garments, 6–7
respiratory adjuncts, 7–8
trauma triage, 8–9
consent and, 856–858
controversial issues in, 3–4
destination and transfer issues in, 859–
862
fluid resuscitation. See *Prehospital fluid resuscitation.*
of head trauma, 168
legal considerations in, **853–864**
levels, 1–2
liability issues, 862–864
medical control and, 853–856. See also
Medical control.
pediatric trauma, 188
penetrating chest trauma, 97–98
providers of. See *Prehospital care providers.*
sequence of events in, 2–3
Prehospital care providers, determining
existence of patient consent, mental
status examination, 857
Parkland Protocol, 856–857
medical control and, communications between, 858–859
legal counsel interacting with, 857
medical director relationship to, 854
Prehospital fluid resuscitation, of trauma
patient, **61–68**
asanguinous, crystalloid versus colloid,
62
hypertonic crystalloid, 62–63
nonprotein colloids and blood substitutes, 63–64
sanguinous, 64
crossmatch method, 65–66
genetically engineered human hemoglobin, 66–67

whole blood versus packed red blood
cells, 64–65
Prehospital index, 21, 23
Priapism, as complication of sickle cell
anemia, 373
Primary repair, of damaged peripheral
nerves in the hand, 664
Private patients, high risk, in Emergency
Department, 911
PRO. See *Professional Review Organization
(PRO).*
Professional Review Organization (PRO),
medical records review by, 889–890
Proptosis, acute leukemia with, 299, 300
metastatic neuroblastoma and, 299
Protective custody, temporary, for abused
or neglected child, 849
Prothrombin complex concentrates, 342
Proximal interphalangeal joint, anatomy,
782
injury to, 787–788
Proximate cause, negligence and, 829–830
Pruritus, 273–274
in cancer patients, 274
PRV. See *Polycythemia rubra vera (PRV).*
Pseudomonas aeruginosa, hand infection
caused by, 602
Pseudomonas aeruginosa infection, in
neutropenic patient, 510
Pseudothrombocytopenia, in differential
diagnosis of thrombocytopenia, 449
Psychiatric disorders, physical disease
masquerading as, 877
Psychiatric effects, alcohol and, 231
Psychiatric patient, 869–871
categorization issues, 871–874
disposition phase issues, 882–885
evaluation phase issues, 875–879
involuntary commitment of, 871
minors, 873–874
restraint of. See *Restraint, of patient.*
staff attitudes toward, 870
suicidal behavior exhibited by, 870–871
treatment/stabilization phase issues,
880–882
violent behavior by, 870
guidelines for dealing with, 881
voluntary versus involuntary categorization of, 872–873
Psychiatry, emergency medicine, and the
law, **869–886**. See also *Psychiatric
patient.*
Ptosis, 301–303
Pubic rami, unilateral fractures of, 152
Public Law 99–272 (Emergency Medical
Treatment and Active Labor Act), 861–
862
Public safety, versus individual's liberty
interests, 883–884

Pulmonary contusion, 83
evaluation of, 83–84
treatment of, 84
Pulmonary edema, following transfusion
therapy, 398
Pulmonary hypertension, hemophilia
treatment causing, 353
Pulmonary infiltrate with eosinophilia
(PIE), 502
Pulmonary leukostasis, cancer-associated,
424–425
Pulmonary nodule, solitary, radiologic
manifestations of, 327–329
Pulse oximetry, 481, 489–490
Pulse rate, in multiple trauma patient, 40
Purpura, disease associated with, 278
idiopathic thrombocytopenic. See *Idio-
pathic thrombocytopenic purpura (ITP).*
"pinch," 288
thrombotic thrombocytopenic. See
*Thrombotic thrombocytopenic purpura
(TTP).*

Quality assurance, assessing institution's
commitment to, 907
medical control and, 855
risk management and, 906–907

Radial nerve, in hand, 581–582
functional anatomy, 654, 655
injury to, 655
Emergency Department management,
662–663
operative management, 663–665
motor function testing, 654
outcome following repair, 666
trauma evaluation, 596
Radial styloid, radiographic evaluation of,
725
Radiation dose, to fetus from CT scans,
218, 219
to ovaries, 218, 219
Radiocarpal joint, 718
changes precipitating DISI and VISI patterns, 731
Radiographic evaluation. See also *Computed
tomography (CT); Magnetic resonance
imaging (MRI).*
in acetabular fracture diagnosis, 154–155
of blunt abdominal trauma, 108–109
in blunt chest trauma. See under *specific
clinical entities.*
of blunt neck injury, cervical cross table
lateral view, 73–74
flexion/extension views, 74–75

Radiographic evaluation *(Continued)*
   three-view versus five-view series, 74
   of genitourinary trauma, bladder, 141–
      142
   kidneys, 144
   urethra, 140
   of hematologic and oncologic disease
      manifestations, 308
   acute leukemia, 322, 324
   adamantinoma, 330–331
   differentiating skeletal lesions, 308–312
   metastases to lung, 326–327, 328
   metastatic bone lesions, 312–320
   multiple myeloma, 321–322, 323
   neuroblastoma, 325–326
   Pancoast tumor, 329–330
   solitary pulmonary nodule, 327–329
   of multiple trauma patient, 36, 37
   of pregnant trauma patient, 218–219
Radioulnar joint fractures, 713–714
Radius, distal, anatomy, 717–718
   fractures. See *Distal radius fractures.*
   radiographic evaluation of, 724, 725
Rapid sequence induction and intubation,
      for pediatric airway management, 195
Record keeping, art and science of, 901–902
Recordmanship, 900–902
Red blood cells, antigenic determinants,
      381–382
   disorders of, **481–490**
   anemias, 482–489. See also *specific ane-
      mias.*
   polycythemia, 489
   effect of incompatibility of, 392, 393
   fragility of, sickling and, 365
   function of, 481
   hemolysis, hemophilia treatment caus-
      ing, 353
   impaired function of, massive transfu-
      sion and, 400
   peritoneal lavage fluid analysis, 112
   in prehospital fluid resuscitation, 64–65
   substitutes for, 402–403
   in transfusion therapy, 385–387
Referral, of alcoholic patient, 232–233
Refusal of treatment, 838–839
   by minor, 845–846
   by parent of child, 846
   religious freedom claims, 847
Rehabilitation, of alcoholic patient, 232–233
   postoperative, flexor tendon injuries,
      633–634
Religious freedom, parental refusal of care
      claiming, 847
Renal cell carcinoma, in children, 523
   metastasis to the skin, 292
Renal failure, in DIC differential diagnosis,
      473
Renal trauma, adults versus children, 144–
   145

causes, 143
   identifying, 143–144
   incidence, 143
   radiographic examination, 144
Replacement therapy, in bleeding
      disorders. See *Factor replacement
      therapy.*
   in disseminated intravascular coagula-
      tion, 473–474
Replantation(s), amputations and, **739–751**
   anesthesia, 751
   contraindications to, 747–748
      age of patient, 751
      crush and avulsion amputations, 750
      multiple level, 749
      single digit, 748–749
   fingertip amputations, 765
   guidelines for, 746
   indications for, 747
   patient selection criteria, 743–744
      history, 744–745
      radiographic evaluation, 745–746
   referring patient to center specializing in,
      743
Residents, in Emergency Department, risk
      management and, 915–917
Respiratory adjuncts, in prehospital care,
      7–8
Respiratory system, and cancer-associated
      mechanical problems, 421–425
Respondeat superior doctrine, 916
Restraint, of patient, awaiting treatment or
      stabilization of condition, 880
   guidelines for, 881
   pending evaluation, 876–877
Resuscitation and intervention, failed,
      perimortem cesarean section and, 219–
      220
   fluid. See *Fluid resuscitation.*
   in multiple trauma patient, 34–35
   prehospital. See *Prehospital fluid resuscita-
      tion.*
Reticuloendothelioses, in children, 520–521
Retinoblastoma, 306–307
   in children, 520
Retinopathy, as complication of sickle cell
      anemia, 374
Retropharyngeal bleeding, in hemophiliacs,
      349
Return visits, risk management and, 909–
      910
Reverse dumping, 861
Revised trauma score, 20, 23
Rhabdomyosarcoma, 299–300
   in children, 520
   orbital, 301
Rh immune globulin (RhoGAM), 391–392
   for pregnant trauma patient, 216
   with multiple trauma, 38

RhoGAM. See *Rh immune globulin (RhoGAM)*.
Risk management, complaint handling and, 907–908
  described, 905–908
  elements of, 908
  high-risk behaviors and, 908
  and high-risk issues in emergency medicine, **905–921**
  identifying system problems in, 906–907
  in-house emergencies, 915
  newer trends in, 906
  on-call physicians, 911–912
  patients ignoring medical advice, 912–914
  patients leaving before examination, 914
  patient visits and transfers in, 909–910
  physician shift change in, 909–910
  practical tips on, 918–921
  private patients in Emergency Department, 911
  programs, 855
  residents in Emergency Department, 915–917
  system failure and, 906–907
  telephone advice to patient, 918
  telephone orders from private physicians, 917–918
  tenets of, 906
Risk manager, role of, 906
Rolando fracture, first metacarpal, 699, 700, 701
Rotational malalignment, of hand, phalangeal fractures and, 672, 673
  proximal, examining for, 681–682
Rubella, perinatal, in thrombocytopenia differential diagnosis, 450
Rule-based ethics, 533–534
"Runaround" abscess, paronychia and, 606
Runaways, requiring emergency treatment, 845
Rupture, aortic. See *Aortic rupture*.
  diaphragm. See *Diaphragm rupture*.
  esophageal. See *Esophageal rupture*.
  myocardial, 88

Sacroiliac joint, fracture near or subluxation of, 152
Sacrum, fracture of, 151
"Safe position," for hand immobilization, 673, 674
Safety issues, medical, airway management in cervical spine injury, 53–54
  physical. See *Security issues*.
Salmonella sp., hand infection caused by, 602
Scald burn injury, of the hand, 798, 800

Scaphoid, dislocation of, 736
  fractures of, 704–705
  rotary subluxation of, 727, 729
Scapholunate angle, in dorsal intercalary segment instability, 729, 730
  radiographic evaluation of, 725, 726
Scapholunate dissociation, 726–727, 728, 729
Scapholunate joint, 722, 723
Scaphotrapezial joint, 722, 723
  radiographic evaluation of, 726
Sclera, hematologic and oncologic diseases affecting, 304–305
Scoring systems. See also *Severity scores*.
  historical perspective, 15–16
  and triage from the field, **15–25**
Seatbelt bruise, in child, 38
Security issues, precautions in Emergency Department, 32
  public safety versus individual's liberty interests, 883–884
Sedation, for multiple trauma patient, 41
Seizures, childhood malignancies and, 519
Self-determination, patient's rights to, 913
Sensory fibers, 658
Sensory innervation, hand injuries, additional tests in non-acute setting, 660–662
  assessment methods, 594–596
  Emergency Department testing, 658–660
  fibers and mechanisms, 594–596
Sensory threshold. See *Localization test*.
Septic arthritis, of the hand, 612–613
  bacteriology of, 602
Sequestration. See *Platelet sequestration*.
"Setting sun" sign, 300, 302
Severity scores, 15
  abbreviated injury scale, 17–18
  anatomic criteria and mechanism of injury assessment, 18, 19, 23
  injury severity score, 18
  physiologic scores, 18–19, 23, 24
    CRAMS score, 20, 23
    Glasgow coma scale, 19–20
    prehospital index, 21, 23
    trauma index, 19
    trauma score/revised trauma score, 20, 23
  trauma triage rule, 21
  theory and evolution of, 16–17
Shamans, 820
Shift change, problems in risk management, 909–910
Shock, management in pediatric trauma patient, 192–193, 195
SIADH. See *Syndrome of inappropriate antidiuretic hormone (SIADH)*.
Sickle cell anemia, complications of. See also *specific conditions*.

Sickle cell anemia *(Continued)*
  acute, 366–373
  chronic, 373–375
  and pregnancy, 373
  economic impact of, 365–366
  presenting manifestations, 366
Sickle cell disease, in DIC differential
    diagnosis, 473
  emergencies in, **365–376**
  heterozygous states, 375
  homozygous state. See *Sickle cell anemia.*
  indications for hospital admission, 375–
    376
Sickle cell pain crises, acute, 366–369
  anatomic patterns of, 366–367
  diagnostic testing, 367–368
  differential diagnosis of, 367
  disease obscuring, 367–368
  management and treatment of, 368–369
  mechanism of, 366
Sickling, biochemical basis for, 365
  and red blood cell fragility, 365
Signature, patient's, against-medical-advice
    and, 914
Silvadene (silver sulfadiazine), in treatment
    of hand burn injuries, 805
Silver sulfadiazine, in treatment of hand
    burn injuries, 805
Single parent, minors presenting for
    emergency treatment with, 843–844
Sister Mary Joseph's nodules, 291–292
Skeletal lesions, in children, 524–525
  radiological differentiation of, 308–312
Skin, altered coloration, and disease
    association, 276–279
  common cancers, 293–298
  cutaneous ischemia, 288–289
  of hand, anatomy, 557–561
    loss in fingertip and nail bed injury,
      760
    repair. See *Flaps, for repair of fingertip
      injuries.*
  hemorrhage in hemophiliac, 345
  paraneoplastic syndromes involving,
    279–292
Skin creases, of hand, landmark features,
    561–562
  relationship to joints, 558–559
Skin diseases, causing eosinophilia, 502
Skin flushing, disease associated with, 278
Skin sweating, in hand trauma evaluation,
    595
Skin wrinkling, in hand trauma evaluation.
    See *Sudomotor testing.*
Ski pole thumb, 793
Skull, myeloma involvement with, 321
  neuroblastoma metastasis to, 325, 326
  radiography of, in head trauma evalua-
    tion, 181–182

SLE. See *Systemic lupus erythematosus (SLE).*
Smith's fracture, 711
Snake envenomation, as cause of
    disseminated intravascular
    coagulation, 477
  as cause of thrombocytopenia, 454
Snowblower injuries, to the hand, 776, 777
  clinical presentation, 777
  treatment, 777–778
Solitary pulmonary nodule, radiologic
    manifestations of, 327–329
Specific consent, 835
Spinal cord injuries, compression type,
    cancer-associated, 417–428
  in children, 523
  metastatic, 313, 318–320
  costs associated with, 244–245
Spine, hemorrhage into, in hemophiliacs,
    348
  radiological manifestations of diseases,
    metastatic, 313, 317–320
  myeloma of, 321
Spiral fracture(s), metacarpal, 698
  proximal phalanx, 683, 685
Splenomegaly, in sickle cell disease, 375
Splinting, distal interphalangeal joint, 677,
    679
  distal phalangeal fractures, 676
  of extensor tendon injuries, 648
  proximal phalangeal fractures, dynamic
    finger splinting, 683, 685, 686
  gutter splints, 683, 686–687
Sporothrix schenckii, causing hand infection,
    605
Sporotrichosis, of the hand, 605
Sprung pelvis, 153
Spurious leukocytosis, 500
Squamous cell carcinoma, of skin, 293, 294
  in situ, 293–294
Stab wounds, abdominal, management of,
    algorithmic approach, 127–130
  back and flank, 130
  diaphragmatic injury, 131
  foreign body in situ, 130–131
  principles, 126–127
  to uterus, 217
Standard of care, legal disputes regarding,
    940–941
  expert witnesses, 947–949
  legislative changes, 941–943
  practice parameters, 943–946
  predictions on, 949–950
  and tort reform, 946–947
Staphylococcus aureus, hand infection caused
    by, 602
"State actor," legal test to meet, 884
Sternum, fracture of, 81–82
Steroids, use with head trauma patient, 170
Straddle fractures, 153

Streptococcus pyogenes, hand infection
caused by, 602, 616
Stress leukocytosis, 499
Stroke, as complication of sickle cell
anemia, 370–371
Subarachnoid bleed, in head trauma
patient, 175, 177
Subdural hematoma, in head trauma
patient, 174–175, 176
Substance abusers, as multiple trauma
patients, 39
Subungual hematomas, 757–758
Sudomotor testing, in hand trauma
evaluation, 659–660
Ninhydrin sweat test, 595, 660
O'Riain wrinkle test, 660
skin wrinkling, 595
Suicide, patient behavior demonstrating
risk of, 870–871
prediction difficulty, 885
Suicide hot line, 874
Sulfamylon (mafenide), in treatment of
hand burn injuries, 805
Superficial spreading melanoma, 295
Superior vena cava syndrome, 275
cancer-associated, 425–426
Supervision, of patient. See *Restraint, of
patient.*
Surgery, to correct nerve injuries in the
hand, 663–665
extensor tendon injuries, care following,
647–648
flexor tendon injuries, rehabilitation following, 633–634
in hand infections, 602–605
Surgical techniques, in airway
management, 56
Surrogate decision-makers, 537–538
bioethics committees, 538
courts, 538–539
family, 538
physicians, 538
Swan neck deformity, 575, 576, 642, 643
distal phalangeal fracture and, 679
Sweating, of skin, in hand trauma
evaluation. See *Sudomotor testing.*
Sympathetic dystrophy, following nerve
injury in the hand, 667
Symphysis pubis, subluxation of, 152
Syndrome of inappropriate antidiuretic
hormone (SIADH), as complication
of cancer, 415–416
clinical presentation, 416
pathophysiology, 415–416
treatment, 416
Synovial spaces, of the hand, 576–577
infected, 609–610
Synthetic dressings, in treatment of hand
burn injuries, 805

Systemic lupus erythematosus (SLE), and
chronic ITP similarities, 453
in DIC differential diagnosis, 473

Tachycardia, in child, 38
TBSA. See *Total body surface area (TBSA).*
Tegaderm, in treatment of hand burn
injuries, 805
Telangiectasias, malignancy associated
with, 279
Teleology, 534
Telephone advice/instructions, to high-risk
patient, 918
placing in medical record, 900
suicidal patient and, 874
Telephone orders, from private physicians
regarding high-risk patients, 917–918
Temporary protective custody, for abused
or neglected child, 849
Tendon injuries, of the hand, extensor. See
Extensor tendon injuries, hand.
flexor. See *Flexor tendon injuries, hand.*
Tendons, evaluating in hand trauma, 589,
597–599
of the hand, 568
repair principles, 627–628
Tenorrhaphy methods, 627–628
Tenosynovitis, flexor, 576
acute signs, 609–610
Terminally ill patient, prehospital consent
controversy over, 857–858
Terry Thomas sign, 729
Tetanus, amputation wounds prone to,
742–743
in hand nerve injury, 663
Thalassemia and thalassemia traits, 484–
485
Thenar flap, 762, 763
Thenar muscles. See *Intrinsic muscles.*
Therapeutic privilege, concept of, 874
Therapy. See also *specific drug therapies.*
factor replacement. See *Factor replacement
therapy.*
replacement, in disseminated intravascular coagulation, 473–474
transfusion. See *Transfusion therapy.*
unwanted, ethical dilemma presented by,
539–540
Thiazides, maternal, in thrombocytopenia
differential diagnosis, 450
6-Thioguanine, pharmacology and
toxicology of, 434–435
Thoracotomy, in Emergency Department,
indications for, 102–103
in pregnant trauma patient, 208
Thorax, abbreviated injury scale for, 18

Thrombin, role in disseminated
  intravascular coagulation, 469
Thrombocytopenia, **445–457**
  clinical presentation, 447
  differential diagnosis of, 447–448
    decreased platelet production, 449–451
    increased platelet destruction, immune
      related, 451–453
        nonimmune related, 454–456
      platelet loss, 449
      pseudothrombocytopenia, 449
      sequestration, 449
  in hemophiliacs, 355
  heparin-induced, 455–456
  idiopathic. See *Idiopathic thrombocytopenic
    purpura (ITP)*.
  laboratory analysis, 447
  neonatal alloimmune, 451
  patient evaluation, 456–457
  and platelet function, 445–446
  and platelet kinetics, 446
  thrombotic. See *Thrombotic thrombocyto-
    penic purpura (TTP)*.
  treatment protocols, 456
Thrombophlebitis, migratory, 289
Thrombosis, hemophilia treatment causing,
  353
Thrombotic thrombocytopenic purpura
  (TTP), 454–456
  distinguishing from ITP, 452
Thumb, anatomy of, 577–581
  flexor tendons of, 623
  human bite wound of, 614, 615
  joints of. See *Digital joints*.
  length of, 562
  movements defined, 578–579
  multiple level amputation injury to, 749
  pulley system of, 579–580
Tinel's sign, in hand nerve injury
  evaluation, 662
TLS. See *Tumor lysis syndrome (TLS)*.
Torres v. City of New York, 876
Tort law, and actions in contract, 825
  and basis of liability, 823–824
  solutions to inefficiencies of, 948–949
Tort reform, predictions on outcome of,
  949–950
  regarding malpractice, 942–943
  and standard of care disputes, 946–947
Total body surface area (TBSA), burn
  injury assessment, 798
  hospital admission and, 807
Touch pressure, in hand nerve injury
  evaluation, 661–662
Toxicology, and pharmacology of
  chemotherapeutic agents, **431–441**
Tracheobronchial injuries, 84
  evaluation of, 84–85
  treatment of, 85

Tranexamic acid, 343
Tranquilization, rapid, in combative
  trauma patient, 56–57
Transcription mechanisms, medical record
  documentation and, 890
Transfer, of prehospital patient, destination
  choice and, 860
  and diversion relationship, 861
  legislation governing, 861–862
  medical records accompanying, 896–897
  risk management and, 909–910
Transfusion hemosiderosis, 398
Transfusion reaction, air embolism, 398
  allergic, 395
  clerical error causing, 393–394
  extravascular hemolytic, 394
  febrile, 394–395
  graft-versus-host disease, 395
  hemosiderosis, 398
  infections, posttransfusion hepatitis, 396
    viral, 396–397
    other, 397–398
  intravascular hemolytic, 392–394
  pulmonary edema, 398
  volume overload and congestive heart
    failure, 398
Transfusion-related illness, as complication
  of sickle cell anemia, 374
Transfusion therapy. See also *Fluid
  resuscitation*.
  alternatives to, 401–403
  for anemia, 488–489
  blood products for. See *Blood products*.
  complications of. See *Transfusion reaction*.
  in Emergency Department, **379–403**
  history of, 379–380
  massive transfusion, 398–401
  thrombocytopenia following, 452
Transient ischemic attacks, as complication
  of sickle cell disease, 370–371
Transplantation center, for replantation of
  amputated limbs, 743. See also
  Replantation(s).
Transscaphoid perilunate dislocations, 734
Transtentorial herniation, 167
Trapezium fractures, 706–707
Trapezoid fractures, 709
Trauma, as cause of disseminated
  intravascular coagulation, 476
  to hand. See *Hand trauma*.
Trauma center, development of, 29–30
  financial issues, 250–251
  organization of personnel at, 31–32
  preparing for patient arrival at, 32
  staff training, 30
  universal precautions employed at, 32
Trauma index, 19
Trauma score, 20, 23
  pediatric, 188–190

Trauma triage, appropriate, need for, 16
    comorbid factors, 22, 23
    complex nature of, 15
    mechanisms of injury as triage tool, 21–22, 23
    in prehospital care, 8–9
    severity scores in. See *Severity scores.*
Trauma triage rule, 21
Treatment, consent to. See *Consent.*
    refusal of. See *Refusal of treatment.*
    statutes concerning minors, 843
Trespass, action of, tort law and, 823–824
Triage, from the field, scoring systems and, **10–25**. See also *Trauma triage.*
    mistriage rates, 18, 23, 25
    overtriage, 16, 23, 25
    in trauma situations. See *Trauma triage.*
    undertriage, 16, 23, 25
"Trigger diagnosis" phenomenon, 940–941
Triquetrolunate dissociation, 727
Triquetrum fractures, 705–706, 708
Tropical eosinophilia, 502–503
Truth-telling, as medical value, 533
    issues raised by, 540–541
TTP. See *Thrombotic thrombocytopenic purpura (TTP).*
Tumor lysis syndrome (TLS), as complication of cancer, 411–412
    pathophysiology, 412
    treatment, 412
Tumors, osseus. See *Bone lesions.*
Two-point discrimination, in hand trauma evaluation, 595
    moving, 661
    static, 659
Two-point threshold. See *Two-point discrimination.*
Typing, of blood, expediting for massive transfusion, 399
Tzanck smear, 616

Ulceration, of leg, as complication of sickle cell anemia, 374
Ulna, fractures. See *Ulna fractures.*
    radiographic evaluation of, 724, 725
Ulna fractures, radioulnar joint, 713–714
    styloid, 713
Ulnar nerve, in hand, 582
    functional anatomy, 656
    injury to, 657
        Emergency Department management, 662–663
        operative management, 663–665
        motor function testing, 657
        outcome following repair, 666
    trauma evaluation, 596
        motor function, 596–597

Ultrasound, in blunt abdominal trauma evaluation, 118–119
    in pregnant patient, for blunt abdominal trauma, 210–211
    confirming placental abruption, 212
Undertriage, 16, 23, 25
United States v. Eide, 899
Universal donor, 385
Universalizability test, in decision-making model, 535–536
Universal precautions, against HIV, 32
Upper airway obstructions, cancer-associated, 421–422
Urethra, trauma to, 139–140
Uterine contractions, following blunt abdominal trauma, 211
Uterus, in penetrating abdominal trauma, management controversies, injuries above, 216
    injuries to, 217
    size at different gestation times, 214
Utilitarianism, doctrine of, 534
Uveal tract, hematologic and oncologic diseases affecting, 305–307

Values, for health care providers and systems, 532–533
    religious, 533
    societal, 531–532
Vancomycin, in treatment of febrile neutropenic patient, 511
Vascular access, in pediatric trauma patient, 195–196
Vehicles, injury associated with, all-terrain vehicles, 259
    automobiles. See *Motor vehicle crashes.*
Vibration testing, in hand nerve injury evaluation, 662–663
Vinblastine, pharmacology and toxicology of, 440–441
Vinca alkaloids, pharmacology and toxicology of, 440–441
Vincristine, pharmacology and toxicology of, 440–441
Violence, by behaviorally disturbed patients, 870
    guidelines for dealing with, 881
Viral infections, following transfusion therapy, 396–397
    in thrombocytopenia differential diagnosis, 450
VISI. See *Volar intercalary segment instability (VISI).*
Vital signs, in multiple trauma patient, 40
    in pediatric patient, ranges for, 190
Vitamin K deficiency, in DIC differential diagnosis, 472–473

Vitiligo, melanoma and, 277
Volar intercalary segment instability (VISI), 729, 731, 733
Volume overload, following transfusion therapy, 398
Voluntary muscle test, median nerve, 652
 radial nerve, 654, 655
 ulnar nerve, 656
Voluntary patient (psychiatric), 872
von Frey monofilament testing, 595
von Willebrand's disease, case example, 338–339
 characteristic features of, 339
 diagnosis and treatment of, 339, 341
 therapeutic agents used, cryoprecipitate, 340
  factor VIII, 340, 342
  fresh frozen plasma, 339–340
  prothrombin complex concentrates, 342

Weight, of pediatric patient, formula for calculating, 190
White blood cells, disorders of, **495–512**
 peritoneal lavage fluid analysis, 112
Whole blood, in prehospital fluid resuscitation, 64–65
 for transfusion therapy, 384–385
Wilms's tumor, in children, 522

Wilson's fracture, middle phalanx, 691, 692
Wiskott-Aldrich syndrome, in thrombocytopenia differential diagnosis, 450
Witch doctors, 820
Withdrawal, alcohol, 202
 evaluating patient with symptoms of, 877
Wringer arm, 770
Wringer injuries, to the hand, equipment causing, 770–771
 pathophysiology, 772
 treatment, 772–773
Wrinkling, of skin, in hand trauma evaluation. See *Sudomotor testing.*
Wrist, extensor tendon injuries at level of, 645–647
 flexor tendons of, 623
 fractures, **703–714**
 ligamentous injuries, **717–737**. See also *Ligamentous wrist injuries.*
Wrist fractures, **703–714**
 carpal, 703–709
 distal radius and ulna, 709–714
Writ, origin of, 822

Zero defects concept, in risk management, 907
Zone of transition, skeletal lesions and, 308, 310

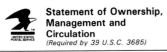

Statement of Ownership, Management and Circulation
(Required by 39 U.S.C. 3685)

1A. Title of Publication	1B. PUBLICATION NO.	2. Date of Filing
Emergency Medicine Clinics of North America	0 7 3 3 8 6 2 7	8/13/93

3. Frequency of Issue	3A. No. of Issues Published Annually	3B. Annual Subscription Price
FEB/MAY/AUG/NOV	4	$82.00

4. Complete Mailing Address of Known Office of Publication *(Street, City, County, State and ZIP+4 Code) (Not printers)*

W. B. Saunders Company, Harcourt Brace & Company
6277 Sea Harbor Drive, Orlando, FL 32887-4880, Orange County

5. Complete Mailing Address of the Headquarters of General Business Offices of the Publisher *(Not printer)*

W. B. Saunders Company
Curtis Center, Independence Square West, Phila., PA 19106-3399

6. Full Names and Complete Mailing Address of Publisher, Editor, and Managing Editor (This item MUST NOT be blank)

Publisher *(Name and Complete Mailing Address)*
Joan Blumberg, W. B. Saunders Company
Curtis Center, Independence Square West, Phila., PA 19106-3399

Editor *(Name and Complete Mailing Address)*
Sandy Hitchens, W. B. Saunders Company
Curtis Center, Independence Square West, Phila., PA 19106-3399

Managing Editor *(Name and Complete Mailing Address)*
Barbara Cohen-Kligerman, W. B. Saunders Company
Curtis Center, Independence Square West, Phila., PA 19106-3399

7. Owner *(If owned by a corporation, its name and address must be stated and also immediately thereunder the names and addresses of stockholders owning or holding 1 percent or more of total amount of stock. If not owned by a corporation, the names and addresses of the individual owners must be given. If owned by a partnership or other unincorporated firm, its name and address, as well as that of each individual must be given. If the publication is published by a nonprofit organization, its name and address must be stated.) (Item must be completed.)*

Full Name	Complete Mailing Address
W. B. Saunders Company stock is owned 100% by Harcourt General Corporation	27 Boylston Street Chestnut Hill, MA 02167

8. Known Bondholders, Mortgagees, and Other Security Holders Owning or Holding 1 Percent or More of Total Amount of Bonds, Mortgages or Other Securities *(If there are none, so state)*

Full Name	Complete Mailing Address
N/A	

9. For Completion by Nonprofit Organizations Authorized To Mail at Special Rates *(DMM Section 424.12 only)*
The purpose, function, and nonprofit status of this organization and the exempt status for Federal income tax purposes *(Check one)*

(1) ☐ Has Not Changed During Preceding 12 Months	(2) ☐ Has Changed During Preceding 12 Months	*(If changed, publisher must submit explanation of change with this statement.)*

10.	Extent and Nature of Circulation *(See instructions on reverse side)*	Average No. Copies Each Issue During Preceding 12 Months	Actual No. Copies of Single Issue Published Nearest to Filing Date
A.	Total No. Copies *(Net Press Run)*	7,525	7,300
B.	Paid and/or Requested Circulation 1. Sales through dealers and carriers, street vendors and counter sales		
	2. Mail Subscription *(Paid and/or requested)*	4,269	4,160
C.	Total Paid and/or Requested Circulation *(Sum of 10B1 and 10B2)*	4,269	4,160
D.	Free Distribution by Mail, Carrier or Other Means Samples, Complimentary, and Other Free Copies	99	103
E.	Total Distribution *(Sum of C and D)*	4,368	4,263
F.	Copies Not Distributed 1. Office use, left over, unaccounted, spoiled after printing	3,157	3,037
	2. Return from News Agents		
G.	TOTAL *(Sum of E, F1 and 2—should equal net press run shown in A)*	7,525	7,300

11. I certify that the statements made by me above are correct and complete

Signature and Title of Editor, Publisher, Business Manager, or Owner

Joan Blumberg Joan Blumberg, Executive Vice President

PS Form **3526**, January 1991   *(See instructions on reverse)*